Montana Adventure

Montana Adventure

The Recollections of
Frank B. Linderman

by

FRANK B. LINDERMAN

Edited by

H. G. MERRIAM

UNIVERSITY OF NEBRASKA PRESS
Lincoln and London

First Bison Book printing: 1985
Most recent printing indicated by the first digit below:
1   2   3   4   5   6   7   8   9   10

Library of Congress Cataloging in Publication Data
Linderman, Frank Bird, 1869–1938.
  Montana adventure.
  "Bison."
  Includes index.
  1. Linderman, Frank Bird, 1869–1938—Biography.
2. Authors, American—20th century—Biography.
3. Montana—Description and travel. 4. Montana—Social
life and customs. I. Merriam, H. G. (Harold Guy),
1883–   . II. Title.
PS3523.I535Z47   1985   813'.52 [B]   85-1051
ISBN 0-8032-7916-7 (pbk.)

Portions of Chapters I, III, and V previously appeared in
Frontier and Midland, Vol. XIX (Spring 1939).

Foreword

I URGE everyone to read Frank Linderman's text before perusing the account of his life and writings at the end of this book, in order that he may feel and understand Linderman through his own story. My account contains additional details and comment on his life and writings.

At the urging of his friends and publisher to write a book about his life experiences, Frank Bird Linderman decided to undertake the task, as he states, with little relish for it. He began it in New York, it would seem, in late 1929 while on a visit there and finished it in 1930. His editor, Richard Walsh of the John Day Company, writing to him about the manuscript on March 9, 1931, suggested that it be made into "the story of Montana . . . in terms of Frank B. Linderman." Herbert Stoops, who illustrated several of his books, commented in much the same vein: "[A] retrospective history of the great Northwest plains that became Montana could be combined brilliantly with the colorful and always interesting episodes in your own life." The hope that he would undertake this more elaborate writing probably accounts for the fact that Linderman's recollections, originally titled "My Camp-Kettle Career," was not published at the time. The idea appealed to Linderman, but he did not set to work on it.

He began his recollections when he was stimulated by success. He had just placed four books with the John Day Company; he had met many persons who, admiring him and his writings, became warm friends; he had had his spirit refreshed and been given new confidence. The suggestion, though, of a more ambitious work came when he was weary and when he had in mind other writings which he felt were more important. His son-in-law, Roy Waller, wrote to Mr. Stoops in July, 1938—about two months after Linderman's death—that Frank had "intended to finish his

v

'Camp-Kettle Career' while in Santa Barbara this spring, but he apparently did nothing to it—as he added nothing since he recorded his experiences in New York in 1929–1930." Whether Linderman contemplated undertaking the sizable task put to him by his publisher and his illustrator or simply filling in the years from 1930 to his death, no one knows.

His publisher thought that in "My Camp-Kettle Career" he was not writing naturally and easily. True, experiencing self-conscious reluctance and embarrassment when writing it, he may have missed out on some of the verve and pleasure in expression that are in his other writings. Yet "My Camp-Kettle Career" reveals his traits of humor, courage, and honesty, and gives clear and interesting—and often exciting—pictures of his varied experiences. And the account is a valuable addition to the literature and history of his time.

A full-length biography of Frank B. Linderman should be written and probably will be when the value of his writings has become fully appreciated. Meanwhile, *Montana Adventure* and the supplementary materials about his life and writings at the end of this book will supply much information and provide an introduction to him as both author and man. Linderman's writing has been retained exactly as he wrote it, except for the words added in brackets, correction of obvious typographical errors, regularization of capitalization and punctuation, and division into chapters. I have also supplied footnotes which furnish additional background information.

H. G. MERRIAM

Contents

A section of illustrations follows p. 54.

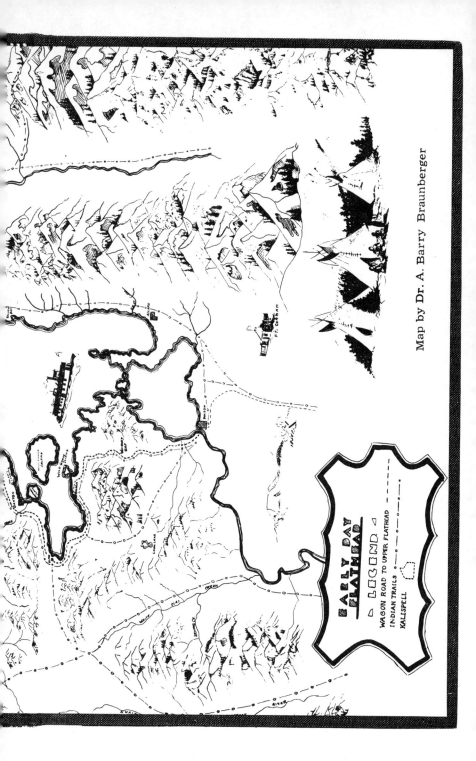

Map by Dr. A. Barry Braunberger

FT. CONRAH

EARLY DAY
FLATHEAD
LEGEND
WAGON ROAD TO UPPER FLATHEAD
INDIAN TRAILS
KALISPELL

MONTANA ADVENTURE

CHAPTER I

A Lad in the Flathead Valley

LAST summer a man stopped me on the street in Kalispell. "Hello, Frank," he said, eagerly offering his hand. Then, wonderingly, "Don't you know me?" he asked.

"No," I replied, giving his hand a good shake nevertheless, because I saw that he was an old-timer.

"I'm Tom Jones," he said. "You used to call me Cayuse Jones; *now* do you know me?"

His eyes were so full of expectancy that I lied. "You bet," I said, trying not to look straight into them until my memory served me better.

"Do you remember when we rode into the Kootenai village at Dayton Creek?" he asked, with a hand on my shoulder.

"I well remember the time that *I* rode into the Kootenai camp on Dayton," I answered, thinking for the first time in years of one of the silliest acts of my life.

"Well, I was with you, at your side, your knee was touching mine. We both rode in together. God! When I saw what we were up against there I was scared good and plenty."

"So was I," I said.

"Wasn't that the biggest fool play ever made this side of crazyland?" he chuckled.

We found a place to sit down and talk over the happenings of a day more than forty years before, when a party of settlers had ridden into the Kootenai village to capture La-la-see, Pierre Paul, and Antley, the Kootenai killers. We did not get them. Instead, we suddenly found ourselves in an extremely difficult

1

situation. So tense were the moments in the big Indian camp that a single awkward move, even a cough or a loud sneeze, might have precipitated a fight that would have wiped us out. And yet I have not the slightest remembrance of Cayuse Jones. I know that he was a member of the party, however. He could not otherwise have talked of it as he did. It was this chance meeting that decided me to write my experiences in Montana before I forget them altogether.

It may be that the blood of earlier Lindermans who pioneered in New York state, Pennsylvania, and Ohio, was somewhat responsible for my boyhood ache to go west, since I cannot remember when I first began to feel it. I know that it came to me very early, and that afterward it never left me. And how I feared that the West of my dreams would fade before I could reach it! At last, however, I won my parents' reluctant consent to leave home and felt that I was free. I believe I should soon have had to go even though their permission had been withheld. Now, when my father, mother, and my only brother are gone, I am glad I waited for it as I did. "Don't worry. He will soon be back home, and then he'll be glad to stay," said my father at the dinner table when finally they had decided to let me have my fling.

I had found a large map of the western states and territories, and that night, for the hundredth time, I spread it upon the floor in my own room to pore over it as I always had, flat on my belly. Long before this I had decided where I wished to go, but now that my dream was coming true I needed to be sure I had made no mistake in my choosing. I had to have unspoiled wilderness, because I secretly intended to become a trapper. I remember that I felt glad when the Flathead Lake country in northwestern Montana Territory seemed yet to be farthest removed from contaminating civilization. I'd go as straight as I could to Flathead Lake.

Another boy of my own age had promised to go west with me as soon as I could get away. His father was a lover of fine horses, and kept a negro coachman who told us that he had served in a cavalry regiment against the Indians "way out yonder in de West."

Besides this, he could make sounds resembling the ringing of distant, sweet-toned bells deep down in his throat. Great as this accomplishment seemed to me, I remember that whenever he rang his bells I turned away so that I might not see his hideously distorted face, his swelled throat, and bulging eyes that threatened to burst. I have never known another human being who possessed this strange faculty. We decided to take this negro with us if we could manage somehow to steal him away without our parents learning about it. This led to much planning in the stables, and I shall never forget how jumpy I got after secret sessions with the other boy and the negro when my mother would sniff and say, "What can you possibly find to interest you in that old stable? Your clothes smell disgustingly of horses."

One night the negro showed us a letter from his mother and asked us to read it to him. The envelope solved our problem, since it had not been properly sealed. I now wrote a letter to the negro myself, put it into the old envelope, and carefully sealed it. My chum then managed to slip it among the family's mail next morning, and a servant promptly delivered it to the negro in the barn. That evening we were jubilant indeed. The negro had been given [two] weeks leave to visit his mother who, the letter said, was very ill in Virginia, and wished to see her only son. Of course, we now had cover for the negro to disappear and wait for us at an agreed place. Now we learned that our partner, the black man, hadn't a red cent to his name. I had saved up $75.00, and out of this sum I paid $67.50 for a ticket to Missoula, Montana Territory, for the negro, which was then as far as a train would carry a passenger over the unfinished Northern Pacific Railroad. My chum had much more money than I and I do not remember why I paid the fare for the negro. I had a pass over the road, and $7.50, when we boarded the train in Chicago bound for the new Northwest. My father had also taken a seat in the coach with us, and not until he got off, after an hour's run, did my chum and I have an opportunity to learn whether the negro was on the train. We found him smoking a cheap cigar in the smoker; and at last we were off, all together.

3

The road was new and rough, often startling in its eccentricities. When we reached the Missouri River, the steamboat *Helena* took us upstream to a landing place, and then turned us over to teamsters, with bobsleds, who hauled us to a point where a train, made up for the purpose, took us aboard again. Landslides along the Yellowstone stopped this train several times, and we got out and shoveled with the workmen to clear the track. I was between sixteen and seventeen years old when, with my companions, I reached the Flathead country on the twentieth of March, 1885, having hired a team and driver in Missoula.[1] But neither the white boy nor the Indian-fighting negro was cut out for life in the new Northwest. After four or five days and nights of bitter grumbling, they left me and returned to "the States."

During their short stay in the Flathead country we had hastily built a tiny log cabin, packing the logs on our backs, on what today is called Nigger Prairie, for the negro.[2] The cabin had no windows or floor, and its door was the green hide of a white-tail deer that I had killed nearby. Its uncovered pole roof leaked for hours after the rain outside had ceased to fall, and there was neither chinking nor daubing between its logs. There was no fireplace, and its only furniture was an old percussion-lock Kentucky rifle that had belonged to my father in Ohio, and the axe. But the thing I most marvel at now is that we had no blankets, no covering at night except our light overcoats.

Each night the wolves howled dismally around our miserable camp, and it was these timber wolves that decided the negro that the States needed him more than I did. The white boy had been thoroughly homesick from the start and would have turned back in St. Paul if the negro and I had not gilded the way westward with imagined adventures. It was well that he came on with me, since if he had weakened earlier than he did the negro would have quit with him. I could not then have built the cabin alone.

[1] The three probably drove to the site of present-day Polson and took one of the lake steamers to Demersville on the Flathead River.

[2] About four or five miles east of the present town of Big Fork. The cabin was "at the foot of the lake about twenty yards from Marten Creek, which joins the Big Fork a little below where the lake and river meet."

A Lad in the Flathead Valley

Our grubstake had been light even in the beginning, and now when my companions left me there was little left except venison. I had had the bad luck, while building the cabin, to step squarely upon the upturned edge of the sharp axe, dropped in tenderfoot fashion among some limbs that had been trimmed from the cabin logs. My light shoe sole had been severed and my foot cut to the bone, not because of my weight alone, but because of the added weight of a green house log, one end of which was on my shoulder; and it was the last log we needed, too. The negro bound up my foot with my only handkerchief and I managed to help put the poles on the roof; but the wound dampened my ardor so much that when my partners left me I felt mighty blue.

It was afternoon when they went away. That night a storm of mingled rain and sleet wet me to the skin before I thought of a way to a little comfort. The front end of the green deer hide was pegged to the top of the doorway. Now I lifted the tail end, and propped it up at both corners with poles, so that the hide sloped downward into the cabin. Then I raked my fire up close to the door *outside* and sat *inside* just under the deer hide—and let her rain. It wasn't long until one side of me was quite dry. Then I turned the other toward the fire, keeping this up all night. My foot, if unused, gave me no pain and I didn't mind the wolves. I rather liked to hear them; I always have. And now when they are gone I like to hear the voices of coyotes in the night.

My grub was all gone by the time I could walk, even with a stick. But this gave me no worry. One could not starve with white-tail deer in plain sight every hour of daylight. I wasn't troubled by worldly possessions either. We had started out with two trunks and a box or two of baggage; but I never got them, and never learned what became of them. I could shoulder my Kentucky, carry my axe and overcoat wherever I went, and I could eat meat until I found a place to work or got out of the country, whichever the Fates decreed.

Nigger Prairie was what we called a park in the heavy timber. The Indian trail that led through it forked not far from my cabin, one branch leading to the Big Fork (Sweathouse) River[3] and the Swan Lake country, and the other crossing the high mountains through Aeneas Pass (named for Big-knife, the then Kootenai chief whom the Jesuits had named), to the south fork of the Flathead River.[4] On the edge of the prairie toward Flathead lake the trail forked again, sending out branches, one to the mouth of the Big Fork, and the other, passing Three Lakes,[5] to the Flathead valley, which it traversed. These trails, all of them, were deeply cut through the bunch grass, showing me that they were extensively used. Following farther into the timber where deer traveled them continuously, I saw that they were often six inches deep, and in dry weather beaten hard and smooth as stone, even the roots of trees being exposed.

My excursions from the cabin had not been distant, and yet they had been sufficient to make me wonder and worry a little. I did not know if the Indians in that remote section were friendly to white men. There was nobody to tell me, and during all this time I had not seen an Indian. Then one morning before sunup when I was rekindling my fire to cook some venison I heard a horse whinny. The sound was friendly enough, and yet I felt a little jumpy, *especially* when I saw twenty-five head of cayuses feeding between my cabin and the skirting timber across the prairie. I knew that they were Indian horses, and the sight of them made me feel as lonely as a hole in a hillside. I forgot my breakfast to watch the horses, and to look carefully for a camp which I confidently expected would be somewhere on the edge of the timber about the prairie.

I had a large bowie knife, which I then fondly believed was the proper thing for a hunter to carry, a glittering mistake with "a sure defense" etched on its blade. The knife was sticking in a log near my fire. I hastily slipped it into its scabbard on my belt,

[3] Apparently the lower end of Swan River after it leaves Swan Lake was then called the Big Fork (Sweathouse) River.

[4] The trail ran from the Flathead valley over Aeneas Pass, beside Aeneas Mountain, by Aeneas Lake to Aeneas Creek, and into the South Flathead country.

[5] Three Lakes probably refers to Echo, Mud, and Loon Lakes, not far from Nigger Prairie.

put on my powder horn and bullet pouch, and picked up my antiquated Kentucky to have a look farther down the prairie. A strip of jack pines grew on a succession of little knolls that extended through its middle, and I hobbled from knoll to knoll without seeing an Indian or a camp. Reaching the last timbered knoll, I sat down near a good-sized jack pine tree, not far from the grazing horses. The sun was just coming up. The whole setting was so startlingly beautiful that I nearly forgot Indians. The snow-capped peaks began to take on color. The frost crystals on the thick stools of bunch grass were sparkling like millions of diamonds, when suddenly the horses stirred like wild things. I saw them all lift their heads, prick their ears in one direction, toward the Big Fork. The light, crisp breeze was coming from that direction. I crept behind my tree, watching the skirting timber with the horses, until an Indian with a rifle across in front of him rode into the prairie on a pinto horse. The loose horses now began to move about restlessly, at last trotting away up the prairie back of my cabin, where the Indian, by riding hard, turned them toward the Big Fork, the whole outfit going lickety-split. "It will soon be over," I thought, when suddenly the Indian reined his horse to a short stop. I saw him look up and down the prairie, nosing the wind like a wolf. Then he rode straight to my little cabin, which was well hidden by jack pines. He had smelled the smoke from my fire.

What ought I to do now? I wondered. My overcoat and the axe were in the cabin. Everything else that I owned was with me. "Let him have 'em," I thought, watching for the Indian to ride away with my property. But he didn't appear. The horses, not being followed, stopped to graze again. I sat down by my tree to wait. An hour passed, or I thought the time that long, before I finally began to hobble toward my cabin without knowing exactly why. Anyway, I saw the Indian before he saw me; and I stopped, fascinated. He was seated on the log beside my smouldering fire, calmly filling his black stone pipe out of a long, slender buckskin sack. His blanket, a white Hudson's Bay, was tucked tightly about his lean hips, his rifle leaning against the log beside him. I thought him a middle-aged man. While I watched, he bent forward, raked a glowing stick out of my fire, lit the pipe, and then settled back with such an air of peace and contentment that I fairly ached to shake hands with him, if he'd let me.

My first step forward was upon a tiny patch of frosted snow among the trees. His ears caught the sound of the crackling snow crust. Without the least startle or show of surprise his head turned slowly until he saw me. Then he stood up with extended hand. "How! How!" he said so pleasantly that I answered, "Very well, sir, how are you?" giving his hand a good shake. What a fine face he had, that red man! We tried hard to talk together, but with little success. However, we smoked together, *my* tobacco in *his* pipe. I remembered long afterward that he had wished to impress me with the fact that he was a Flathead and not a Kootenai, telling me this in the sign language over and over again. But of course the sign language was Greek to me then. There was good reason for his wanting me to know that he was not a Kootenai. The Kootenais were unfriendly to white men. We had trouble with them later on.

My Indian visitor instinctively knew that I was a rank pilgrim. His smile said as plainly as words that he thought me a babe in the woods. However, he was exceedingly polite, and tried to treat me as he would a grown man. This made a deep impression on me. From that day I frequently fibbed about my age. I did this so consistently and for so long a time that I finally forgot the true number of my years. It was only when I saw my mother again more than twenty years afterward that I learned exactly the date of my birth. I remember that when I attempted to argue with her, my mother said with a grim smile, "I was present when you were born, my son, and therefore I ought to know."

For many years after our meeting I knew my first Indian intimately. His name was Red-horn, a renowned Flathead warrior who had counted several "coups" and had taken more scalps than any other living member of his tribe. It was Red-horn who gave me my first glimpse of what men in the old Northwest called the "moccasin telegraph." I cannot prove that old-time Indians transmitted messages through thin air over long distances, and yet I have more than once believed that only by some secret means could Indian news travel as it seemed to. Several years after my first meeting with Red-horn I was camped alone in an Indian lodge at the foot of Swan lake. Red-horn and his woman and two young sons reached this camping ground at about sunset. Knowing my lodge by sight, Red-horn came at once to visit me. He stayed until late in the night. The next morning he came again, sitting exactly where he had sat the night before, talking signs and pidgin English as he had before, till suddenly he stopped short, lifted his eyes to the smoke-hole, and sat motionless, as though listening. His attitude, so suddenly assumed and so tense, caused me, now a hunter like himself, to strain my ears to catch the sounds that disturbed him. But I heard nothing unnatural. When I again looked at Red-horn's face his eyes met my own.

"My friend killed. Bad work," he said in signs.

"When?" I asked, wonderingly.

"Now," he signed, positively.

"What name?" I asked in the sign language. He told me, but I have forgotten it.

"Where?" I asked. He pointed south.

Fortunately I happened to know the day of the week and month, which was out of the ordinary. I had no watch, but by the sun I thought the time of day to be about nine o'clock in the forenoon. Later in the year when I visited the lower country I learned that Red-horn's friend *had* been murdered on that day, and approximately at that hour. I have experienced other seeming exhibitions of the efficiency of the "moccasin telegraph," but I will leave them and get on with my story.

A white man named Alvin Lee had staked a claim on the Flathead River. I had seen him once, and that had been when we came into the valley. I had liked him at first sight. Now I made my way to his cabin, which was quite distant from the river. He told me he intended building a new shack by the stream and that he would operate a ferry on the river. "I'm not a boatman," he said. This offered me an opportunity. I knew boats, having been

9

around them all my life, so that we quickly made a deal. I helped him build his new cabin and run his ferry, the first "boat" being a raft of logs. I often think of the days and even weeks that passed without a customer, white or red. But soon settlers began to come into the Flathead Valley, and then business picked up a little. By fall I had, by trading some goods which I had received from my father, obtained some cayuses, steel traps, and a camp outfit, and became a trapper as I had intended.

Instinctively I was a hunter and trapper. From early boyhood birds and animals interested me; learning their habits occupied much of my time. I owned a shotgun and a rifle almost as soon as I could carry them, old muzzle-loaders, of course. My collection of birds' eggs was the largest, and perhaps the best, among the boys in Elyria, Ohio, where I lived for years. Saturdays and vacation days found me in the woods by daylight, for nobody who has not been often in the open country before sunrise can ever know the birds and animals of any country.

Looking back, I marvel at my lust to kill game. Even though I've never been a wanton killer, I'm sorry now that I ever killed at all. But one has to kill to live in the wilderness. However, my rifles have long been laid away. Only hunger now could induce me to kill an animal or a bird. Even as I write these lines the snow outside my window is thickly tracked by deer and grouse that were about the house last night and early this morning. Sometimes deer come so close that one might easily touch their backs from our windows at Goose Bay, and yet I am not tempted. Of all the animals I know, there are but two whose lives I would yet take without a qualm—the mountain lion and the lynx, both rivals of the white man as game destroyers. And yet both the lion and the lynx kill that they themselves may live.

Hank Jennings was, unconsciously, my first teacher of the trapper's art. With my newly acquired outfit I intentionally camped near him, spending my evenings at his fire. I remember that when I apologized for my rusty traps he looked surprised. "Wo'th more'n new ones, son; lucky to git 'em that-a-way" he said, as though fortune had spilled treasure into my lap. One night when he condescended to eat supper in my camp, I gave him a copper penny that I had saved. "Half of it'll be on my rifle before noon tomorrow," he declared. "Best front sight in the timber, except mebby bone, but bone breaks too easy." He went on, happy in the possession of the penny, a scarce coin in the Northwest.

Accompanying Hank on his trap lines, I learned how to "set" for lynx and marten, as well as for fishers and wolverines. The fisher, or pekan, has always been rare in Montana, his pelt, during my trapping days, bringing more money than any other. Wolverines were plentiful, their reputation for cunning being greater than they deserved. They are fighters, powerful animals, considering their size, and yet I found them easy to trap. They are, however, great trap robbers, sometimes devouring not only a trapped animal, but the trapper's bait as well. I have known a wolverine to follow my trap line and eat, or destroy, everything in my traps, besides helping himself to bait here and there. Once a trapped wolverine got away with a trap of mine. I followed him for two days without seeing him. When I gave up he was going strongly with a Number Four Newhouse beaver trap on his right front paw. His hide was worth about $6.00, and the trap $3.50. Trapped, the wolverine does not sulk, as the big cats usually do. He is on the fight, straining the trap chain to get at the trapper, his gasping growl fierce indeed.

Hank Jennings always talked to a wolverine in a trap. Setting his rifle against a convenient tree he would approach the enraged animal with a club. "Waitin' fer me, be ye?" he would say. "Ha-ha; dad *burn* ye! Didn't rob me this time, mister; wa'n't so damned cunnin' as usual, hey? leetle keerless whar ye set yer foot last night. Whope! Dodged that one, did ye? Well, how's *this* one? Thar!"

Telling of Hank's talking to a trapped wolverine has reminded me of old Left-hand, also known as Dominick. Early one morning while hunting deer I heard an Indian's voice in the thick timber ahead of me. It was so animated, so plumb full of fun, that I stopped to listen eagerly for a replying voice; but none reached me, the same voice going merrily on, punctured with strong exclamations, none of which I understood. I was interested. (Indians seldom talk to themselves.) Making my way carefully, I came out of the timber into a little meadowy patch where I saw old Left-hand dancing about a trapped wolverine, with a willow switch in his hand. He had used a "spring-pole," bending a young fir sapling to the ground so that when his trap was sprung the young tree, released, would spring erect, thus obliging the wolverine to stand on his hind legs, his imprisoned front paw held about his head. Seeing me, Left-hand began to use pidgin English: "You stealum my bait," he laughed, lashing the angry animal with the willow. "Me w'ip you por dat, oui, plenty w'ip you, me!" The old fellow was in high glee at having caught the wolverine, his willow switch more an expression of his merriment than of his wrath.

My first real trapping was on the Big Fork, known by early trappers as Sweathouse River, where George Lakin taught me to set for beaver. Here is an animal that is truly cunning, that is, if trappers have lately been working on a colony of them. They quickly learn to avoid traps, especially if the trapper is careless about leaving "sign" of his visits. Stories of beaver sagacity are of course exaggerated, furnishing entertaining campfire yarns, and yet every trapper of wide experience has met cunning in beaver kind. There is always danger, if one beaver is carelessly caught, that the whole colony may leave the country, so we worked upstream, taking care not to disturb even a stick or a stone above our traps. There are many "beaver medicines," bait that attracts the animals to traps. The medicine that I used was a portion of beaver castor, cinnamon, allspice, and cloves, equal parts—about what would remain on the point of the small blade of a pocket-knife—mixed thoroughly with beaver oil from the glands. This mixture, and others, will serve in any colony of beavers, furnishing a scent that is naturally of beavers, and yet foreign to any colony. If only beaver castor is used, the beavers may not recognize the scent as being foreign, and so let it alone. Strange beaver musk, scent, attracts them always, hence the trapper's medicine. Even after thirty-nine years of disuse the medicine in my old birch bottle is strong, reminding me of trapping days as nothing else can. Skinning out a beaver is quick work for an experienced hand, but fleshing a beaver skin is careful work for anybody. This is generally done in camp. Fleshing times were always ceremonial feasts for my dog, Mike.[6] Whenever I fleshed he sat directly across the fire from me, his eyes watching every stroke of my curved knife, his mouth drooling in anticipation of the fleshings, which he never failed to catch and swallow in a gulp; and he would never leave his place until the last hide was fleshed. Then, licking his chops, he would lie down with a sigh expressing so much satisfaction that I always wished I had another hide to flesh for him. Beaver hides were stretched and sewed in willow hoops in the form of the letter *O*, and hung up to dry.

Taking land fur is different from beaver trapping. Trap lines are blazed into the forests, often before the snow comes, the blazes made high enough on the trees so that they may be seen after snow has fallen deeply. Wherever a trap is set along these trap lines, which may be many miles in length, a tree is blazed peculiarly, so that the trapper may know when he is approaching a set.

I always enjoyed getting snug for a winter's trapping, building the cabin, getting in dry wood, blazing trap lines, and killing meat. Heads, necks, and offal were saved for bait. These, and whatever other meats we used for bait, we often dragged along our trap lines to attract fur-bearing animals, leaving bits at sites selected for future sets.

Once, because we built our tiny cabin during extremely cold weather, a partner and I covered it outside and inside with deer hides. We soon regretted the interior finish, however. Wood mice built luxurious nests between the pole roof and the deer hides overhead, so that deer hair got into everything, even into our bannocks and beans. We came near to starvation that winter, even though we at first had plenty of meat. Late snows came on suddenly, falling so deeply that deer and elk left the country. We had lost supplies in the fall through the swamping of our canoe in the Big

---

[6] Linderman wrote a book-length manuscript (unpublished), entitled "Mike, the Story of a Trapper's Dog," about this dog.

Fork rapids, and instead of returning to the valley for replenishments we thought to make out with what he had left. Up to the time when the big storm struck the country we might have gone out for supplies on snowshoes; but once started, the snow fell continuously for two weeks. It was so light and so dry and deep that even with bear-paw shoes on our feet we sank to our waists; one could not travel a half-mile in an hour. Our grub was nearly gone when the storm began. When it was over we had nothing to eat, and felt foolishly trapped. We wallowed into the timber looking for a shot at anything in the form of meat, finding nothing; and we were out of tobacco, to make matters worse. Kinnikinnic mixed with tobacco is a fine thing, but when smoked straight it quickly loses its good qualities. We knew that there must have been plenty of deer in the upper country when the storm began, and that they must have worked their way out, making deep snow trails. We decided to travel toward the foothills and try to find one of these snow trails. If we succeeded in this, and failed to get meat there, we could follow the trail out to the lower country, without snowshoes. I have seen these trails so deep that the deer traveling them could not be seen by a man twenty yards away. After making our decision, we turned in to get some needed sleep. In the night I heard Jack Bartlett, my partner, get up and put on his snowshoes. Thinking that he must be dreaming I asked, "Where are you going, Jack?"

"I've got a hunch," he said, in the dark. "If you hear me shoot, an' then whistle, fetch a knife. I aint goin' to pack a knife, fer luck."

"What foolishness," I thought, as the door's wooden hinges creaked dismally. I must have slept; anyhow, I was aroused by a rifle shot that in the keen air sounded like the crack of a whiplash. Then there came a shrill whistle. Hopping out of the bunk I put on my bear paws, grabbed my belt and knife, and began wallowing toward Jack, whose rifle flashed four times after I started. He was not far, not more than one hundred yards from the cabin, and he had broken the back of a whopping big buck with his first shot. The others were fired to finish off the animal.

14

I need not say that part of that deer was in our camp kettle almost before it had quit kicking. But how came the buck to be there in the deep snow, so near our cabin? Why had he left the snow trail that he must have been traveling? Jack answered these questions easily. "He was sent; that there buck was sent," he said with finality.

Anyhow, the deer saved us a hard struggle, and perhaps our lives. Jack Bartlett was a superstitious Missourian who would not believe that the world was round. Nevertheless, he was an honest man and a good partner. A week later a chinook came roaring through the forests, settling the snow so that with bear paws traveling was easy. We found the snow trail and plenty of meat, which we ate straight for two more weeks, without a bit of salt. However, we managed to get a little tobacco, such as it was. Jack chewed, as well as smoked; and while we were building our cabin we had camped down the river a little way. In this camp, intrigued by a deep hole in the stump of a broken spruce tree, Jack had pitched his tobacco cuds into it, instead of tossing them into the fire as usual. One day my deep desire for a real smoke inspired me. I remembered about the hole in the spruce stump. With thoughts of the treasure that this hole might yet contain, I put on my snowshoes, located the site of the old camp, found the spruce stump, and dug down beside it to the hole—and there safe and sound were the tobacco cuds, like little balls that crumbled when I touched them.

I have said that I have seen snow trails made by deer so deep that the traveling animals were hidden in them. I have, and they were sometimes so narrow that in them a man had little room between the walls of snow, worn smooth as glass. Deer, in many places, could not have turned around in them. At such points mountain lions and lynx and wolves made great killings. Trapped by snow, deer sometimes "yard," trampling wide patches where they browse on bushes until relieved by a change of weather; sometimes they die in their "yards." Nearly always when snow threatens to shut them in they make their way through the deepening snows to a less snowy section.

15

Lincoln Lee, who lives with us at Goose Bay, and whose word is beyond question, tells of watching a band of mule deer breaking a snow trail. When the leader, tired by bucking the snowdrifts, stopped and bent his head, the deer next behind him leaped over the leader to take his turn. Lee declares that three or four large bucks successively jumped others to relieve the trail breaker, and that several fawns at the tail end of the band only kept their places, leaving the heavy work to the older deer. I have never witnessed this myself, and yet I have no hesitancy in recording it here, having intimately known Link Lee for forty-five years.

Nowadays, when in winter I look out of our windows at the snow-laden fir thickets, at saplings bent like old, burdened women, all headed in one direction as though striving to leave the country behind them, I wonder how we stood the game we used to play. With a heavy rifle weighing from twelve to fourteen pounds, some jerked meat, and perhaps a few traps, we traveled on snowshoes for days, looking for "sign," a new location for a winter camp where fur was more plentiful. When night came on, we camped beneath some old spruce tree, only to go on with daylight. We never suffered, were always healthy and strong. And we were meat eaters. If I were to try to tell how much meat we consumed, I would not be believed, I am sure. However, the old ration for French *voyageurs* was ten pounds of meat containing bone, eight pounds without bone, or four ducks, or two geese, per day, per man; and we were generally as hungry as French *voyageurs*.

We wore moccasins both summer and winter, buckskin in the summertime and often raw deer-hide moccasins in the snow. The latter we made rather hurriedly, sewing the raw deerskin around our feet for the day, or the trip, turning the hair side in. They kept our feet warm, and dryer than buckskin, although our feet were always wet in winter, excepting in very cold weather. Then, sometimes, if one did not keep traveling, his feet would get cold. I remember one morning when I had hastily fashioned a pair of these rawhide moccasins that were shapeless, my partner, Black George, walked around me looking down at my creations. "Be right damned careful not to git yerself lost with them things on,"

16

he said, sarcastically, "because if ye do ye'll never be able to backtrack yerse'f. Ye won't know which end's the toe of 'em."

Becoming a trapper was like joining a fraternity. A pilgrim no longer, I began to know the men of the old Northwest, a type unlike any that lives today. They were mostly in their late forties and fifties. Some had grown gray on the plains and in the mountains, and all talked even then about the end of the good days. I began to see, and understand, that three lures—fur, gold, and grass—had brought three thin waves of white occupancy into the wilderness of the Northwest, that each had been distinctly epochal, each peculiarly selective of its own disciples, and that all had been as evanescent as the wilderness they had invaded. Their footwear characterizes the cohorts of each:

Moccasins—For more than half a century after Lewis and Clark ascended the Missouri River, fur was believed to be the only source of wealth in the Northwest, and this was supposed to be inexhaustible. It had steadily increased throughout generations of meat-eating red men who, numbered by many thousands, depended entirely upon the game and fur of their country for food, clothing, and sheltering homes, and yet a mere handful of white men wiped it nearly all away in a single generation. The immense herds of buffalo that had constantly increased in spite of Indians and packs of hungry wolves were annihilated by these whites who slaughtered buffalo by thousands for their tongues alone. I have heard white men boast of killing fat buffalo cows "just to see 'em kick," and I have seen white men kill deer by the dozen and feed them to their hogs. No wonder the Indian believes the white man to be the natural enemy of all natural things. That he kills for the thrill of taking life is a certainty, and he is shortsighted in his killing. For instance, one might as well call all men Christians as to declare that every member of the several species of the genera *Accipiter* and *Astur* are *hawks*, in the sense that the white man knows these birds; and yet he kills them all indiscriminately, even when some of them are his friends. He has nearly exterminated the badger, and now the ground squirrels, in spite of all he can do to keep them down, are destroying his crops to the tune of millions of dollars each year. In these enlightened days gun clubs give prizes and dinners to winning teams for killing the largest number of hawks and whatnot, without regard to the natural habits of the destroyed birds.

The cowhide boot—When the heyday of fur finding had passed, gold was struck on Grasshopper Creek in what is now Beaverhead County, Montana. Never before had the Rockies attracted white men in considerable numbers. Now the stampede to the gold diggings was immediate. There were two reasons for this: the Civil War had just begun and American families were divided by the questions of slavery and the South's secession; men fled from service in either of the contending armies to find peace in the wilderness, and perhaps gold. Unlike the trappers and traders, these placer miners were a heterogeneous lot, and they were gregarious as well. They established mining camps wherever they found "pay." Many of these camps grew into sizable cities that vanished with the gold in adjacent gulches. Several, more fortunately located, survive to this day. Three—Bannack City, on Grasshopper Creek, Virginia City, in Alder Gulch, and Helena, in Last Chance Gulch, served in turn as the capital of Montana Territory, the last remaining the capital of the state. This settlement by white men, that had so suddenly come to the mountains, ignored the plains. From its smugness in the East, civilization jumped across the vast stretches of grasslands to set itself up in the Rockies, and not until the pay gravel in their more famous gulches had all but petered out did many actual settlers come to the plains of the Northwest.

The riding boot—The seventies and eighties brought great herds of cattle up from Texas to Montana, the finest summer range on earth. Now the cowboy, last of the plainsmen, came into the picture. The cow-girl did not come to the cattle ranges until after the cows had gone. Every white woman who rode a horse in cowland used a sidesaddle, and wore a skirt that would make a score of the modern garments.

In the beginning the cowman was scarcely an actual settler. Like the trapper and trader and placer miner, he did not, at first, intend to build or to settle in the Northwest. Like the others, he hoped to enrich himself and then leave the country to the Indians and hungry wolves. But the glamor of the untamed wilderness laid hold of him. He fell in love with the grasslands and could not leave them. Instead, after the surveyors came, he availed himself of the Pre-emption Act, "desert-claimed," bought scrip, and in every possible way extending his landholdings until his home ranches grew into vast proportions. Prompted by him, his cowboys, always loyal to an employer and his "iron," often claimed and proved up on lands adjoining the home ranches. These cowboy claims nearly always became additions to the cowman's domains, usually "for and in consideration of the sum of one dollar to him in hand paid, etc.," so that when at last the sheepman arrived he found land barons to dispute his way.

However, it was the farmer, the "drylander," the "nester," who finally brought a new era to the Northwest that forever ended the day of the cowman. Sentiment, more than greed, set the cowman against the nester's coming. He had grown to love the wide, unpeopled plains and his life upon them. Having established himself there in the face of obstacles, he resented the entrance of farmers as an invasion of his rights. He had hated the sheepman, who, with his bands of sheep, was far more nomadic than himself. But the nester plowed and fenced the ranges which the cowman had freely used for years.

I remember riding with an old cowman along a fence that had lately been erected by a nester. Gazing sorrowfully at the freshly broken sod on the other side of the wire, my friend said: "Well, lookin' back a bit, I can see that the sheepmen wa'n't so awful bad after all. These here drylanders have made gentlemen out of 'em, by comparison." And once I saw an old cowman walk up to an aged Indian and shake his hand warmly. "Do you know him?" I asked, surprised. "No," he replied, "but I sure as hell know just how he *feels*. We cowmen run him an' his kind off the ranges, an' now the nesters have run us cowmen off."

Not many men are now living who took part in the settlement of the Flathead country, and even these do not always agree in their recollections of the events that stirred them most. They may differ from me, and yet be right. However, I was much younger than any of them, and the happenings of early Flathead days impressed me deeply. Time meant nothing to me then. As I have said, I seldom knew the day of the week or month. Sometimes I kept a notch stick, but was never slavish in my attention to it, and I usually lost it before very long. Dates will therefore not figure prominently in this story.

I have said that my first Indian acquaintance, Red-horn, had tried to tell me that he was not a Kootenai, and that he had good reason for this. The Kootenais, or Kootenahha, as they call themselves, resented the settling of the Flathead country by white men, and I began to hear stories of missing trappers. Nobody knew whether these stories were true or false, because the trappers were as nomadic as the Indians themselves. The missing men might easily have left the country. Nevertheless, these reports were disturbing. There were but few trappers in the forests and mountains of the Flathead. None of them believed strongly in danger from Kootenais, and yet all were cautious. We used no horse bells, avoided Indian camps, and were careful with our campfires.

The first real evidence I had that the Kootenais were ugly came to me one morning when with two or three pack horses I was coming down the Indian trail on Swan Lake. A band of young Kootenais crowded me and my horses off the trail, jeering as they passed. Two days later while I was in the valley a Kootenai threatened a white settler who was building a fence across an old trail. And so things drifted until the spring of 1888 (I believe) when Kootenais killed three white men on Wolf Creek and burned their bodies. Nobody in the Flathead knew that these men were in the country, so that they were not missed. Chance led to the discovery of their murder. Nearly as I can remember, a Flathead who understood the Kootenai tongue came suddenly upon a camp of these Indians at night in thick timber. Seeing their fire, Indian-like, the Flathead crept near enough to learn who had kindled it. Hidden by bushes, he overheard the Kootenais counting coup, boasting of having killed three white men on Wolf Creek, after first disarming them. Upon his arrival at the Ramsdell Post on Tobacco Plains, the Flathead told Ralph Ramsdell what he had heard at the Kootenai's fire, even furnishing the names of the killers. Ramsdell, who spoke the difficult Kootenai language fluently, mounted his horse and rode to Demersville without stopping, a distance of about ninety miles.[7] Reaching the town, he raised a posse, and with it set out to capture the killers, who were known to be camped on the ground now occupied by the Flathead County poor farm.

Led by Ramsdell, the posse silently entered the Kootenai camp, where there were several lodges; but nobody knew which lodge held the killers. The night was black dark, so that in the light of the fires inside the lodges the men could easily count the Indians in each, and yet were unable to recognize any of them. To call out would warn the culprits of their danger; to lift a lodge door and enter might prove fatal. By now the Indians had become alarmed. There was no more time to waste. The men slashed open the lodges with their knives, stuck their rifles through these openings, and in the light of the fires captured two of the wanted Indians. While the posse was securing these prisoners, a running horse with a Kootenai rider dashed out of the camp into the night. Ramsdell sprang onto his jaded horse that he had ridden from Tobacco Plains, and gave chase, firing two shots at the flying Indian, who escaped uninjured. This was either Pierre Paul or La-la-see. The others were hanged by settlers and trappers across the Flathead River from the then sprouting town of Demersville, that no longer exists. I took no part in the hanging and will not go into its details.[8] However, one of the Indians who had been hanged was a son of a Kootenai chief. We all expected real trouble now, so that when word reached us that the Kootenais had declared open war, we gathered to stand them off.

[7] Demersville, then pronounced *Demarsville*, was the terminus of steamboat travel up the Flathead River before the Great Northern Railroad came into the region in 1891. It was four or five miles southeast of present Kalispell. It was named for Jack Demers, a storekeeper there.

[8] A brother of La-la-see had been killed by a white man several years previously. In the Public Library in Missoula, Montana, is a copy of the sheriff's invitation to the hanging there on December 19, 1890, of four Indians—La-la-see, Pierre Paul, Pascal, and Antley.

I went first to Lee's Ferry (Lee's Landing), where there were now two Lees, Alvin and his brother Lincoln, who now lives with me. We decided that if the Kootenais attacked they would not attempt to cross the big Flathead River, but would come up the east shore of the lake and cross the Big Fork near its mouth, if they came into the valley at all. Both Alvin and Link Lee were natural sons of the West, and were dead shots. They declared they could take care of that point of entry into the lower valley and advised me to help the folks at the Big Fork ford. I found several men (seven, I think) and two or three white women in George Lakin's cabin near the mouth of the Big Fork, and there Lakin was elected captain of the company. He dispatched me at once to warn a family of Swedes who were building a cabin farther up the Big Fork, saying that he would send a bobsled to fetch them out. I think the month was February. Anyway, there was deep snow in the timber, where I got a bad fall. My horse, going as fast as he could in the snow, struck covered glare ice, and, bunching his feet, slid across it to pile up at its end, on top of me. I helped the man and woman pack up their belongings, mostly children and feather beds. We were ready for the bobsled when it arrived with two men. On the way out to the valley Jim Bartless and I rode ahead, John Allison walked behind the sled, and the frightened Swede drove the team.

There was no road through the country. We followed the old Indian trail that, after crossing Nigger Prairie, climbed a heavily timbered hill. Bartlett's eyes were poor; he could seldom distinguish objects at a distance, and now the light on the snow all but blinded him. "You'll have to be the eyes of this outfit, Frank," he said disgustedly, "I can't see a damned thing but snow." The bobsled and team had already marked the way in the snow when it had made the trip to the Swede's cabin, so that Bartlett and I had now only to follow the sled tracks. Sometimes, because of down timber, these tracks led us away from the Indian trail and then back into it, often making sudden turns among the firs and tamaracks. Most of the trunks of fallen trees were snow-covered, their outlines seeming to lift themselves into view on every hand.

Our walking horses made almost no sounds. Once, just after we entered the thick timber, I heard one of the children in the sled whimper and the mother rebuke it in a frightened tone.

My eyes were everywhere. Near the top of the hill the sled tracks turned suddenly out of the trail. Looking ahead, I saw where the tracks swung back again. Instead of following them in their detour, I kept on the trail. Bartlett for some reason swung off with the sled tracks, and for a moment was out of my sight. On the crest of the hill and off a little to my right was a thicket of young fir trees. In front of this, toward me, there was a huge snow-covered tree trunk. I saw that something had tracked the snow along this tree trunk on the hillside, and that whatever had made the tracks had stepped across the trunk, scraping the snow from it in a manner unlike a deer. Without taking my eyes off the down tree and the thicket, I reached the point where the sled tracks came back into the trail just as Bartlett joined me there. The down tree was not more than seventy-five yards away now, and I could see that the tracks did not enter the fir thicket. I thought it wise to ride over and learn what had marked the snow. I hadn't ridden ten feet when an Indian's head was lifted cautiously over the down tree. Instinctively I swung my horse sidewise, got down, and threw my rifle barrel across my saddle's seat. But the head had disappeared. Instead, I now saw a white capote made from a Hudson's Bay blanket.

"What it is? What is it?" whispered Bartlett, swinging from his horse.

I didn't answer. I was drawing a bead on the shoulders, when "No shoot! no shoot! Me no Kootenai! Me Plathead" relieved the situation and, I believe, saved a life. Today I have no doubt that the Indian told the truth, and yet at that time I thought perhaps he was lying like a circus bill.

Allison, who was a born pioneer, had at once turned the team around, thus sending the Swede and his family back toward Nigger Prairie, and had then hurried up to help Bartlett and me. This episode put reality into our mission. The rest of the journey was made with even greater caution, but nothing happened. We

23

reached the Lakin place with our refugees and settled down to wait for the Kootenais. The little cabin, partitioned by blankets, was overcrowded. Children fretted and men, tired by guard duty, snored on the floor. The trail up the lake crossed the Big Fork a little above its mouth. This ford was our bugbear. We watched it night and day. My tricks were from 5:00 to 7:00 P.M. and from 4:00 to 6:00 A.M., both being in dim light in the heavy timber. The river, running over shoals, made considerable noise. The wind diminished or emphasized the rippling of the swift water, so that I imagined I heard horses' hoofs across the stream. I was very young, and believe that I really wanted a little brush with the Kootenais, against whom I then felt revengeful. Standing behind a large yellow pine near the ford, I felt all the thrills a youth can know on guard duty. My orders were to fire two shots, if I could, and then make my way back to the cabin, if the Indians came. But they didn't show up, and after several days and nights of waiting we disbanded, more or less fearfully.

When I again visited my cabin on Nigger Prairie it had been entered. Some grub, steel traps, and a rifle had been stolen. Left-hand, a Flathead friend, told me that Kootenais had taken my property, and I have always believed that they did. This mention of Left-hand has stirred remembrances of two characters of early Flathead days. Left-hand, or Dominick, as he was often called, and his brother Baptiste had different portions of white blood. The former was a typical Indian, very tall and straight, with graying hair that was long and always neatly braided. Baptiste was short and portly, with bobbed hair and rings in his ears. On his chin there were perhaps two dozen long gray hairs, which he seemed to cherish, being "'ap-w'ite-man." Both spoke a most delicious pidgin English, and Chinook as well. Both were expert sign-talkers, and both belonged to the most picturesque class of breeds. They were good friends of mine. I could write a book about them.

The way was far to water on Nigger Prairie. I had to have a well. One day, after John Bartlett and I had dug twenty-two feet in search of water, old Left-hand rode out of the timber into the prairie. Seeing me at the windlass, he came to the well and, dismounting from his cayuse, looked gingerly down at Bartlett. Lefthand had never seen so deep a hole. He was astonished. "No strikum hell?" he asked, covering his mouth with his slender hand, the sign for astonishment.

"No," I said, "No strikum."

"Huh!" he grunted, again bending his long body to look down into the well. "Mebby priest damn liar. She's tell hit H'injin hell down dis-away. Tst! Tst! Tst! Twendy peet mebby, and no strikum hell. Huh!"

The old fellow sat down and lit his stone pipe, watching me hoist the dirt that Bartlett dug from the well's bottom. At last, as though he had settled a perplexing problem, he got up, and, dropping his brass-mounted Henry rifle into the hollow of his arm, said, "No 'orsses, no 'oomans, no chilluns, no meat; I guess by gar *dis* hell. Mebby priest damn liar. Mebby priest no good!"

Baptiste had a deep voice that was in perfect keeping with his bearing. He often gathered bits of United States history from me. These he would always repeat in my presence, and, like many old men of his kind, he could make a good speech. One day while I was eating my dinner alone in a new cabin farther up the Flathead valley, both Left-hand and Baptiste rode their ponies inside and began shooting up through the roof. They had been attending the first celebration of the Fourth of July at the store in the upper valley, and they were tight. I saw their condition and went on with my meal, wondering how on earth they had managed to ride their ponies through the door. The shack was filled with powder smoke and the reek of sweating horses.

"You ha'nt praid, Prank?" asked Baptiste in his deepest tones, letting another bullet tear through my pole roof.

"No," I laughed. "No good, breakum my roof," I said.

"No, no good," he laughed. "Wot's hit mean, dis pourth July, huh?"

"You savvy King George-man (Englishman)?" I asked.

"Yah."

"You savvy Boston-man (Yankee)?" I asked.

25

"Yah."

"Well. mebby one hundred snows gone now, Boston-man and King George-man, she's fightum seven snows."

"Tst, tst, tst," he clucked, deeply impressed. "Seven snows fightum! Seven snows! God! Plenty kill hit; big wan, dat fight. Me savvy pourth July. Me tell hit H'injin."

The Kootenais continued ugly. Unproved stories of their killings persisted until all trappers looked upon the Kootenais as enemies. No doubt there was truth in some of these tales, and I believe that there was some bushwhacking on both sides. Finally, a detachment of United States regulars was sent into the valley. The soldiers camped on the outskirts of the little village of Demersville, where their presence had a quieting effect throughout the whole section. I heard no more about Kootenai killings in the timber until July, when we got proof of the murder by Kootenais of at least one more white man. There was to be a celebration of the Fourth at the store at Egan[9] and another at Demersville across the river, during which the men from the lower country were to play a game of baseball with the men from the upper country. I played left field for the former.

We drove to Egan in an eleven-passenger Concord coach and a fast team of six horses belonging to Eugene Sears. Reaching the post early in the morning, we found twenty-five or thirty men assembled for the celebration there, some of them already a little tight. A big half-breed by the name of Bill Finlay was quite drunk, and on the fight. When intoxicated, Bill was a bad man. He emptied his six-shooter in all directions, swearing lustily until Ralph Ramsdell, who was acting marshal of the day, sent a Flathead Indian whom we called Antoine to quiet Finlay. I saw Antoine walk up to the big breed, saw them tussle a little, heard a muffled shot, and saw Bill double up like a ball on the ground, and roll. The Indian had shot him in the bowels. Several men carried the big man into a cabin, where he died a few hours later. And then somebody proposed that Antoine be arrested. I do not remember

9 Egan, no longer in existence, was across and down the Flathead River a short way from Demersville.

who ordered the arrest, nor do I know whether there was any legal authority present. Anyway, Antoine was handcuffed, and, to make a good job of it, "the authorities" also laid hold of a Kootenai whose name I have forgotten. These Indians were tied together and stretched out on the floor of Wilkes' saloon. "Let's hang 'em both to top off the celebration," went round for a while; and then somehow a free-for-all fight started in the saloon.

Standing on the billiard table, my moccasined feet spread wide, I watched the wildest row one can imagine. Men struck other men without cause or perceptible provocation. This madness spread like fire in a dry forest. I felt the urge to punch somebody myself. Soon shooting began. I saw the floor splinter beside the captive Indians and heard glassware shatter back of the bar. In a twinkling Charlie Wiser, who throughout the fighting sat laughing on the corner of the billiard table, and I were the only occupants of the saloon, except the now thoroughly frightened Indians on the floor. I witnessed some brutal acts during that fight. I saw one man knock another down and then kick all his teeth out with his boot heels. The poor wretch had been looking for a fight since early morning and yet did not deserve such punishment.

Outside, the fighters seemed suddenly to have come to their senses. One by one they returned to the saloon. It was now that Antoine, realizing his own danger, wished to talk. He told us where a white man (named Dunn, from Ida Grove, Iowa, I believe,) had been killed on Angel Hill.[10] Several white men saddled their horses and at once set out to prove Antoine's story. They found the remains of Dunn, partly devoured by wolves, exactly where the Indian had said. Upon the party's return to Egan, we, the celebrating citizens, signed a paper telling the world that Antoine had been tried for the killing of big Bill Finlay, and "honorably acquitted." Besides this, Antoine was so liberally treated to whiskey that he fell asleep in the street.

A Kootenai, whose Indian name I have forgotten, but who was

[10] Angel Hill is eighteen miles from Kalispell on the west side of the highway around Flathead Lake. A mile and a half farther on is Goose Bay, where the Lindermans later lived.

called Pascal, had shot Dunn late in the fall. His body had lain all winter within half a mile of my own camp on the shore of Flathead Lake, where I live today.

Now there were four known killers in the Kootenai village at Dayton creek. If I remember correctly, these were Pierre Paul, La-la-see, Antley (or Antler), and Pascal. I knew them all. Pascal was a cripple who walked with one foot turned in and on its side, the result of a bullet wound. Besides this, I think he had been shot in the knee.

About a month before we learned of the murder of Dunn, while Jim Hughes and I were yet in the camp near Angel Hill on the lake, Pascal had ridden up to our fire. Jim, who hated Indians and wanted the whole world to know it, was a hundred yards away getting a camp kettle of water from the lake. I was frying some venison when Pascal stopped his horse beside me. Standing up to talk to him in a friendly fashion, I put my hand on his pony's neck. The animal bit me savagely on the breast, and the Indian laughed. Jim, dropping his camp kettle of water, came running. "Knife him! Knife the dirty blankety-blank!"

But the Kootenai was gone into the thick timber by the time Jim reached the fire and gave me his private opinion of a white man who would permit a Kootenai to laugh at him and live.

These four Kootenais were finally hanged, and it was his remembrance of our abortive attempt to arrest them that led Jones to jog my memory that day on the street in Kalispell.

Jim Hughes' old rifle hangs over my desk as I write.[11] On its short shotgun stock is an inlay of bone which I happen to know commemorates what I have always believed to have been a revolting occasion, the so-called Fight in the Cypress Hills, where, in the hands of Jim Hughes, this rifle played a leading role.

Writing unfavorably about an early acquaintance isn't often done by decent old-timers in Montana. Many a time I have sat beside the same campfire with Hughes. Therefore I shall first confess prejudice here, and then make my story short. I gathered

[11] The rifle is now in the Johns Collection in the Montana Historical Museum in Helena. Jim Hughes later operated a lumber mill at the foot of Angel Hill.

what I know of the Fight in the Cypress Hills from Jim himself and from Black George, who had once been his partner and was later my own. I was young and impressionable then. I knew and felt Jim's attitude toward the Cypress Hills affair, and this, I am sure, forever fixed my own. Speaking of the Fight in the Cypress Hills, I have more than once heard him chuckle, "Our old buffalo guns could reach them dirty devils farther'n they could ride in half an hour."

A sketch of the story has been told, published in the second annual *Scarlet and Gold*, the magazine of the famous Northwest Mounted Police. The sketch was evidently written on the testimony and evidence introduced at the trial of Jim Hughes, Philander Vogel, and George Bell, whom the Northwest Mounted Police had arrested and taken to Winnipeg, charged with "wanton and atrocious slaughter of peaceful and inoffensive people, unsuspicious of attack, and without warning [having] shot down forty Indians in cold blood."

They were acquitted for lack of evidence. There is no doubt in my mind that our Canadian brothers, on this occasion, at least, were very lenient with their offending neighbors. My short account of the affair will differ from that of the Canadian writer, who, as I have said, got his information in court. Mine is firsthand.

Jim Hughes and twelve other white men—wolfers, buffalo hunters, and whiskey peddlers—lost some horses through theft by Indians. To avenge themselves, and at the same time secure horses, they crept, before dawn, upon an unsuspecting and guiltless camp of Crees in the Cypress Hills, during the last days of May, 1873. Here they waited for daylight, and then, when the first Indian showed himself, opened the ball. According to Black George (I am not certain that I ever heard Jimmy give the number killed) these thirteen white men killed eighty Indians (not forty), including some women and children. I will leave off here.[12]

---

[12] J. K. Howard, in *Strange Empire* (New York: Morrow and Company, 1952), p. 266, states that sixteen men from Fort Benton, after trading with Assiniboines and getting them drunk, accused them of stealing the horses, but, he asserts, the Crees actually stole them. The white men killed forty men, women, and children and wounded many others. Wallace Stegner, who as a

I should add, however, that prior to the arrest and trial of Jim Hughes, Vogel, and Bell, in Winnipeg, there had been some legal proceedings in the case at Helena, and that anybody forming his opinion from the testimony in either court might well believe the Fight in the Cypress Hills to have been a very gallant action, thirteen against many.

------

boy lived near the Cypress Hills, writes interestingly of the massacre in his book *Wolf Willow* (New York: Viking Press, 1962), pp. 74–80.

CHAPTER II

Trapping and the Free Life

ONE spring my partner and I needed a canoe for trapping beaver. There were no cottonwoods available that were of sufficient size, so we cut down a large pine tree at the foot of Swan Lake. The foot of the fallen tree was swelled, that is, the tree trunk was so ill-shapen at its base that we cut off a log sixteen feet long and then took the next cut for our dugout. The following fall I went up the Big Fork alone with this canoe, intending to trap what we then called Marten Creek, just below the foot of Swan Lake (Johnson Creek now). Reaching the foot of the lake very early in the afternoon, I camped by the log that we had cut the spring before and built my campfire against it. I intended to stay there for some time. To be comfortable, I pitched a wagon-sheet tent, without ends, besides making myself a fine bed of selected fir boughs. It was late in November. The days were bright and pleasant, the nights so wonderfully beautiful that I hated even to sleep. I had not seen an Indian on my way up, nor had I heard a rifle shot. That night, lying on my bed, belly down, my chin on my hands and my moccasins toward my fire, I was looking at the quiet water in the lake that was spattered all over with stars. The firelight did not reach more than halfway into the tent and was not reflected in the lake, and yet, back of me, I was conscious of its light and warmth. Up the lake, loons were laughing; back in the forest a timber wolf had howled two or three times. I was wondering if this wolf's voice was that of Old Sandy, a timber wolf I had more than once tried to get. I was straining my ears to catch the next howl when, as suddenly as one snuffs a candle, my firelight

31

went out, or seemed to. An Indian, a Kootenai, bent over, was standing straddle of my body in the tent, between me and my fire. Turning my head, I looked squarely into his painted face.

"How!" he said, and backed outside, seemingly a little surprised.

"How! How!" I answered as soon as I could find the words.

He knew me. We smoked together before he went away from my fire. He may not have meant mischief, and yet I feel sure that had I been a stranger, a pilgrim in the country, he would have killed me. As it was, he frightened me out of my night's sleep. Next morning I found that ten lodges of Kootenais had camped a mile or so below me, having reached their camping ground after I had passed it.

Many a time while hunting white-tail deer in heavy timber I have known that a Kootenai was following me. This always got on my nerves. Once while hunting a cedar swamp in the upper Swan Lake country I caught a Kootenai in the act of trailing me, and made him come out from behind a big tree.

At about this time I first met Black George, a trapper, who became my partner. I had ridden into Demersville, consisting then of a store owned by Jack Demers, and the saloon of Johnnie Foy. The early spring day was stormy. Sleet, driven by a north wind that iced the grass and stung my face, obliged me to ride with my head bent downward. Near the saloon my horse shied at a canvas-covered bedroll that was sheathed with ice. Leaning against the roll I saw a Winchester, its muzzle up and exposed to the storm.

"Somebody has gone on a spree and forgotten his rifle," I thought, getting down to attend to the gun that might become rusted. There was no ice in the barrel. Throwing a cartridge into its chamber, I fired it. Then, after wiping the piece as well as I could on the tail of my buckskin shirt, I shoved the rifle into the bedroll among the blankets. My horse had turned his rump to the storm. When I turned him back to lead him to the store, I saw Black George staring drunkenly at me from the saloon window. He came to the door.

"How!" he called, coming out into the storm to stand before me, his lower legs encased in tattered "Red River" leggins that had once been very fine ones. He was just under six feet tall, with long, black hair and beard that were both streaked with gray. His buckskin shirt, almost black with wear, was open far down, exposing his hairy chest. His hat was pulled down over his eyes. I noticed that his knife scabbard held no knife. Later on I learned why.

"Old hand, ain't ye," he sneered, sticking his hands under his cartridge belt flat against, his stomach. "Takin' care of my rifle for me! A damned pilgrim takin' care of Black George's rifle!"

But by now I had caught a twinkle in his half-befuddled eyes. "You'd do it for another man," I said.

"How do you know I would?" He smiled and we were friends.

Black George was a good partner. Little by little I gathered bits of his story, even his real name. He was a gunfighter. On the other side of the range where he hunted buffalo he had made a killing or two. In one of these affairs he had used his butcher knife in deadly fashion.

"I felt her go bump, bump, bump over every rib the feller had," he told me. Afterward when on a spree Black George never packed his knife. "It ain't a white man's weapon nohow," he said when he told me this story, which I have purposely abbreviated. It was said that Black George had fled from the other side—that the hangmen of 1884 had nearly "got" him in the Basin.[1] And this may be true.

The story of the doings in Montana Territory during the year 1884 is a wild one. Men whom I have known hanged more than twenty cattle rustlers in the Basin and along the Missouri and Musselshell Rivers. Besides this, they so thoroughly frightened others that they went back to the States and stayed there. Cowhands on the ranges, trappers and hunters in the Rockies, westward, differed widely in opinion regarding the action taken by these vigilantes of the cow country. Many openly called them "a bunch of dirty stranglers." Others, equally well informed, spoke

[1] Judith Basin, in central Montana.

of them as "deliverers." Nobody talked loudly, however, especially against the vigilantes. Everybody knew that Granville Stuart of the D. H. S. outfit had been chief of these plains policemen, knew about Flopping Bill, and others, on both sides of the questionable business.[2]

I knew Granville Stuart quite well. One day, years after most men had forgotten 1884, I was discussing his exceptionally exciting career with a friend who said: "I will never forget the first time I ever saw Granville Stuart. I was in a saloon at Gilt Edge with some other cowpunchers who were talking about the recent hangings on the Musselshell. One of the boys was a little tight. He kept trying to horn into our group, who had our heads together. 'What you all whisperin' fer?' he demanded. 'Granville Stuart is a dirty, murderin' old —— —— ——!' He struck the bar with his fist, for emphasis. And just then a roan horse stopped in front of the open door. I saw an old man get down from his saddle. In he came, a wiry old fellow of fifty, I reckoned. 'Will one of you point out the man who just said that Granville Stuart is a dirty, murdering, old —— —— ——?' he asked, looking us over as calmly as he might size up a bunch of culls from a beef herd. I could hear my watch ticking in my pants pocket while I waited for somebody else to ante. But nobody there wanted Graybeard's game.

"'Perhaps my ears played me a trick,' said the old man, evenly. 'Have a drink, all of you, on Granville Stuart. Set 'em up, Billy.'"

---

[2] The vigilantes of 1884 engaged in what James Fergus called the "Horse Thief War." Fergus, for whom the county in which Lewistown is located was named, wrote: "It would be well . . . to understand that the hanging, etc., of horse thieves has not been done by bands of lawless cowboys, but was the result of a general understanding among all the large cattle ranges of Montana" (Ernest Staples Osgood, *The Day of the Cattleman* [Minneapolis: University of Minnesota Press, 1929], p. 160). Theodore Roosevelt was present at the meeting of the Montana Stock Growers Association in Miles City on April 20, 1884, and supported the Marquis de Mores in his demand for a "rustlers' war." The conservative members' counsel prevailed, however, and the Association voted to take no action against the rustlers. What might be called the standard account is in Granville Stuart's *Forty Years on the Frontier* (Cleveland: Arthur H. Clark Co., 1925), II, 193–226. A good account is also in J. K. Howard's *Montana, High, Wide and Handsome* (New Haven: Yale University Press, 1943), pp. 125–137.

Black George was a slave to whiskey. I have known him, in the dead of winter, to snowshoe fifty miles to get drunk. And once after trapping all winter I heard him say to the trader who had bought his furs, "Gimme a sack of salt for a grubstake, Bill. I'll take the rest out in drinkin'-whiskey."

In his cups he was a little disagreeable, apt to be quarrelsome; yet he was always "white" with me. When at last we split the blanket because he wished to go further north, I asked him to write to me if he found fur plentiful in a country he expected to visit.

"Nope," he told me, "I ain't never wrote no letters, and I ain't goin' to begin with you."

He was a coolheaded man. I shall never forget one night when he was fighting a burly half-breed, rough and tumble. The fellow was down and had somehow managed to get Black George's right-hand thumb between his teeth. Men were thick around the pair, so that when they went down I could not see them on the dirt floor of the little saloon. Black George made no sound. I did not know what was happening until it was over. Black George never packed a six-shooter, and, as I have said, never wore a belt knife while he was drinking. Now, being unable to force the breed's jaws apart, Black George managed to get out his jackknife. This he was calmly trying to open with his teeth when somebody kicked his elbow, knocking the jackknife into the crowd. It was now that I learned what was going on. We soon made the big fellow let go the thumb, which was badly mangled. Nobody in the Northwest had then ever heard of infection. Even the worst wounds got little attention, and yet they nearly always healed quickly. Black George's thumb gave him trouble, however; it refused to heal and kept growing worse until we appealed to the surgeon who was with a detachment of United States Regulars. To show our appreciation for his services we gave him a fat cub bear.

I have said that Black George was coolheaded. He was, and yet I once saw him when he seemed to have suddenly lost his natural calmness. The cats, all of them, generally sulk in a trap. Their eyes, greened with fright, follow every move a trapper makes. Their ears are aback, their mouths open to a hissing growl, and their bodies are crouched as though for a leap. Fearsome as they appear in a trap, they are nearly always dispatched with a club. One extremely cold day George and I, who had met where our trap lines crossed each other, came to a trap that held a large lynx, not far from our cabin. "Big feller," said George, striking the animal a sharp blow on the head. "Let's us pack him to the shack where we can skin him out in comfort."

Taking a buckskin thong from his pocket, he speedily tied the near front paw to the off hind paw, and then lifted the animal up so that he might poke his own head through the loop made by the tied legs. The body of the lynx was thus under George's arm against his body, nearly halfway down his side. The head of the beast was in front, so that its tail end was towards me when I fell in behind my partner to go to the cabin. The jostling, upside down, revived the lynx. If its head had been where its tail was I might have noticed signs of returning life in time to have warned my partner; but as it wasn't, the first I knew, George's hat went flying. I cannot describe what followed. Both George and the lynx moved too swiftly for any recorder. I know that the lynx bit, spat, clawed, and growled, and that George swore strange oaths, all in a whirl of flying snow, before they came apart. "Kill him! Kill the —— ——! What you laughin' at? Want to see a feller gutted? Hell!"

I sobered instantly, and, limp from laughing, killed the lynx. Then off I went again into gales of laughter, while George, muttering, made a hurried examination of his bloody arm and breast. His buckskin shirt had saved him much, perhaps his life.

The only medicine that he packed was turpentine. I used this freely on his wounds at his direction. "I'm sorry I laughed, George," I said, honestly enough, when the cabin began to smell like a paint shop.

"S'll right, Pardner. It must hev looked right funny fer a spell, I reckon."

"It did; it *did*," I said, remembering the start and the finish, particularly.

"Hell," grunted George, pulling his shirt away from his deeply scratched breast.

I turned away from him, holding my breath against a return of my mirth. George saw this, and somehow it tickled him. He began to laugh himself, and what a blessing this was to me! We had it out now, each furnishing a new start occasionally by mentioning some incident of the fight.

"Don't never fool with 'em none," said George at last, very soberly. "Kill 'em plumb dead before ye take 'em out of a trap. Their cussed toenails can raise more hell with a man than a sharp butcher knife."

Telling about Black George and the lynx has reminded me of a winter I spent trapping on the Big Fork with another partner. Lynx, wolves, and wolverines were especially plentiful, and deer suffered accordingly. The lion is the greatest deerslayer of them all, and yet I do not believe that the mountain lion or the lynx, cats though they be, kill as wantonly as wolves and coyotes. Old Indians say that a wolf kills for fat, and a lion for meat. I know that the cats, especially the lynx, nearly always remain near a kill, which they partly cover with dirt, sticks, and leaves, until eaten.

I once took ten full-grown lynx in ten nights at such a bait. A wolf or coyote does not often lie near a kill. They eat their fill and then go on to kill again when hungry. They will, however, if meat is scarce, return to a kill. Deep, lightly crusted snow and glare ice are their allies. On the one, deer break through and flounder. On the other, they can scarcely stand, let alone run, notwithstanding the naturalist and big-game hunter who declared in the *Saturday Evening Post* that when chased by wolves in winter, deer seek the glare ice on forest lakes where their "sharp little hoofs dig in" and beat the wolves. This is a mistake. Instead of harassed deer *seeking* glare ice, or any kind of ice, they instinctively *avoid* it, and only take to it when driven there by wolves that instinctively know their quarry cannot get away from them when once they are on ice. It is always the wolf and not the deer who chooses ice for such a chase, when he can. I do not mean to say that the wolf can run *well* on glare ice, he cannot; but the deer cannot run at all.

During this particular winter I saw a lynx spring from a spruce tree onto the back of a large doe standing on glare ice. The doe had been trying to get a drink of water, I think. Anyhow, when I first saw her she was walking gingerly on the glare ice toward a narrow strip of swift-running open water that was between icy spaces on either side, the center of the river itself. I was dragging a deer to camp along the ice across from the deer, which paid not the slightest attention to me. She was in the open with nothing between us excepting the ice and the strip of rushing water, the whole distance from the doe to myself not exceeding sixty yards. I had stopped to watch her awkward, slipping steps, and did not notice the leaning spruce tree until, like an arrow, the lynx shot out of its top onto the doe's neck and shoulders. Down she went, of course, floundering desperately for her footing, the teeth of the lynx tearing at her throat. I shot the lynx. The doe, relieved, scrambled to the shore, and into the timber, leaving a little blood and much hair on the snow. All this happened quickly, within thirty seconds, perhaps; and yet if my bullet had not ended him, the lynx would have killed the doe, even though she carried him into the timber before she died. The lynx had been in the leaning spruce when the doe came beneath its top, which was out over the ice quite a distance. He had been so intent on killing the doe that he had not seen me; or if he saw me he gave my presence no consideration. I have always believed that where man is concerned the lynx is bolder than the mountain lion, who, though much larger and stronger, seems to be a greater coward.

I got a needed lesson in woodcraft that winter. My partner had gone to the settlement for a spree. So far as I knew, there was no other white man in the country. The river was frozen over for more than two miles above our camp and for several miles below it. Across from our cabin there was thick spruce timber. One day while my partner was away I crossed the river on the ice, and then put on my bear paws to hunt a deer for fresh meat. Sign was scarce. It was late in the afternoon when I ran across a deer that appeared to be in good condition and killed it. Darkness was coming on when I cut straight for the river, dragging my deer. It was pitch-dark when I came out onto the frozen stream that ran in every direction through the heavy forest. I knew that I was downstream from camp and that I must go up the river, but which way was the stream running? The snow-covered ice was perfectly level. Either way might be upstream as far as anybody could see. The sky was as black as the timber itself, so that there were no stars. I noted the trees, but they told me nothing. I even began to hack a hole through the thick ice with my butcher knife, intending to feel the sluggish current; but this proved too great an undertaking. Finally, on a dead guess, I started out, dragging my deer. I turned bend after bend in the river, some of them regular oxbows, in the dark forest, without seeing a familiar thing until near midnight, when I began to recognize the country. An hour later I reached the cabin. Imagine my surprise to find a bright fire burning in the mud fireplace, and Hank Jennings, the red-headed giant, seated on my bunk.

"Git lost?" he asked kindly, "I been a-listenin' fer a shot ever since it got dark."

"No," I said, "I wasn't lost, but I couldn't tell which way this confounded river was running when I struck it miles below here. It was all snow-covered and alike, so that I couldn't tell. It was too dark to see the mountains. I knew, of course, that I wanted to go upstream, but there was no way I could learn which way the river was running, you see."

"Humph!" grunted Hank, cutting tobacco for his pipe.

"And this river is so darned crooked here in this timber that it takes a long time to get anywhere," I added, hanging up my snowshoes.

"Humph!"

"Besides, I knew I ought soon to recognize the country. If I hadn't, I should have had to turn back."

"Humph!"

By now I realized that there had been a trace of disgust in all

39

these "humphs" of Hank's. "Could *you* have told how this river was running?" I challenged, a little irritated.

"I reckon," he said, lighting his pipe. "Whoa! Now don't let yer critter's tail git over the dashboard. Listen, an' answer, so's ye'll l'arn. This here's the *same* river ye git yer cookin' water out of, ain't it?"

"Yes, of course, but——."

"Hold!" Hank pointed his pipestem at me, a smile on his thin lips. "When ye dip yer camp kittle into it, which way's the water runnin'?"

"To my right," I answered, shortly.

"If, when ye crossed it this mornin', you'd stopped an' dipped in yer kittle through a hole in the ice, which way would the water a-been runnin', you bein' on 'tother side from here?"

"To my left," I answered, sorely irritated.

"Did ye cross the river *ag'in, anytime* today, Pardner?"

"No," I said, wondering a little by now.

"Then, no matter when ner whar ye struck it, above this here camp, er twenty mile below it, this here river would a-been runnin' to yer left, wouldn't it, Pardner?"

"Thank you, Hank! I'll remember," I promised, feeling very small and incompetent just then.

Often since that night I have submitted the problem of the snow-covered river to others for solution. Nobody has correctly solved it, and yet a good woodsman ought to know.

I believe it was the spring I met Black George that the Kootenais stole four horses from me, took them from their winter range on the shore of Flathead Lake. I determined to recover them. Having a good horse and a little Spanish mule on another range farther up the country, a long day's walk from my camp on the lake, I went after them afoot. Securing the pair, I returned to camp, put a light pack on the mule, and struck out for the Kootenai country. The month was April, the weather unusually stormy and cold. I had long intended to "squat" on a piece of land about where the little village of Rollins stands today, so that when I reached this coveted spot I camped for the night, with the sun yet two hours high. I used the remaining daylight to lay up a foundation three logs high all around, snaking in the light timber by the horn of my saddle. I cooked and ate my supper, spread my blankets, tied my horse and mule to a big pine tree at the head of my bed, and turned in. The main camp of the Kootenais was at Dayton Creek, only a few miles away. I counted on reaching it very early in the morning. We never undressed to go to bed in those days, except our feet. That night I wore all my clothes, even my chaps and six-shooter. A strong northerly wind made breakers roar on the beach of the big lake not far from my bed, and soon a fine rain began to fall. I had whittled some fat pitch shavings for a quick fire in the morning, and now when the rain began to fall on my face I scraped them under the edge of my blankets to keep them dry. I had felt tired when I bedded down, and in a few minutes slept soundly. Sometime near midnight I was wakened by the thud of horses' hoofs. The night was black as the inside of a buffalo bull when I sat up to listen. The only thing I saw was a single glowing ember of my campfire, about as large as one's fist, which the gusty wind had kept alive.

"How!" came a voice out of the blackness and rain.

"How—How—Ho-hi-eee!" I replied cheerily, getting up with the pitch shavings in my hand. These I dropped on the live ember of fire, and then walked up to the shadowy form of a horse a few feet away. Stepping up close, I put my hand on the horse's neck to look into the rider's face. My hand felt a roached mane! Indians never roached their horses. One of my lost horses had had a roached mane when I turned him out in the fall. He was a white horse, my pet pack animal; but a white horse is difficult to see at night. Suspicious, I bent down to look at the animal's head—and just then the pitch shavings caught fire. The Kootenai was riding my horse, Old Stub! The other visitor was a woman, who, in the bright light of the burning pitch shavings, smiled at me from the back of the best horse I ever owned. But we didn't get along. They left my camp with their saddles on their own backs.

Tying the recovered horses to the tree with my horse and mule, I turned in again. My bed was dry. I had taken care not to

41

uncover it when my callers arrived; yet I did not sleep any more. I fully expected the trouble that came with the daylight—forty Kootenais, who surrounded my camp, tore down and burned my foundation, and otherwise misbehaved. One even slapped my mouth with the back of his hand. My back was against the pine tree, and when he slapped me the muzzle of my cocked Colt six-shooter wasn't two inches from his belly. He counted a fine coup on me, did that Kootenai, and now when I look back, I respect him for his bravery. But at the time, in my anger, I ached to kill him in his tracks. However, I saw that no matter how far I got with my Colt they'd get me in the end, and took his insult.

"De Chief (called Aeneas; Big-knife was his name)[3] she say you gotta go 'way prom 'ere now," said a half-breed on the outskirts of my circle of entertainers.

"You tell him I'm going on down to the Frenchman's at Dayton Creek. Tell him I'll wait there till his people bring in two more horses they stole from me. When I get my horses I will go back up the country where I came from. You tell him," I replied.

"She say you gotta go now de odder way, de Chief," came the cheerful message, after the breed had repeated what I had said.

While they jabbered among themselves I saddled up, got the pack on the mule, and pulled out, the recovered horses "tailed" to the mule. The Kootenais followed me to the Frenchman's camp, where they did some fancy riding and wild shooting; but in the end they brought in my missing horses.

When I left the Frenchman's with my outfit, the Kootenais

[3] Linderman wrote in the "Tenth Annual Report of the Water Department of the City of Kalispell" (December 31, 1923): "Aeneas was the old chief of the Kootenais, a full-blooded Iroquois. Probably named by the missionaries because, like Aeneas of the Iliad, he was a man without a country. He was probably employed by the Hudson's Bay Company to carry messages to parts in the West as far as the Pacific Ocean. He counseled peace, even when his son had been hanged by white men, yet he hated the white man. I do not hold Aeneas in high regard, for of all Indians I have known he was the only one with whom I had trouble."

Jean P. Smith records this incident: "I asked the author [Linderman] as he stood beside his open fire in his red voyageur's cincture about the portrait of Aeneas [that hung on the wall]. 'Oh, he slapped my mouth once. That's Big Knife. He wanted me to leave the country.' Linderman chuckled reminiscently, 'And by George, I did!'" (*Frontier*, XI [November 1930], 59).

followed me every step of the way to the foot of Angel Hill, singing lustily just behind me in the drizzling rain. The way was for the most part through heavy timber, with now and then an open patch where the trailing chorus was sure to swell in volume. I knew they were singing because they felt they had won a victory. I did a little *humming*, myself, and I wasn't at all sorry when they turned back. Riding alone through that timber in the rain, handling five horses and a mule, with a band of singing Kootenais behind me hadn't been a joyful business.

Having nothing to do until it was time to join Black George in our winter quarters, I worked for a cow outfit owned by half-breed brothers named McDonald, in the Little Bitterroot country, which was not far from the Kootenai camp. A man called Little Joe and I occupied a cabin near the foothills. During the summer we saw no white men; and every Kootenai that came our way was ugly as a tormented badger. All through the summer, which was hot and dry, I felt worried, and at last I got a good scare.

I had a Sharps rifle, .44-77, which would sometimes pull the head off a discharged shell. One day I killed a deer with it, not far from the cabin occupied by myself and partner. When I discovered that the headless shell was stuck fast in its chamber, I packed the rifle to camp and laid it on my bunk, intending to dig out the shell as soon as my deer was cared for, but forgot it until midnight. Then I remembered with a pang of regret I shall never forget. The month was September. The moon was full and very bright when I was aroused from sleep by a yell that sent shivers up my back. Springing from my bunk, I ran to the open door. One look was enough. A long line of horsemen was riding toward the cabin, yelling like madmen. Kootenais! We were in for it; and there was a shell stuck fast in the chamber of my Sharps. "Joe! Joe! Turn out. We're jumped!" I called.

There was a bar that one could drop against the closed door, and another which fastened a hinged window shutter. I slammed them both into place.

"What's the matter?" asked my sleepy partner, mechanically reaching for his Winchester.

43

There was no need for a reply. The cabin was surrounded. I could hear the heavy breathing of horses and the tramping of their hoofs. I remember that a thin streak of moonlight came into the dark cabin through a crack between the logs and shone on the stock of my crippled Sharps. I had a good Colt six-shooter, however, and was buckling its cartridge belt about my waist when a voice outside said, "Oh, Frank! Oh, Mex-skim-yo-peek-kinny!" (Iron-tooth, my Piegan name).

But they were Kootenais, outside. They *must* be. The only white man within a day's ride was a Frenchman on Dayton Creek, and he spoke very little English.

"Don't answer," I whispered, trying desperately to see through a crack between the cabin logs.

"Oh, Mex-skim-yo-peek-kinny!" called the voice again. "Open hup de door, Frank! Sacre Bleu! We're 'ongry lak hell."

A chorus of wild laughter greeted me when I finally opened the door to Big Angus McDonald, whose brother, Archie, owned the cabin we occupied. Ten other breeds were with him, and each led his string of horses to be used in the roundup which we began next morning. The eleven riders, each leading extra horses, the tricky moonlight, my sleepy mind, my crippled Sharps, and no doubt my thoughts of the threatened trouble with Kootenais all contributed liberally to make the prospects for a fight seem very real. For more than a year the joke was on me. But the jokers never knew how remarkably well their joke functioned that night on the Little Bitterroot.

A man's life is but a short span of the years, and Montana is a vast country. No one man could see all that happened here, even in his own time. I have never wished to write these memoirs, but having told these episodes, I can see that I have much more to tell of the times when the wilderness was being cut to the measure of civilization.

Montana became a state in 1889.[4] Up to this time the Flathead country lying on the western slope of the Rockies in the state's northwestern corner had attracted few white settlers. For the

---

[4] Linderman later reported that on this occasion Alvin Lee, with whom he worked, said, "Now she's gone to hell"; and he added, "And I believed him."

most part it was a heavily timbered section, so that its grasslands were not extensive enough for large cow outfits; and in it there was no gold. Besides, it had never been buffalo country. Its Indian tribes, the Flatheads (Salish) and Kootenais, or Kootena-hahas, had always been obliged to cross the mountains for buffalo. These excursions had kept them at war with the plains tribes, particularly with the Blackfeet, for generations, and at the same time strengthened the friendship between the Flatheads and Kootenais. Besides a few trappers, buffalo hunters, and "Cayuse" or "Coyote" Frenchmen who had spent years on the "east side," the first white settlers of Flathead valley were mostly quartz miners from Nevada and Butte City. Without the least knowledge of farming these men, many of them confirmed bachelors, took up claims and became farmers as though they had reached the realization of a lifelong dream. In handling horses, swinging an axe, or killing their meat in the forests most of them were pitiably incompetent; and yet in questions where law and order required a hand these men were never wanting. Their cabins began to dot the beautiful valley in the middle eighties. Finally, small patches of plowed ground fenced in by fir rails appeared, the only section in all Montana where old-fashioned stake-and-rider rail fencing was used exclusively. These miner-farmers not only respected a neighbor's claim to land, but in the claimant's absence were ready to defend it.

I remember an instance of this loyalty. One of their number had gone "outside" to work in the mines of Butte, so that he might earn money with which to purchase a team and farming machinery. While the fellow was away a pilgrim jumped his claim. A few days later five or six of the absentee's neighbors rode to the jumped claim and called upon the jumper.

"Do you claim this land?" asked their spokesman, pleasantly.

"No, sir," replied the jumper, realizing that behind the softly spoken words of his callers there was something ominous.

"Right nice day, aint it?" offered the first speaker, getting down from his horse. "I should think that in such nice weather you'd rather camp outdoors instead of in that cabin."

45

"I would. I'm going to move camp down to the Big Fork this afternoon. Was there something you men wanted?" he finished a little nervously.

"Yis, by Gob, there is, there is," blurted one of their number who had wearied of his leader's diplomacy. "We hear that ye've jumped old Bill's claim, and by Gob we're here to lynch yez off'n it. Git!"

All supplies came into the valley from Missoula, about 140 miles distant. Freighters and packers brought most of the goods to the foot of Flathead Lake, where it was transferred to the little steamboat *U. S. Grant*, that had lately been the sailboat *Swan*. The boat carried it to the head of the lake, and then up the Flathead River to Demersville. I did a little of this freighting myself. The man who owned the outfit that I handled had made a killing back in the States, and had changed his name upon coming to Montana Territory. The Indians called him Crazy-horse, and Crazy-horse will do here as well as any other name. He had two ten-horse teams of cayuses on the trail between the railroad and the foot of Flathead Lake, each pulling a lead and a trail wagon. The freighter (driver) rode his near wheeler and handled a jerk-line and the brake-rope from his saddle. Late one afternoon when a drizzling rain had soaked through my clothes, and the wagons were crawling like turtles through deep mud, Crazy-horse, who was his own wagon boss, rode up alongside of me with a half-breed.

"Let this man have your gun, Frank," he said. "He's in bad trouble. The Indians are after him because he told who killed some white men on the Jocko."

"No," I said, "I'll keep my gun. Let him have yours, if you want to heel him."

"Mine's in the other wagons, and they are somewhere between here and Post Creek," declared Crazy-horse.

At this the breed, badly frightened, began to blubber. Nevertheless, I kept my six-shooter, and the breed headed away toward the mountains.

Crazy-horse continued beside me until I pulled into camp on

Crow Creek. He slept with me. In the middle of the night he shook my arm. "Frank, Frank," he whispered, "the wagons are full of Indians."

I sat up in the drizzle, everything about our blankets black as the bottom of a camp kettle. "What?" I whispered, thinking that I could not have heard correctly.

"Wagons are full of Indians, and I haven't even a knife. Lemme have yours. Here, gimme—Come on!"

He began to creep in the direction of the wagons, invisible as though they were in China. I followed with my gun, every step of my knees settling deeper into the oozy mud and water. I saw nothing, heard nothing, except the slither of mud beneath my hands and knees, until we reached the trail wagon. We crept along its mud-caked wheels to the trail-tongue, where Crazy-horse stopped so suddenly that my face bumped his hip pockets.

"By God," he said, in a natural voice, standing up, "I'd have sworn I saw 'em." He had been dreaming.

I believe it was the spring of 1886 that Henry Therriault, a Canadian Frenchman, opened a store at Selish, a few miles below Demersville on the Flathead River, where the steamboat *U. S. Grant* landed required freight. One day in '87 or '88 Therriault sent for me. I went to the store to see him. I do not remember ever having spoken to the man before, and yet after an hour's conversation he engaged me to handle his business for him while he visited the Coeur d'Alene country. He was gone two months.

Next to the store, which was built of hewn logs, there was a rough cabin that Therriault used as a saloon. His brother George, who could neither read nor write, kept the little ginmill, and Henry's final instructions concerned his brother, the saloonkeeper: "You take and count his money every night. Try to keep his business straight for him," he said. This did not mean that George needed watching, but that in keeping accounts the fellow was incompetent. This arrangement threw George and me together evenings, and our friendship grew strong. He was a powerful man, and I think would have done murder in my behalf. The patrons of both the saloon and store were few, so that I spent

47

much of my time hunting ruffed grouse and deer across the Flat-head River, which is about one-quarter of a mile wide at that point. Sometimes when I returned from several hours in the timber on the other side of the stream I found a pack train waiting for supplies. There was never any faultfinding, however. Men then had plenty of time. When finally the goods were ordered and paid for I always helped my customers pack their horses, visiting with them while we worked.

One day two strangers came to the saloon. One of them, a very tall man of about thirty-five years, got tight within an hour and began to shoot out through the door into the river, and even through the glass of the single window. His partner, seemingly afraid of him, kept out of his way, slumping down on a log stool in the saloon's corner, pretending to sleep. I wanted a drink of fresh water. Taking the pail from the store, I walked to the river a few yards back of the saloon. Returning with the water, I passed the saloon's front door, where the obstreperous stranger hailed me. "Come in, an' have a drink with me, Pardner," he called.

"Thank's, but I don't drink," I replied, going on with my pail.

"Whoah!" The big fellow sprang out of the door and grabbed my arm. The water slopped, and the pail slipped from my hand, soaking my left leg and moccasins.

"Come on, son," he growled, pulling me backward through the saloon's door to the rough bar. "Whiskey!" he demanded.

George set out the bar bottle and two whiskey glasses, but the stranger was dissatisfied. "No, no. None o' that size. We want a drink, me an' my pardner," he said, stepping around the end of the bar for a beer glass. This he nearly filled with whiskey. "Here ye are, son. Down her," he laughed in seeming good nature.

I began to explain.

"Down her!" My host's manner changed instantly. His hold on my arm tightened. "Down her!" The muzzle of his cocked six-shooter was pressed against my cheek.

I drank the whiskey at a gulp, and never felt it. While the glass was at my lips I heard a thud; the big fellow was on the floor. George Therriault had struck him with a beer bottle.

Tableau. The fellow's partner, now quite awake, stood with George and me looking down at his fallen companion, whose forehead was bloody. The badman's hat, with its rattlesnake hatband, had fallen into a box of sand used as a spittoon.

"Where's my horse?" he whimpered when he began to recover from George's blow. Sitting up, he reached dizzily for his six-shooter that was lying, cocked, on the floor near him; but I beat him to it. Setting its hammer, I walked to the back door of the saloon and sent it flying out into the Flathead River. He didn't even protest. I heard afterward that he attributed the blow that felled him to me, and that he declared he'd "get" me. But his threat did not worry me.

The Flathead country, being the last section of Montana Territory to settle, attracted many shady characters. Nobody asked questions of strangers. I have been intimately acquainted with men whose names I never knew. There were Shorties and Fatties and whatnot, who appeared and disappeared like spring flowers. One morning I was raking hay for a half-breed on the Flathead reservation at the foot of the lake. Beneath my seat on the rake I had swung my rifle, an old Henry .44-40 rim-fire. The trail from the upper country cut close in to the fence that enclosed the small hayfield. When I turned my mule on one of my rounds I saw a horseman waiting for me at the fence.

"What you shooting, partner?" he called.

"Henry .44-40 rim-fire," I answered, stopping my mule.

This information seemed to disappoint the fellow, who wore new store clothes and looked very fine. His saddle was new and squeaky. His rifle, lying across in front of him, was a brand new Winchester.

"Got any cartridges for your Henry?" he finally asked.

"Yes," I replied, "about a beltful."

"How'll you trade rifles?" he asked, getting down and climbing the fence to fetch his rifle for my inspection. It was a .45-60 Winchester, '76 Model, without a blemish.

"Even," I said, suspecting that the fellow was out of ammunition, and that this was his reason for proposing the trade.

Pumping a cartridge into the chamber of my Henry, the stranger tried a shot at a spot on a rail of the fence. "All right," he said, handing over his rifle, which was worth three of mine. "There's a cartridge in its chamber, and one more in the magazine," he told me, getting onto his horse.

Where he came from, or whither he went with my old Henry, remain unanswered questions. I have never doubted that he was "on the trail" and sorely needed ammunition.

Demersville, at the head of navigation on the Flathead River, had grown a little by now. There were perhaps fifteen or twenty permanent citizens in the village when a Kootenai Indian ran amuck there. Crazed by whiskey, the Indian tried to enter a cabin after dark where a woman, named Mrs. Rich, and a little boy were alone. Rich himself was away from home. The Indian had his knee in the doorway, and the frightened woman and little boy were trying desperately to shut the door against him when a rifle shot rang out. The Kootenai crumpled into a heap outside. The door, relieved of the pressing knee, went shut with a satisfying slam. Nobody then knew who had fired the shot. Mrs Rich said that she had seen its flash through the window, but declared that she had seen nobody outside.

News of this killing sped to the Kootenai camp on Ashley to goad its young bloods. Burning for revenge, a party of these rode into Demersville and demanded the person of George Rich, who was supposed by them to have fired the fatal shot. But Rich was not available. I have often wondered what might have transpired if he had been about, since the villagers were badly frightened. To appease the Kootenais, who threatened to burn the town, they promised to locate and deliver Rich at daylight the next morning; the Indians were to come for him at daylight. With this understanding the Kootenais took the dead man and departed to await the morning.

The Indians gone, the citizens of Demersville lost no time in sending for help. Several messengers were dispatched in as many directions. These horsemen engaged others, so that news of the situation in the valley's metropolis was quickly spread. I was camped on the Big Fork, near its mouth, and lost no time getting to Demersville, where pickets stopped me on its outskirts near midnight. The Missoula Mercantile Company's store, that had only lately been taken over from its founder, Jack Demers, was headquarters for the town's defenders. A shadowy man, with a candlestick all lumpy with candle grease, tiptoed behind the counter there and gave me one hundred rounds of ammunition to fit my rifle and a blanket. I thought he looked frightened as a cottontail rabbit. I filled my cartridge belt, and my pockets besides, leaving the empty cartridge boxes on the counter. War or no war, ammunition cost money. My blanket smelled new and was prickly. Nevertheless, I stretched myself on the floor for a nap, wondering how many men had already reached the town. I remember that a new arrival who entered the store in the darkness stepped squarely upon my stomach. A 3:30 I felt a hand on my shoulder. "Guard duty," whispered a voice whose breath smelled of whiskey.

Slipping quietly outside, I met a trapper whom I knew, and who I believe is yet living. He was standing by the door as though waiting for me. "Want to see you a minute," he whispered, falling in beside me to walk toward my station. "Ten of us mountain men have made up our minds to settle this Kootenai question this time," he went on. "You are the eleventh and last man to be let in on it. I'm goin' to shoot the old chief right where his belt buckles as soon as they come in after Rich. We'll make these farmer-folks fight today, and have this thing over with, or get licked. Soon's you see 'em comin' git as close to me as you can; then we'll all be together. And don't say a word about this to anybody."

I was rather glad of the scheme. The Kootenais had been a menace to us who spent much time alone in the hills. I realized that if the ten conspirators confided their plan to others, somebody would block it; and yet I did not like the idea of forcing a fight in this manner. However, I went out to join my companion, who was to stand guard with me, without knowing if he, too, happened to be one of the chosen. I've forgotten the month. However, I know

51

that it was early fall and that daylight came on between five and six o'clock. It was yet too dark to distinguish objects very far away when my partner, Michel Therriault, said, "Look, here they come."

Looking toward Ashley Creek, where the Kootenais were camped, I saw horsemen coming. Without further investigation we ran back, as ordered, to join the men at the store, who were up and outside the building. I saw my trapper friend and stopped beside him. But the horsemen we had seen proved to be several half-breeds who had been in the Indian camp. They had come in to tell us that the Kootenais, having seen reinforcements enter Demersville, had decamped in the night.

Relieved of the tension, some of the men now got drunk at the town's expense. I remember that somebody drew up a set of resolutions. The preamble was quite flowery. When they finally reached the "resolves," one line declared that if the government did not take immediate steps to curb the Kootenais, the settlers would do so themselves, "and so protect our homes from the ravages of a savage foe." I wish that I had a copy of those resolutions before me.

The arrogance of the Kootenais in demanding the person of a white citizen of Demersville thoroughly aroused the settlers in the valley. The Indian's threat to burn the town hung over the infant community night and day. The men on the little steamboat *U. S. Grant* carried rifles, and when traversing the river, flowing mostly through heavy timber, expected to be attacked. Nobody, especially those who were in the hills or in the timber, felt secure.

I was serving as hunter (killing fresh meat) for a government outfit that was surveying the valley when word reached me that a party of men was going at once to try to capture the Kootenai killers, who were supposed to be in the Indian camp at Dayton Creek, and that Bill Houston, the sheriff, had come up from Missoula to lead it. I felt that I ought to go with this posse, but my horses were all out on the open range. The engineer in charge of the outfit refused to let me have a horse, saying that I was employed by the United States government and must not leave him.

Nevertheless, I struck out afoot for the Ramsdell store at Egan, where I arrived quite late at night. Billy Ramsdell readily staked me to a horse and saddle, and I went on to Demersville. But the party had already gone. It must have been nearly eleven o'clock when I headed away for the trail down the big lake, riding as fast as I could and yet save my horse for the long trip. Entering the dark timber I kept my cayuse on an "Injin trot" wherever the going would permit, thinking of the other posses that had tried to capture the outlaws.

There had been two attempts, and both had failed. The first had been captained by carelessness. I have forgotten many of the details now. However, I am sure that the month was February, and that forty-five men left Demersville on the same errand that we now had in hand. I cannot fix the date. But it was very soon after the execution of the Indians just across the river from Demersville, because the bodies of the Kootenais were yet hanging when the posse left the valley. Armed mostly with Winchesters, the posse rode without cartridges in the chambers of its rifles until the Indian camp was sighted. Then, upon being commanded to load, one of the men (I well remember his name) shot Billy Ramsdell's horse, breaking a leg. If this blundering accident had occurred after the posse had entered the Indian camp, the shot would have been mistaken for a signal to fight, and then none of the party could have escaped. As it was, the whole outfit was trapped like a rat. Its members were defied and insulted. To show his contempt for white men the Kootenai chief seized Billy Ramsdell, the interpreter, and shook him until his ribs rattled. Words from the old chief's tongue were hot.

The situation was tense as a fiddlestring when Ed Truman, who was as deaf as a boulder, blurted out, "If she's goin' to start, gimme a sign, Bill. I got three of the dirty beggers dead in line." There were several half-breeds within hearing, and besides these, there were full-bloods there who understood English. Instantly the gunlocks began to click, the black eyes to blaze. Raising his hand for peace, Billy Ramsdell began to speak rapidly in Kootenai. Somehow he managed to patch up the trouble. Forgetting his ignominious shaking by the chief, he not only saved himself but the whole company. Billy and the chief parleyed. Then the Indians and the posse lined up, facing each other, to fire a salute celebrating the peace between them. But some of the angry Kootenais fired rather low, so low that their bullets barely missed the heads of two white men, I remember.

The second posse, like the one I was following now, riding at night, reached the Indian camp at daybreak only to find the Kootenais waiting for it. The whites were told that the killers were somewhere in the mountains. There was nothing for the company to do except to turn back for the upper valley. Such was the temper of the Kootenais and such had been the fortune of the other posses that had tried to take La-la-see, Pierre Paul, Antley, and Pascal. I wondered if we, led by the sheriff, would have better luck. I wished that Billy Ramsdell were with us. However, I was riding Bill's horse. There might be luck in this. The men ahead of me had taken the old Kootenai trail about midway between the valley and Dayton Creek. I caught up with them at Big Lodge, where the little village of Rollins now stands, falling in behind.

Just as day was breaking we came to the camp. The sheriff divided us, and we surrounded the lodges, riding in closely, as ordered. Chosen men began at once to search for the killers; but they were not in the camp. However, because he had been protecting outlaws, the sheriff arrested the chief himself. I shall never forget the scene. Coming out of his lodge, the old man snapped his rifle in the face of a deputy sheriff. Luckily the cartridge was defective, or the gun spring weak, so that the primer did not explode. It was all over in a minute. The sheriff, with several picked men of the posse, started at once for Missoula with the Kootenai chief a prisoner. But at the foot of the lake, where the city of Polson stands now, the old Indian weakened. Promised his liberty if he handed over the culprits, the chief sent out several Kootenais, who brought in but one of the killers, Pascal. Nevertheless, the sheriff let the old chief go. Later on, the other killers were taken, delivered up by the chief, who saw at last that he could not harbor them. They were all hanged in Missoula.

Frank Linderman at the age of sixteen, just before he went west.

The cabin which Linderman and his future brother-in-law, Sam Johns, shared, built in 1886. Pictured is Sam Johns.

Demersville, Montana, about 1890.

Frank Linderman and Mrs. Linderman at the time of their marriage in 1893.

The office of *The Chinook*. Linderman is standing in the doorway, in the long printer's apron.

Contemporary cartoon showing Senator Thomas H. Carter knocking down the "Indians." Linderman is at lower left.

The Lindermans' home at Goose Bay, on Flathead Lake.

Frank Linderman, from a drawing made by Carl Link in 1937.

All the men in this posse, excepting myself, were deputized before leaving Demersville. We who turned back from the Kootenai camp did not then know that the chief had weakened, that he had promised the sheriff to give up the wanted men, so that our accomplishments did not seem very satisfying. Almost the first man I saw in the posse, after catching up to it, was my bitterest enemy, a man I distrusted, and feared not a little. Somehow one does not expect to find his enemies espousing a common cause with himself. This man's presence gave me something to think about besides Kootenais. He was a Spaniard of unusual proportions. I watched him constantly.

Earlier that year I had had to cross the South Fork of the Flathead in flood water. My partner had not relished the prospect of using a raft for our packs on the swift stream. To appease him I borrowed a canoe from a friend who had lately built a cabin just above our camp. I had tried to buy the canoe, because I expected to take several pack trains up that way during the coming months. But my friend had not then wished to sell it. "The canoe is here for you anytime," he had said. "Consider it your own whenever you wish to use it."

First swimming our horses, we crossed our goods in the canoe, and then left it, going on up the South Fork to some coal claims that we had located the year before. My claim had been jumped by a confederacy of which this Spaniard was a member. There had been high arguments, stirring up bad blood between us; but I had, nevertheless, managed to hold my claim. A month later I came back down the South Fork trail alone with eight pack horses whose only loads were the pack gear and my camp equipage. Reaching the crossing place where I had left the canoe, I unsaddled the horses and then jumped them into the river, watching until they had all climbed out on the other shore. Then I went after the canoe, intending to load it with the packsaddles, mantles, and camp outfit, and take them across in one load. But the canoe was gone. Somebody other than my friend had moved it from its hiding place. Hurrying along down the shore in search of the canoe, I came suddenly upon a camp of men sitting around a fire, among them this Spaniard. I didn't stop to talk with any of them. If I lingered my horses might travel toward the valley. Then I should be obliged to follow them afoot. Seeing the canoe pulled up on a gravelly beach, I walked straight to it. I had no sooner taken hold of it than the big fellow, who evidently thought I was unarmed because I packed no rifle, confronted me.

"Get away from that canoe!" he called, angrily, drawing a bowie knife from its sheath on his belt.

I'd left my rifle with my packs, which, as was custom, I had strung in a circle on the ground, each saddle and gear by itself. However, I had a .44 Smith & Wesson six-shooter on my belt that was hidden by my mackinaw jacket. I pulled it. "Stop where you are!" I said, the gun pointed at him.

He stopped and then began to roll up his sleeve, showing a huge hairy arm. "Put away your gun, and fight me like a man," he challenged, stooping a little, and again moving toward me.

"Stop!" I said, a second time. "If you take another step I'll kill you."

I knew I could not alone manage both the canoe and the Spaniard, so that I began to back toward my outfit, followed by the man with the knife. Stepping, at last, within the circle made by my packs, which in those days was considered a man's own ground, I again stopped the Spaniard. Keeping him covered, I called to a friendly Frenchman in the camp. He came gingerly into view. "Felix," I called, without taking my eyes from the Spaniard, "put my outfit into the canoe for me." The Frenchman complied, even taking my rifle, which I had had no opportunity to pick up. Backing to the river and into the canoe, I kept the big fellow standing where he was until we were safely across the river. I dared not even turn my head. If I had given him the chance the fellow would have raced to the camp for his rifle. On the way over the river, which is not very wide, I spoke to my friend, the Frenchman, who was just behind me with the paddle. "Felix," I said, "why do you, a white man, travel with a low-down character like that Spaniard?"

His reply furnished me with thought for a long time. "Well,

Frank," he replied in pidgin English, "she's halways pleasánt wid me, dat man."

I did not know that the Spaniard had bought the canoe from my friend while I was up the river. And the Spaniard did not know that my old-fashioned Smith & Wesson contained but a single cartridge in its cylinder that rolled about whenever it pleased, that I might have had to snap the weapon five times before the hammer found the cartridge, thus giving him time to use his knife. If I had known that the canoe belonged to the Spaniard I would have crossed the South Fork as I have crossed many another stream, without a canoe. But he did not wish me to know that the canoe was his property. He had deliberately planned to quarrel with me, and to have the question of my taking the canoe without his permission as an excuse for killing me, which I am sure he would have done if he had known about my six-shooter's condition.

There was now talk of a railroad coming into the Flathead. Demersville began to boom. New boats appeared on Flathead Lake, the *Pocahontas* (afterward the *Dora*), the *Tom Carter*, the *State of Montana*, and the *Crescent*, the last two quite pretentious. Demersville saw a rosy future and preened herself accordingly. The town grew rapidly. It incorporated, had a mayor, and became tough. "A man for breakfast every morning," seemed to be its motto; and it lived up to it. But the unromantic railroad builders didn't come near it. Instead, a new town, Kalispell, was located a measly three miles up the valley from Demersville; and the new town was not even on the river. The railroad builders had not only ignored Demersville, but they had given no thought to the possibilities of steamboat transportation, and Demersville was at the head of navigation.

After its amazement passed, its breath came back. And then Demersville began to move. Hotels, stores, and residences were promptly hauled to Kalispell. I well remember seeing Demersville's second largest hostelry drawn by a score or more of horses on its way to Kalispell, with its regular boarders eating their dinners in its unsteady dining room. On January 1, 1891 the

57

railroad reached the new town, and then Demersville gave up the ghost. It had been a boom town with wild and woolly ways. Its passing was as spectacular as its heyday, when hundreds of men, unable to find better accommodations, slept upon its billiard tables. Today only one building marks the site of Flathead's first city. A little church, white and prim, stands there alone as though to prove the constancy of its faith. I have a kindly feeling for old Demersville. I met and courted Mrs. Linderman there.

CHAPTER III

Quitting the Free Life

FOR a time, after I met and became interested in Miss Minnie Jane Johns, I found it difficult to quit the old life of a trapper, and yet I knew that I must if I expected to marry her. More than once I made brave attempts to settle down, working in the store of G. H. Adams in Demersville, where my lady was postmistress, and in the town of Kalispell. Sometimes I hung on for several weeks, or until some old partner showed up. Then away I would go again into the mountains for a time. My job was always waiting for me when I returned to town, and each time I came back to it I promised myself that I would stick, and make a home. One day, after the lady had promised to marry me, I met an old partner in Kalispell. He was delighted to see me, gave me a glowing description of some new beaver country he had found, and urged me to go to it with him. "Ketch up yer hosses, an' we'll pull out o' here quicker'n hell would scorch a moccasin," he said.

"I've quit, Red," I declared. "I'm never going to set another trap."

Even while I was speaking I realized that there was but one way for me to quit the old life, and that was to leave the country.

He pretended that he had not heard me. "Look yonder," he pointed to an Indian lodge half hidden by quaking aspens. "That's my camp," he said. "I'll run in your hosses fer ye, an' hobble 'em. Let's us pull out tomorrow evening so's nobody'll know where we're headed fer."

"No, Red," I said, leaving him to go back to the store where all the afternoon I "fought my head," imagining the smell of the smoke of Red's lodgefire in my nostrils. I could not hold out, and knew it.

"Just this once more," I told my lady, and left her. I do not believe she felt very sure that I'd come back.

Red and I left the valley the next evening. I had six horses in the outfit, besides traps, saddles, and camp equipage, seven years' gathering. We camped after a two-hour drive in the moonlight, moving on again next morning at daybreak to a meadowy country not more than fifteen miles from Kalispell. Red wished to kill a couple of deer here and dry the meat enough so that we could keep it, saying that where we were going there were no deer to be had. I was lucky, killing two bucks before dusk. And yet all the time I was looking for deer my mind was wrestling with my problem, so that when Red came to camp I was ready with a plan to leave him.

"I'm going back to Kalispell and have a tooth attended to," I told him. "It might give me trouble later on."

I am not certain that he understood I was quitting him. Anyhow, he tried to insure my return by advising me to ride his top horse. "Take Spot," he said. "He'll git ye there an' back quicker'n any hoss in the outfit."

I made no objection, rode Spot to Kalispell, stripped him, and turned him loose on the range. Then I called on my lady. "I'll always be a trapper unless I go away from this country, and go now. I'm leaving in the morning," I told her.

"Where will you go?" she asked.

"I will look up some men whom I once took into the mountains. They will know where I may find work. My first stop will be in Missoula," I answered, as though my plans were all made.

We spent several hours trying to lay out our future. But everything seemed so chaotic that we were unable to bring any kind of order to the necessary moves we knew must lie ahead. "Anyhow, I shall go to my home in New Richmond (Wisconsin) and wait there until you are settled," said my lady, finally.

When I bade her good night I began to feel low-spirited. The urge to catch up old Spot and again join Red was strong. I'd quit him rather indecently, and this began now to bother me. However, I had left him six rather good horses, and all my outfit, seven years' gathering. This ought to square me with him; and old Spot would take the back trail to Red's camp, I was certain. Then, as though to further torment me, some outstanding quality of each of my horses came into my mind. I'd grown fond of them, especially of old Stub. What would eventually become of him if I left him in this manner?

Reaching my room, I found my dog, Mike, lying beside my saddle and rifle. I'd raised him from a fuzzy puppy. He had stuck to me like gumbo to a saddle blanket. I lighted the lamp and sat down on the bed as full of rebellion against civilization as a young man could be. Mike, sensing that I was in trouble, came softly to me. Poking his muzzle under my hand, he nosed it sympathetically. How could I leave Mike? He could not endure civilization, I knew. He hated dogs, all dogs of all sizes. In any town he would have fifty fights a day until he was finally killed. I could not take him with me. He would prove a great troublemaker, might land me in jail.

His nose nudged me. How many times I had dug porcupine quills out of that cold nose! I had cut in to get hold of them, and then pulled them out with my bullet mould. He had never whimpered during these painful operations, and yet never learned to let porcupines alone, or skunks. He could kill a skunk in five seconds. He had killed scores of them, hunting them on his own hook to play even with the tribe. And always, after he had killed a skunk he felt hurt because I scolded him for trying to crawl into the blankets with me. There was nothing alive that he would not tackle, and tree, if the animal could climb. He had his faults, it is true. He would fight every dog that showed up, and would break if not carefully watched. But his nose would lead me to a deer any time. Somehow he knew by the way I walked whether I wanted a ruffed grouse for supper or a shot at a deer, and always acted accordingly.

A good dog must sometimes wonder if his master's mind is sane. I know that Mike often did. One day when I was running a trap line, I came to a place where I had set a trap for a lynx. The trap was gone, clog and all. The ground was frozen hard and was bare, so that there was almost no "sign" to follow. The trap had been clogged with a small fir sapling, and both trap and clog were gone, leaving only faint "sign" that led me about fifty yards from the set.

There it ended, near a large fir tree. I went over the ground a dozen times without being able to follow the "sign" farther than before. At last I went back to camp for Mike. I never permitted him to follow me on trap lines, because I was afraid that he might somehow get into a trap. But now I brought him to the set, showed him what had happened, and said, "Go get him!"

Away he went to the very spot where the "sign" ended. There he sat down, looking wise. In a minute I was beside him. "Where is he?" I asked disgustedly. Mike looked first at me, as though to make sure of my words, and then, lifting his head, looked up into the fir tree. "Boo," he barked.

And there, not fifteen feet up, was the lynx, trap, clog, and all. I hadn't dreamed that the animal could climb a tree with the heavy trap and clog. In fact, I had not once considered the tree. Now I must either climb the tree, or shoot the limb off that held the clog. I decided upon the latter. Mike would be waiting to seize the lynx when the animal came down. He might get badly scratched, and to no purpose. "Go back to camp!" I said, and shall never forget the expression Mike gave to his beautiful black and white tail as he left me to settle with the lynx.

Sitting there, with Mike's head on my knee, I thought of another time when the dog must have believed me silly. I was crawling through haw brush that bear had pulled down and broken, when Mike, knowing that bears were near us, broke. In a minute I heard him bark, not twenty yards to my left. Making my way through the difficult bushes, I came to a large cottonwood tree about which Mike was capering anxiously. I saw a black bear high up in the tree and shot it. The heavy animal struck the ground with a thud that might have been heard a long way. But Mike paid no attention to the kicking bear, a fact that should have warned me that the game was not yet played. Pushing my way through the tangled bushes to the tree, I seized the dead bear's hind paw and rolled the animal away from the tree trunk. Mike came dashing up to me barking furiously, as though to tell me to look out for myself, although there was no danger. Looking up, I saw another bear in the tree, not six feet above my head. Stepping backward to get a little distance between me and my mark, I fired too quickly. My bullet broke the animal's lower jaw, knocking him out of the tree. In a second Mike was upon him. The animal could not bite the dog because of his broken jaw, but he could, and did, cuff him terribly while I tried to strike the bear with a club I had picked up. I dared not shoot again for fear of hitting Mike in the twisting, whirling blur that was tearing up bushes and distributing fur. At last I succeeded in landing a blow upon the bear's snout just below the eyes. This stunned him so that I could stick him with my knife. The fight ended, Mike lay down, exhausted. His white ruff was red with blood, and his eyes green with fight. He never knew that I had struck the bear, but believed he had killed the animal alone, I'm sure. And he must have thought me silly to have shot the higher bear first.

His loyalty to me was astonishing. He would permit no man to handle or even touch my rifle or any part of my camp outfit. His pride in my string of pack horses was laughable. Trotting back and forth from lead to trail, his tail up and his head high, he inspected every horse as though he owned the outfit. Sometimes when the water was cold in the streams I would offer him a seat in my lap when fording. He would always spring lightly into the saddle with me, and then when I put him down on the other side he would shake himself as though he had had to swim, even rolling as dogs do after being in cold water. He seemed never to understand that a dog might cross a river without getting wet.

He was almost arrogant in his attitude toward the horses, and he worked hard all day long keeping the trail they were traveling clear for them, even of woodchucks and chipmunks. And how he did hate an Indian! (All Indian dogs hate white men, too, for that matter.) He often embarrassed me by his open hostility toward Indians. Once when a Kootenai was trading me a horse for a rifle the Indian reached for a cartridge I held in my hand. Instantly Mike seized the man's wrist and held it, his eyes fired by unbelievable hate. The Kootenai did not cry out or struggle, even when his blood began to drip to the ground. I had difficulty in making Mike let go. A white man would have demanded the dog's life; not so with this Indian. "The dog's heart is strong," he said, while I was prying the set jaws from the wrist. "I will trade you a good horse for him." As though Mike would have accepted an Indian master!

I have had many Indian friends, and one Indian partner, who were as genuinely fond of me as I was of them. However, this has not blinded me to the natural, and thoroughly deserved, dislike which Indians hold for the men of my race. I am, of course, speaking of the old-time Indians, especially those of the Northwestern plains, whose ancient customs perished with the buffalo, and whose existence became uncertain with the advent of white men. Mike, like many men of my acquaintance who never admitted a just cause for the Indian's enmity toward white men, instinctively knew there was bad blood between the races and was only too anxious to prove his loyalty to me and my kind. He never grew accustomed to my Indian partner. He would sometimes romp with him, and yet when bedtime came he would not permit the Indian to go peaceably to bed with me. There was always a show of white teeth at the red man, and a few reproachful looks in my direction before we all settled down. Mike slept on my side of the bed, and I believe always fitfully, with one eye on Koonsaw, the Indian.

Koonsaw was young and handsome, always rode a snow-white horse, and wore a scarlet blanket. He was a renowned wrestler among his people, possessing many admirers among the young women of his tribe. His youthful body was perfect, and in summer naked, excepting moccasins and breechclout. One day while we were camped on the lake shore where the city of Polson stands now, a white man came to our fire. His name, I believe, was Kelley. Anyhow, I knew him later as Cockeyed Kelley, a wrestler of some reputation. In our camp that day on the lake shore Kelley challenged Koonsaw for a wrestling bout. The Indian was willing enough, but had no money, so that I put up five dollars against a like sum by Kelley, as a purse for the winner of the match. Kelley, quite sure of his prowess, took some time preparing for the affair, even going carefully over the ground itself. At last he stepped forward to meet the Indian, who simply dropped his bright blanket and stood forth. Koonsaw's attitude now became one of seeming menace that was beyond a dog's understanding. The white man was a stranger, and yet to Mike, the color of his skin was a bid for any dog's fealty. Besides, here was a glorious opportunity to get even with Koonsaw for presuming to sleep with me. No sooner had the Indian's hand touched the white man's body than Mike had Koonsaw by the breechclout; he would have gone deeper if I had not instantly prevented him. I was obliged to hold my dog while my partner wiped up the beach with Mr. Kelley, so that in the end we were satisfied. I had my money back, Koonsaw had Kelley's five dollars, and Mike had again shown his preference for white men at the expense of my partner.

Koonsaw was murdered a little later, the five dollars which he won from Kelley being in a measure responsible for his taking off. The country was settling rapidly now, so that whiskey was more easily obtained, and Koonsaw loved liquor. One day soon after the wrestling bout he got a half-gallon of whiskey from a freighter who was hauling goods from the railroad to Flathead Lake. When I learned that Koonsaw was rapidly becoming irresponsible, I hid not only his Winchester but my own rifle and six-shooter, so that if he declared war on anybody he would find no ready weapons in our camp.

The day was sizzling hot. I was sitting in the shade of our lodge when I saw a horseman appear on the crest of the hill toward the railroad, thirty-six miles away. The horseman, leading an extra horse, was coming slowly down the trail toward the lake when Koonsaw came to the lodge and entered it. I heard him muttering stupidly to himself while he lifted and turned things upside down in the lodge, guessing what he was seeking. Presently he came out and asked me for his rifle. I told him that I had hidden it, that he was drunk and might get into trouble if I let him have his gun. He begged for it, for my own, for even a butcher knife, his eyes lighted strangely with mingled fear and hate. "No," I said. "I am your friend. A gun is bad for you now."

Slowly sinking down to his knees, his arms about my own, he whispered in pidgin English; "Angus, she's comin' now. Me seeum. Angus' heart no good pour me. Gimme gun, ah, gimme gun."

"No," I said, flatly, and shall never forget the look in his eyes at my refusal.

He got up, and went away from the lodge before the horseman reached the lake. I believed that he had hidden away from the man he feared. However, I soon heard loud talking in English. Walking around the lodge, I saw Angus McDonald,[1] a half-breed whom I knew very well, and old Jack Fisher, a white man who had a cabin nearby, holding a powwow. Both had been drinking. I heard Koonsaw's name spoken by both. Jack, who, besides Koonsaw and myself, had been the only man, red or white, at the foot of the lake before Angus came, must have known where Koonsaw was hiding, because I saw him point to a patch of willows below our lodge and say, "Go get him!"

I ran to my horse, which I had staked near the lodge, quickly half-hitched his lower jaw with the stakerope, and sprang upon his back. I found Koonsaw in the willows, lying flat on the ground. "Here, get onto this horse and ride," I said, getting down to hand him the rope.

He needed no urging, and dashed away for the high hill. I wished now, most heartily, that I had had the time to get his Winchester for him. But there hadn't been a moment to spare. Even now, Angus, riding the horse he had been leading, was pressing Koonsaw, who was quirting his mount with the rope's end. The horse that Angus was riding was a famed runner, having won many races in the valley. The race now was short indeed. Watching, half breathlessly, I saw the naked Indian turn on his barebacked horse to face the breed, saw the breed lean over, stab the Indian in the back, and dash by him in a cloud of dust. Then I saw my horse running loose, and Koonsaw on the ground.

I ran to him, meeting Angus. He was signing, and seemingly satisfied. Koonsaw was not badly hurt. The knife blade had been a short one. It had been the blow, more than the wound, that had unhorsed him. After dressing his hurt, which was below the shoulder blade on the left side, I sent him away on another horse, armed this

[1] This Angus McDonald should not be mistaken for the Angus McDonald who was a Hudson's Bay Company factor.

time with his Winchester. I never knew all the particulars of his murder by an Indian of another tribe at Ravalli or Arlee. However, I feel certain that the Indian who killed Koonsaw had been hired to do the office. I know that the murderer invited Koonsaw to smoke with him in his lodge, and that, when Koonsaw stooped to enter, the wretch who had offered his hospitality shot him twice in the breast.

All this, and much more, came to me while I sat on the bed with my dog's nose on my knee. But I had to leave him, and made arrangements with Sam Johns, my lady's brother, who was managing the Adams business, to care for him. Next morning when the *State of Montana*, the finest boat that has ever been on Flathead Lake, left old Demersville I was aboard, wearing a suit of store clothes. My buckskin outfit was in a sack with other belongings, including my belt knife. Of all the things I learned to use in the wilderness, a belt knife was the most difficult to forget. For months I caught myself reaching for my butcher knife to do every chore that a jackknife does for more civilized men. Steaming down the Flathead River, I felt the first pangs of homesickness I had ever known. What a wonderful country this had been! What sights I had seen! Months are as years to a boy, and I was yet but a boy. It seemed to me that I had been in this wilderness for a lifetime, that I belonged here, that I could never leave the forests, the sight of big game, the grand rivers and mountains, for civilization.

Just below Selish the steamboat passed several lodges of Crees. How well I remember my first meeting with these Indians. I had seen them soon after their battle with Canadian troops at Duck Creek in 1885. Some of them were wounded, and all had seemed to me to be upstanding men. Since our first meeting we had been warm friends. Many a day I had hunted with the Crees and Chippewas of the band. Now I saw Muskegon, a particular friend, standing beside his lodge. I waved my hat. He answered with his hand, although I am sure that he did not recognize me, dressed up as I was. I had gathered many Cree legends from Muskegon, and hoped to get others. I had many friends among the Blackfeet and Flatheads, and even a few Kootenias called me "friend." Now I was leaving it all—and for a girl who weighed less than ninety pounds.

And where was I going? What was I to do, who had neither a trade nor profession and very little schooling? Several years before this I had acted as guide for Governor Sam Hauser, Judge Frank Woody, Hon. A. Sterne Blake, and G. A. Wolf,[2] all pioneers and prominent in the young state's affairs. One night while we were sitting around our campfire the Governor quoted Shakespeare. "Isn't that right, Frank?" he asked, to banter me.

"No, Governor," I replied, much to his surprise, I'm sure, "Not quite right," and I corrected him.

"By Gad, the boy's right. He's right! I remember now, he's right! What's the rest of it, Frank?" he asked getting up to sit down again, beside me.

I knew little of Shakespeare, but thanks to my mother, who was well versed in the works of the great Englishman, I could go on with the quotation. This seemed to impress the Governor.

"Boy," he said, kindly, "Don't spend too much time running wild. What you have already done has been good for you, but quit this life within another year. You don't belong in the wilds. How old are you?"

"Twenty-one," I told him.

"Just right to begin," he chuckled, tossing a stick onto the fire. "When you come out of the wilderness look us up, any of us. We'll help you get your stride, some way."

I had liked these men so much that I had refused to accept any pay for my services, which had included horses, camp outfit, and even a sailboat and canoe. However, they had had a beautiful rifle made especially for me, a Ballard, Union-Hill. The rifle had come to me months after they had gone to their homes. Now I would look these men up, tell them I had quit the old life, that I was going to marry and settle down. I felt certain this information would impress them. Anyhow, I felt that it ought to.

By the time the *State of Montana* had steamed out of the river onto Flathead Lake, whose shore line was yet wild, unsettled forest,

---

[2] Samuel T. Hauser was Territorial Governor of Montana from July, 1885, to February, 1887, and had organized banks in Virginia City and Helena. Judge Woody was prominent in the development of Missoula. G. A. Wolf was a Missoula banker.

I had reviewed my associations with these men whom I now intended to find. Major Pete Ronan, the Indian agent on the Flathead reservation, had advised them to employ me, had even sent a messenger into the upper country with a note telling me that the party would meet me at the foot of Swan Lake, taking it for granted that I would take care of them. Somehow, the Indian messenger had been delayed, or was willfully slow in his riding. There was little time to spare for what I must do before the party arrived. I rode to the foot of Swan Lake, stripped my horse, turned him loose to go back to the valley, and cached my saddle, intending to paddle my canoe to the head of the lake and fetch back my sailboat for the expected party. I had thought to go without eating until I reached my upper camp at the head of the lake; but I grew hungry. Remembering some flour and a little jerky that I had cached in a sack a few months earlier, I went after it, purposing to fix a little of the flour with water, in the sack itself, and to bake a bannock on a rock. Even in the darkness I had no trouble finding the sack, which I had hung in a fir tree, with a large, flat rock placed carefully over the string to prevent squirrels from cutting it. I forgot all about the rock. Standing beneath the hanging sack, I jumped up a little and cut the string with my butcher knife. The next thing I knew, Mike was pawing my face; and it was cut from my right temple diagonally downward to my mouth, so that my tongue was sticking through my upper lip. I forgot my project of bannock baking and tried to bandage my wound with a red bandanna handkerchief, but could not make it stay in its place, finally leaving it off. Next morning, by looking into the calm water, I saw that my wound was shallow on the upper part of my face, and that while my temple was sore, only my lip had been cut deeply.

The next night when I was coming down Swan Lake with the sailboat, towing the canoe, the wind was blowing half a gale. In the darkness I could not make out either shore. Tearing along at a great clip, I suddenly saw the flare of a fire off to my right. Was I befuddled? I felt certain that I was not more than halfway to the lake's lower end, and yet here, nearly abreast of me, was a fire on the shore. It must have been built by my outfit. It must be at the foot of the lake. Fires were uncommon in that country then. "Funny," I thought, hauling my sheet as close as I dared and heading for the fire, wondering how I should fare, since I dared not leave the tiller to lower my sails. My boat's rudder needed attention and hadn't had it, so that if I left the tiller, in the sea that was running, my rudder would jump out and away. I was unable to judge how far the shore really was. I beached the boat with a crash that nearly tore the spar out of her. Lowering my sails now, I picked up my rifle and headed toward the fire.

"Halt!" a loud voice commanded.

Startled a little, and yet believing that this was some joke, I kept on.

"Halt!"

This time I distinctly heard a rifle slap down into a man's hand. I halted, stood stone-still, bending a little so that I might see better.

"Merely form, friend," said a cheery voice; and then I saw brass buttons shine in the firelight. Two soldiers in soiled blue uniforms, one a sergeant, the other a private, and both negroes, came to meet me, escorting me into their camp.

Soldiers! Never before, and never since, did that country see soldiers. But here they were, an exploring party, lost as a band of bats in daylight. I helped them out a little, drew a rough map of the country for them, and should have enjoyed taking them to the head of the river, as they proposed; but because of my present engagement I could not. In a few minutes after I entered the camp the commanding officer was called from his bed. He was a young and very important lieutenant who called me "my man," I remember. I did not like him. But I did like the gentle white-haired surgeon who laid me down in the firelight and patched up my battered face so nicely that today only a faint scar on my upper lip shows.

The soldiers, all negroes, helped me get my boat off the beach when finally I was ready to set out again, with strips of plaster and several stitches making my face feel stiff as a board. I had been right in my belief that the fire was but halfway down the lake, so that now I let the boat go with the wind until I came to another fire, this time at the foot of the lake. I made a decent landing, spread my blanket, and went to sleep, leaving Mike in the sailboat, because I had seen two bird dogs in the camp. Mike would half kill them both before morning if I permitted him to come ashore with me.

At daybreak I heard a jolly voice calling "Frank! Frank!"

Thinking that it was I who was being called, I sat up. "Yes, sir," I answered.

"No, not you," the laughing voice went on.

And then I saw a white head lift itself out of some soft blankets spread near a fir tree. "What's the matter; why not let a fellow sleep?" growled the white head in mock anger.

"Look, look, Frank, at what the good Lord sent us in the night," laughed the first voice. "He's our guide, Frank. He *must* be, and I'll bet he eats grizzlies raw. My God! Look at his face, Frank!"

This had been my introduction to the men I now proposed to ask for help. I remembered one other incident of the trip. Knowing that Mike would never stand for the bird dogs being in the sailboat, I left him to watch a frying pan, thinking that we should return to the foot of the lake within a few days.

"Will he stay with that frying pan, do you think?" asked Mr. Blake, who, in spite of Mike's arrogance, seemed to admire the dog.

"Yes, sir, I think so," I said. Ten days later Mike greeted me upon reaching the foot of the lake. He looked as lean as a snipe's bill, and yet he thrashed both the bird dogs before I could get hold of him.

When the *State of Montana* landed me at the foot of the lake, where there was yet no settlement, I tried to collect fifteen dollars from a half-breed who owed me the money. However, I did not get it, and took the stage for the railroad, with twelve dollars in my pocket. Judge Woody and Mr. Wolf lived in Missoula, the Governor in Helena, and Mr. Blake at Victor, in the Bitterroot valley. But when, with my rifle, saddle, and sack, I finally reached Missoula, I learned that the Judge and Mr. Wolf were out of town, that they had gone to the horse races in Helena and Mr. Blake had gone with them.

"When will they return?" I asked Mr. Wolf's Chinaman.

"No can tell. Mebby him stay long time, mebby two, tlee week," replied the Chinaman, as though time meant nothing at all. I was turning away when he said, "Me savvy you. You Flank Linnamon. You ketchum my hat. Membah?" He laughed merrily.

I remembered. He had been the cook for the party. One day while we were in my sailboat the Chinaman's hat had blown off in a vicious squall of wind. The hat landed far from the boat.When I started to trim sails so that I might recover it, Mr. Wolf objected. "No, no," he shouted above the wind, "let the darned hat go, and get us to shore." I had taken the party to camp, and then with a canoe recovered the hat, much to the Chinaman's satisfaction.

"You likeum pie?" he asked, ducking inside to bring out nearly half an apple pie, baked to a nicety. "I savvy you; you ketchum my hat."

I wished heartily that I were in Helena with these men who had been in camp with me, but I did not have enough money to go any farther. I must somehow wait for them to return to Missoula, and in the meantime find work, if I could. Times were hard. The far-off Flathead began again to call me. "Why not go back?" was uppermost in my mind when a man asked me if I would help him drive a band of horses to Billings. He had trailed the band from some place in Oregon, forty-five head of heavy mares. His helper had quit him that morning, after a quarrel, he told me. I have forgotten the man's name, and the bargain we made, except that he was to furnish me a saddle horse for the trip, and then pay my way back over the Northern Pacific from Billings to Missoula.

There was nothing eventful about the undertaking, except that while camped a little above Billings on the Yellowstone I met Plenty-coups, the Crow chief, for the first time. He was then in his forties, a perfect specimen of manhood. Through an interpreter and with sign language we talked of the Flathead country and about the three forks of the Missouri, where he had had several desperate battles with Flatheads years before. He told me that excepting the Cheyennes, whom he called "the-striped-feathered-arrows," the Flatheads were the bravest warriors. I saw Plenty-coups several times after our first meeting, which he always remembered. It was he who gave me my Crow name, "Sign-talker." Two years ago I wrote the story of his life, entitled *American* and published by the John Day Company, of New York.

Returning to Missoula, I found Judge Woody, Mr. A. Sterne Blake, and Mr. Wolf. "You are the very man I want," said Mr. Blake, as soon as we had shaken hands. "Sam (meaning Governor Hauser), Dan Floweree, and I are going into the Clearwater country after elk. You are the very man to take us there."

"I've quit, Mr. Blake," I declared, earnestly. "I'm afraid to go back into the mountains. If I do, I may never be able to break away from them again. Besides," I added seriously, "I'm going to marry and settle down right away."

My seriousness caused much merriment. "Well," laughed Mr. Blake, "you are not going to get married today, so get your gatherings. We've got to be rustling if we catch the train up the Bitterroot. I'll wait here for you—and hurry."

Times were hard, I have said. There was nothing else that I could do. Aboard the train, a triweekly combination freight and passenger service, I told Mr. Blake that I would take him into the Clearwater country if he would get me some permanent employment upon our return to civilization. He said that he would, that between himself and Sam the task would prove to be easy. Then he took up the proposed trip, talking of nothing else until we reached his home near Victor.

Besides his ranch just outside Victor, where he lived, he owned a quarter interest in the Curlew mine, on Big Creek. This property had paid well and was yet being worked. In earlier days Mr. Blake had married a Snake woman. Unlike many other white men, he had kept her, even after the country settled, so that now he was living in his new house with his family of mixed-blood children. Their home was neat and orderly and the children well-behaved. Mrs. Blake was a good woman; and I have never known a better man than Sterne Blake. If our second daughter had been a boy, he would have borne the name Sterne, for Mr. Blake. Being a girl we named her Verne, which was as near as we could come to Sterne.

That night I thought for a long time about my having to go again into the mountains. I wanted to go badly enough, and yet I dreaded the ordeal of having to leave off. When morning came, however, I rounded up some of the Blake horses and began to break one of them that Mr. Blake wished me to ride on the trip. There was no trail up Big Creek to the Clearwater country. I had to blaze a way myself; and there was need to hurry, since Governor Hauser and Daniel Floweree were to arrive in time to reach the Clearwater before the full of the moon in September, when the elk begin to "run." It was already September when I set out, with a helper named Bill Cook and one pack horse. We returned to the Blake ranch in about ten days, having located a fairly good course over the range of mountains to elk country.

Governor Hauser and his young son, Tom, were already at Mr. Blake's home when I returned. Dan Floweree could not come. Instead, he had been obliged to go to a hospital to have a bullet that he had carried for years removed from his leg. The Governor had brought with him a negro cook, who proved to be the most worthless man, white, black, or red, that I ever saw around a campfire. Besides this negro cook the Governor insisted upon engaging a packer named Shinn, who, with the cook, completely spoiled the hunting trip. Shinn was drunk when he arrived and managed to remain in this condition throughout the journey, on the Governor's whiskey, which he stole at will. I slept with Mr. Blake. One morning just as day was breaking I saw Shinn slipping from his blankets toward the packs. I nudged Mr. Blake. We watched our packer lift the Governor's little keg to his lips and hold it there for an unbelievable time. "The damned rascal," whispered Mr. Blake. "He'll drown himself in Sam's whiskey." The negro was little better. Both continually stole the liquor, and so kept themselves thoroughly pickled.

One night when we had reached a camping place that I had selected Shinn and the negro were nowhere in sight. We had traveled over rough country, so that the pace had been slow. I believed that the pair would show up a little later. But when black darkness had come on I began to worry a little. The missing men had the mess pack, so that we would have to go to bed without supper. Besides this, the pack horse that carried the Governor's keg was with them. I had visions of trouble. At ten o'clock I set out to find the wayward ones, sometimes creeping in the darkness on my hands and knees to save my neck. At last, after more than an hour's traveling, I saw a bright fire far below me in timber. When I was within hailing distance the way became dangerous in the dark, with the firelight blinding me. "Douse the fire, Shinn, so I can come in!" I called.

There was no answer. I must have been nearly half an hour going two hundred yards to their camp, if one could dignify their layout by such a term. Before I even saw Shinn or the negro, who were both dead drunk, I saw that not a pack had been removed from the tired horses and that one of them, a fine mare, had a broken leg. How long these two wretches had forced her to travel in this condition I never knew. I hurriedly unpacked her, and then ended her sufferings. My shot aroused Shinn a little, enough so that he began to abuse me. But the Governor's dining-car cook slept peacefully on, lying flat on his back over a boulder as large as a camp kettle.

There being no grass for the horses, I unpacked and tied them up to trees, knowing that if I let them run loose they would set the outfit afoot by going on down to the valley. I had promised to fire three shots in quick succession if I found Shinn and the cook. Now I climbed well up the mountainside and wasted that much ammunition, since neither Mr. Blake nor the Governor heard my signal of success. After this I made myself some coffee and then bedded down with the drunks to wait for daylight.

Two days later we stopped hunting because of bad weather. The equinoctial storm, which in Montana is sometimes severe, brought mimic winter to the mountains within a few hours, obliging us to make hasty preparations for an indefinite stay not far from the summit of the mountain range. The days dragged—I've forgotten how many. However, the Governor loved to hear echoes and amused himself trying to raise them, not knowing that echoes are asleep in such storms and that even when wakened are weak. One night in this forced camp after his voice had worn out calling to the echoes, the Governor asked, "Why don't you help me out a little, Frank?"

"Because," I answered, "we are near our elk country. Yelling isn't good tactics in game country, Governor."

I shall always remember his chagrin at my reply. "By golly! I hadn't once thought of that. Why didn't you stop me before now?" he asked humbly.

Rain, sleet, and finally snow held us in this camp for several disagreeable days and nights. And yet I remember them with pleasure. Governor Hauser and Sterne Blake were even then the only living members of the unfortunate Yellowstone Expedition of 1863.[3] Sitting by our fire they told me the whole story of that terrible experience, of the night attack by Indians who had followed them for days, of the awfulness of the moments when, according to agreement, several of their wounded comrades killed themselves, and the final escape of the rest of the party. The Governor, wrought up by his remembrances, walked, even ran, about the fire showing, in pantomime, many unwritten details too revolting to record. In his telling of their leader, Jim Stuart, and his defiance of the Indian chief, the Governor was dramatic indeed. The quick little man enacted the leader's part during the Indians' visit to the Expedition's camp so faithfully that the more placid Mr. Blake got up to walk about, his hands fumbling aimlessly in his pockets, as though for his pipe.

"The chief sat *here*," said the Governor, sitting down, "and Jim sat *here*," he went on, getting up only to sit down again facing the spot that he had just vacated. "He had ordered me to tell the men to saddle up; but as soon as a bridle was put on a horse an Indian would cut the bridle reins with his knife, and not more than two inches from the holder's hand. Besides, one or two young braves were pointing their arrows, fitted to their bowstrings, at the men's chests, letting the arrows slip a little, to start a row. Our men were

[3] Under the leadership of James Stuart, two groups of men planned to "prospect the valley of the Yellowstone River and the tributaries flowing from the Big Horn Mountains." The two groups failed to meet at the appointed rendezvous, and both were attacked by Crow Indians. In one group were Henry Edgar and Bill Fairweather, who discovered gold near present Virginia City. Edgar "gave the name of 'Alder Gulch' to the area." See Merrill G. Burlingame, *The Montana Frontier* (Helena, Mont.: State Publishing Co., 1942), pp. 86–87.

ugly, especially George Ives. I was afraid they'd start the ball, so I told Jim what was going on. He was smoking with the chief, the pipe going from one to the other, while both talked in Crow, as though we were having a pleasant party.

" 'Tell the boys to keep cool, to watch me, and do as I do,' Jim said. But when I told the men they were disgusted. 'Tell that squaw-man to hurry up, or I'll start this thing, myself,' growled Ives. I was afraid they wouldn't wait, and was picking my man, when like a flash Jim sprang to his feet, his heavy rifle leveled at the chief's heart—like this; instantly we all covered an Indian. Mine wasn't three feet from the muzzle of my rifle. And then there were breathless seconds that seemed hours. 'Call off your men, or I'll kill you!' Jim's voice was as cool as though he had asked for a drink of water. And the Chief *did*, by God, he *did*." The Governor's slight form seemed actually to sag with relief. " 'Boys, he's weakened,' Jim said. Whew! I wanted to yell."

The Governor sat down now to tell of the dramatic death of Geery, one of the party who had been wounded. "Both Jim and I examined Geery's wound," he said. "I knew that it was fatal, but there wasn't a chance for any of us to get away, so I begged him not to kill himself. 'We might as well all fight it out here, Geery,' I said. He wouldn't listen. 'Jim,' he said, 'you tell the boys that I am mortally wounded, will you? I don't want them to think that I'm committing suicide.' Then he held his six-shooter's muzzle against his right temple and pulled the trigger—and by God, the cap *snapped*. Yes, sir, it *snapped*, and yet to me it sounded like a cannon."

The Governor leaped to his feet. "Wait! Wait, Geery," he cried, leaning over an imaginary form, his voice husky with emotion. "Take this as a warning, Geery, for God's sake!"

Sinking down beside the fire as though weary, he said, "But it didn't do any good. The poor fellow, to keep us from staying there to defend him, again cocked his six-shooter and sent a slug into his brain."

Both the Governor and Mr. Blake were certain that the attacking Indians were Crows. They might have been Arapahoes, however. While there are a few instances where parties of Crows

77

attacked white men, the tribe itself has always been friendly, except for horse-stealing. The fact that their leader, Jim Stuart, conversed with the "chief" in the Crow tongue is not perfect proof of his tribal relationship. Nevertheless, the attack upon the Yellowstone Expedition of 1863 has always been charged to the Crows, who may have been guilty.

It was in this camp that Shinn, the packer, was attacked by delirium tremens. I shall never forget his misery, nor ours. Coming out of his spells, he would whimper, "Frank, don't try to pack me out of here. Just bury me so's the wolves won't pull me around, right here, anywhere."

He made this request so often that Mr. Blake, worn out and deeply disgusted with both Shinn and the negro, said: "Hell, no! If you die, Shinn, we'll pack you out. We'll kill that damned worthless Pullman-car cook so's we'll have two side-packs of cussedness. But for God's sake hurry up and die—or get well, one or the other."

Shinn's condition was such that on the fourth or fifth day both Mr. Blake and the Governor thought it best to abandon the hunting trip and take our patient back to civilization. I cannot forget the great pile of supplies they decided to leave on that camp ground. This seemed to me a sinful waste. I was sorely tempted to cache it and someday return for it. Viewing the rich pile of grub that would have lasted me two years with the meat I would naturally kill, the Governor said, "Frank, if you will take Tommy, and go on into the elk country while Sterne and I get Shinn out of here, I'll give you a twenty-dollar gold piece for every time he shoots at an elk, hit or miss."

I needed the money. "I'll do it," I said, at once making up a pack of the best grub out of the pile before us. Then, saddling two good horses and packing one, I said, "Come on, Tommy," leading off.

The boy mounted his horse and followed me for perhaps a mile when, looking back down the mountain, he saw his father and the others riding in the opposite direction, leaving him alone with me. This settled things quickly for my young friend. "I guess I don't want to go," he called to me, stopping his horse. And there was now nothing to do but to turn back. Many years afterward I reminded Tom Hauser of this episode. He told me that he had never ceased to feel sorry for not having stuck.

The others had now got out of sight. Tommy and I could travel faster if we unloaded our pack on the grub pile with the rest of the supplies. This decided, I stopped and added our pack to the pile, wondering what would eventually become of it all. Grub was grub in the mountains, I well knew. I hated to leave so much for bear bait. I had scarcely unpacked our horse when an old prospector came leisurely down the gulch leading a white pack horse. I wanted to shout what I had in mind for him.

"Howdy," he said, biting off a chew from a meagre plug that I knew he had been hoarding.

"Going out?" I asked, knowing his answer.

"Yeah. Got to git me some grub an' pack it in. I've struck a little placer prospect I want to work on over yonder. Got to git it in 'fore snow comes, too."

"Well, here's grub for you, enough to keep you packing for some time. You're welcome to it, Partner," I said.

I remember how he stared, first at the grub pile and then at me. "Whose is it?" he asked, picking up a can of fancy peaches.

I explained matters. "The grub's yours, Partner," I told him again. "You need go no farther for your outfit."

"Golly, Golly, God!" he laughed, taking up a jar of honey, "I been a-wonderin' if I could stand old Amos Buck off fer a bill o' grub; an' now here 'tis, within a day's drive from my prospect. I'll bet I've struck it *rich*. Luck's changed, an' caught up to me at last. It *must* have."

I never saw the old fellow again. I've even forgotten his name. I remember, though, that I almost envied him with his big pile of fancy grub, such as had never before been seen in those mountains, and his "little placer prospect over yonder."

Tommy and I caught up with the others before noon. When we all finally reached the Blake ranch the Governor began to talk at once of leaving for Helena.

"How much do we owe you, Frank?" he asked, in his quick, decisive way.

"Nothing," I told him. "I'm not a professional guide. But remember that I want work of some kind."

"Sterne will attend to that," he said, dismissing the subject that was of most importance to me.

When he had gone, Mr. Blake gave me a letter that the Governor had written in the worst handwriting I had ever seen. It was addressed "To Whom it May Concern," and declared that without me on the trip just concluded the party might never have returned to civilization, that my "ambition was greater than my strength." Besides this he had enclosed one hundred dollars. He must have been overly worried during the trip. There had never been a time when any man who possessed common sense might not have returned to the valley, afoot if necessary. However, I prized the letter, which is now lost.

CHAPTER IV

Job After Job

ONE day a week after the Governor had gone I rode up to the Curlew mine with Mr. Blake. On the way he told me that I was to be the watchman at the company's concentrator at $3.00 per day, and that I was to begin watching at once. There was nothing for me to do except to stroll around the premises. I quickly tired of this, feeling that the job was a sinecure. However, I began to help the assayer a little, and enjoyed the work. I quickly learned that the Curlew was not then paying, so that I was not surprised when a month later Mr. Blake told me the company intended to reduce the force of miners and do whatever else it could to cut down expenses. He appeared to be worried. "Can you keep books?" he asked.

"I'll try," I said.

"Do you think you could do the assaying, too?"

Silver and lead were the only determinations required at the Curlew. "Yes, sir," I answered, without hesitation.

"This is the tenth," he mused, stuffing tobacco into his cob pipe. "You may tackle both jobs on the first of the month. There will not be very much work at either; and we'll pay you $125.00 per month. I'm going to lay off a whole shift in the mine on the first. The pay streak has pinched out on us."

His buckboard had scarcely disappeared down the gulch when I began to worry over my new jobs, especially over the book-keeping. The first of the month was distressingly near when I thought to send to Mr. Wolf in Missoula and have him order some books on both subjects. Nevertheless, when the first of the month came I took over both jobs, becoming the assayer and bookkeeper. How I managed them I cannot tell. I remember that my first reports to the company's secretary in Helena were promptly returned for corrections and that a friendly letter came with them. I have that letter yet. Little by little I mastered the bookkeeping and the monthly reports; the assaying gave me no trouble from the beginning.

Hauser, Holter,[1] and others operated the Helena & Frisco mine and mill in the Coeur d'Alene country. The regular manager of the Curlew had been sent there to take charge of a troublesome situation resulting from a strike of the miners and millmen, so that I was alone in the Curlew office for months. I had several times heard miners in our boardinghouse express the opinion that the Helena & Frisco Mining Company and the Helena & Victor Mining Company, our outfit, were one and the same concern. This was not true. Nevertheless, I was disturbed by our own miners' attitude toward our company on account of the trouble in the Coeur d'Alene. Then one day news reached us that the Helena & Frisco mill had been blasted, blown to bits, and that there had been fighting on the company's premises. Now, in the boardinghouse, our miners talked of little else, often declaring the two companies to be one outfit under two names. Even with all this I could not see how any of the Coeur d'Alene trouble could visit us.

The Curlew's manager, who under the present arrangement was superintending affairs for the other company, sometimes wrote me short notes telling me what to do. One forenoon a tall, dark-complexioned man of about thirty-five years of age entered the Curlew office and handed me one of these notes. "Put this man to work," it said; and it was signed as usual.

"Miner?" I asked the fellow, thinking quickly of a winze between the four- and five-hundred levels where a man might be used to advantage.

---

[1] Anton M. Holter, first a miner, later turned to lumbering and merchandising and became an influential person in Montana. He and his partner, Evenson, had brought in the state's second sawmill, from Denver, in 1863.

"No, sir," he answered. "Anything else will do me, if it's outdoors."

The concentrator was shut down just now. However, the tailings had lately been running wild, so that I set the fellow at sacking tailings and building a dam with the filled sacks. While I was instructing him how to sew and place the sacks, the mine whistle blew for noon, and the day shift of miners came running down the hill toward the boardinghouse.

"Come with me," I said. "I'll show you where to get your meals. And you had better get some overalls and a jumper," I added, noticing that the fellow's clothes were too good for such work.

On the way to the boardinghouse his walking led me to ask, "You've been a cowpuncher, haven't you?"

"Yes, sir," he replied, shortly, "an' I reckon you have, too."

A mine is the last place one would expect to find a cowpuncher. I could not imagine what circumstances had brought the fellow to the Curlew. The chairs at the table, where I had a sort of reserved seat, were filled, so that I found my man a place at another. I did not see him again until the next day.

I slept in a room in the office building that had originally been intended for a dwelling house. In one of its rooms a trapdoor in the floor let one down steep stairs into a dark cellar that was unused. On the day after the stranger's arrival I was writing some letters in the office when the mine whistle blew for noon. Glancing up the hill to see who was ahead, through habit, I saw the shift of miners come tearing down the trail, with Big Paul, who had the largest head imaginable, in the lead, as usual. I had left my chair to go to the window to watch the finish when the back door opened and shut with a bang that shook the whole building. Turning, I faced the stranger, who had an axe in his hand. "They're after me," he said, glancing nervously at the open door of the office. "Gimme a gun, quick!"

"I haven't a gun here," I said, knowing that somehow the fellow was in a desperate situation. "Come!"

I led him into the room with the trap door in its floor, lifted it, and sent him down into the black hole, with his axe. I had acted quickly, without conscious thought; now I must get out of that room.

Running back into the office, I picked up the only weapon in sight—a chunk of galena ore, worn smooth as glass on one side, that weighed perhaps six pounds—and faced the doorway just as a group of excited miners reached the steps.

"Stop!" I called to them, the chunk of ore raised. I believe it was the sanctity of the office of the manager that worked the miracle; anyhow, they stopped in their tracks.

"What do you want here?" I asked, feeling mightily relieved.

"We want that damned scab, that dirty gunman," answered a voice back in the group.

They must have known that the fellow was somewhere in the office building. But I could not turn him over to them unarmed, no matter who, or what, he might be. And I knew nothing about him. I managed, somehow, to laugh, and to do a good job of it, too. My counterfeit merriment brought a change of expression to the miners' faces. "Men," I said, evenly as I could, "this is silly business. Go to your dinners. You'll not be troubled with scabs or gunmen around here."

There was a stir among them at this. "Frank wouldn't shelter no damned scab," said somebody. "Come on, boys. We'll lay for the skunk!"

They began to move away, but with tormenting backward glances toward the office. When they had gone I lifted the trap door and spoke down into the black hole. "You are safe for a time," I said. "But stay where you are."

"Get me a good six-shooter, Partner, an' let me get out of here. I'll slip into the timber and take care of myself."

"I'll saddle a horse and get you a six-shooter after the miners have gone back into the mine," I promised. "But why are they after you? What have you been doing? Who are you?" My questions were thick and fast now that immediate danger was past.

"I hired out to watch the Helena & Frisco mill in the Coeur d'Alene," he told me. "The night they blew it up I killed one of the dynamiters. That's why they're after me here. They're all branded with the same iron. Get me a six-shooter an' let me get out of here an' take care of myself."

No wonder the miners were after him. Nevertheless, I decided to get a gun for him and let him go his way. Watching, I saw the shift of miners go back up the hill, missing none. A ride of four or five miles brought me to Mr. Blake's ranch, where I told my story.

Mr. Blake was angry. "Mac had no business to send that man to us," he declared. "But we can't let him be lynched," he added. "Ride down to the M. M. store and get him a six-shooter. Charge it to the company, and when you come back I'll go up to the Curlew camp with you."

Both Mr. Blake and Frank Tudor, who was part-owner of the Curlew, went back with me to the office, where I called the fellow out of the hole and gave him the gun.

"How does it come that you, a gunfighter, are not heeled?" asked Mr. Blake, when we four were seated in the darkened office, expecting trouble.

The fellow chuckled. "They jumped me so sudden that I had to slip out of a window without my belt. I was comin' here, anyway, so I just kept comin' after I got out of the window," he said.

After two hours spent in the dark with rifles in our laps, the stranger observed, "If they are sure I'm in this building, they'll dynamite it."

"No, they won't," Mr. Blake declared, positively. "There are some white men in our crew of miners, old-timers who would hang a dynamiter as quick as we would."

Our conversation was low-spoken, and the hours dragged on until at last the sky showed signs of coming day. Then I let the fellow out of the back door, watching until he disappeared into the timber. I never saw him again, nor did I ever hear a word spoken of him, even in the Curlew boardinghouse.

The demonetization of silver caused the Curlew to shut down completely now.[2] Most of the miners went away to Butte. Curlew

[2] The Panic of 1893 and the repeal of the Sherman Silver Purchase Act forced the shutdown of many western mines and was marked by large-scale unemployment and labor strife.

Camp was almost "too dead to skin." This presented to me an embarrassing situation. The date had already been set for my lady to meet me in Missoula, where we were to be married. The shutdown worried me not a little, since the company had not paid me a cent for several months. I was flat broke. There was every reason to believe that the Helena & Victor Mining Company would some day pay me the $706.50 that it owed me; but I needed it *now*. And what a pile of money it seemed to me then! To postpone the date of my marriage seemed out of the question.

While I was struggling with my problem, the mine foreman, who had been with the Curlew ever since it began operations, proposed that several of us lease the mine and together work out a shoot of high-grade ore that had been left in a stope on the four-hundred level. This shoot was small, so that considerable waste material had to be mined in order to get it out. However, we decided to get the lease. It was readily given.

I worked, night shift, in the mine for more than two months. By this time the pay shoot had pinched. Even the low-grade ore that we had been mining along with the other had been "horsed" out, leaving nothing of value in sight. To get Christmas money we started the concentrator, running our ore through the mill. My share of the proceeds was in truth to be matrimonial money, and at the end of our milling proved to be just $26.00, after our bills were paid.

My disappointment was great. Besides the miserable amount of money that had fallen to me as my share for more than two months' hard work, I had met with an accident that came near crippling me for life. As soon as we started the concentrator I went to work in the mill. The shells on the Cornish rolls were so badly worn that they had to be changed. Luckily, there were two new shells in the meagre list of supplies on hand, and we decided to use these. In driving the old ones off the journals with heavy sledges a flying piece of the steel, chipped from the edge of a shell, struck me on the knee cap, breaking off in the bone.

I drove to Victor, where, after probing the wound and removing the bit of steel, the Doctor said, "You may have a stiff knee during the rest of your days. You must go straight to bed and stay there."

"I *can't*," I said, positively. "I'm going to Missoula to be married tomorrow, if I can manage to get some money," I added, intending to ask Mr. Blake for a loan

Doctor Handbidge was then a bachelor. I shall never forget his surprise at my statement. Cocking his head on one side, a mannerism of his, he said, "I'll let you have $100; but if you go to Missoula tomorrow, or a week from tomorrow, I will not be responsible for your leg."

"I've *got* to go, Doctor," I told him. "The lady is already on her way to Missoula, you see."

"Well, well," he fretted, "if you are bound to be foolish, to take such chances and go to Missoula, I'll have to go with you, I suppose."

And he did go, the good fellow, actually holding my leg in his lap part of the time on the train. Together we went to the station in Missoula, where, being on crutches and not wishing to show myself too suddenly, I commissioned him to help the young lady into the station and to tell her as carefully as possible about my accident. I could not believe that I would be permanently crippled, and yet did not think it fair to my intended wife to hide the fact that my injury might have a bad result, so I told her what the Doctor had said about my knee.

"We shall get along well enough," she smiled bravely. And we always have.

The next day we bought our household goods with what was left of $155.00, our entire capital, and began housekeeping in the Curlew camp, where we remained until the next winter. By this time the company of leasers had decided that the Curlew would not pay, and gave up the lease. The Frau and I had had no money since we were married. I remember when we first settled in our house in the Curlew camp she had required an extra closet for her clothes and that I laughingly warned her that a cigar box would soon hold all her apparel if my luck did not change for the better. Now winter was at hand and we were flat broke. I did not get my back pay from the company for more than a year. Everybody who was in search of work went to Butte. Accordingly, I moved the Frau to Victor, made her as comfortable as possible, and then went to Butte myself.

The "silver bill" that demonetized silver and crippled the Curlew had made work very scarce in Butte as well. I rustled the mines and smelters for a whole month without a single gleam of success. I was down to my last borrowed dollar when I was given work weighing calcine at the Butte & Boston smelter. The superintendent had himself engaged me, saying, "I want the weight of every buggy and barrow of calcine that go to the blast furnaces on the night shift."

He handed me a little book and a pencil, and then to impress me with the importance of the required figures he added: "Understand me; I want the weight of *every* buggy and barrow of calcine, or none at all."

A platform scales had been set up in the calcine yard, with a single electric light hanging directly over it. These, with my book and pencil, were all the appurtenances belonging to my office. The night was windy and cold, with thick flurries of soiled snow. The red-hot calcine wheeled upon the scale's platform gave off copious clouds of bluish-green sulphur fumes that inflamed my throat and irritated my nose almost beyond endurance. Nevertheless, I weighed each load as rapidly as possible, carefully noting the weight and the number of each buggy and barrow. So rapidly did they come that I had no time to exchange words with even the English-speaking wheelers. About midnight I noticed that a certain buggy had not shown up to be weighed for some time, nearly an hour. The numbers of all the others appeared in my list quite regularly. This worried me. The wheeler of the missing buggy might be loafing, which was none of my business. But if he was wheeling his charges regularly and was avoiding me and my scales, it was my business to put a stop to his game at once.

The electric globe hanging over my head made a bright circle of light around me. Beyond this, all was black darkness filled with sulphurous fumes and snowflakes. I could not leave my scales, because the loads were coming nearly as fast as I could weigh them. Suspicious of the wheeler of the missing buggy, I kept my one eye on the darkness directly in front of me till I caught the greenish glow of a load of burning calcine that was slipping by just beyond the ring of light.

There was a load already on my scales. "Wait right where you are a minute," I told its wheeler, not knowing if he spoke any English. Snatching up a five-pound scale weight I stopped the recreant buggy. I did not wish to make any trouble, but dared not lose my job through weakness, with times so hard and a baby about to be born into our household. "Go back to the scales," I said, without anger in my voice.

The fellow was an Italian. "No, me no go back," he retorted stubbornly, and started on again.

I took hold of his shirt sleeve. The buggy nearly upset. "Go back," I said, my voice rising.

Snarling, he sprang at me. I let him have the scale weight between the eyes, and down he went. Wheeling the buggy to the scales, I weighed it, watching for the Italian the while. All this brought the smelter shift boss, a young man who was then a little upstage, although he later made a name for himself in the smelting world.

"These men will not stand for your weighing their loads," he told me imperiously. "It takes too much time, anyway, and must be stopped."

"I'm doing the best I can," I told him. "I have orders from the superintendent to weigh every buggy and barrow of calcine that go to the blast furnaces on this shift, and I'll do it."

I did do it, and yet next morning I was let out. "I've got all the figures I require just now," said Mr. Allen, the superintendent. "I'll keep you in mind," he added. "I may have something better to offer you by the first of the month."

Discouraged, my nose and throat raw as fresh meat, I left the Butte & Boston works feeling low-spirited. There was now no good in my rustling for work at this plant, I knew. I began looking for a position in the stores uptown, without once thinking that the first of the month might bring me good news from Mr. Allen, whom I liked. I had tried to secure employment at nearly every store in Butte without feeling the least encouragement when I luckily got a job cleaning old brick from a dismantled smokestack. Being paid by the thousand, I did rather well while the brick lasted, sending fifteen dollars of my earnings to the Frau.

One day soon after my brick-cleaning job had played out I met Mr. Allen on the street. "I've heard that you are an assayer," he smiled. "Come down to my office in the morning. I'm going to put you on as first assistant in the Butte & Boston laboratory."

I was not an assayer. I could determine the amount of silver or lead in an ore, but had never been inside a laboratory where regular analyses were made. I told Mr. Allen this, quite frankly.

"I'm going to try you, anyway," he declared. "You are the kind I like to have around me. I'm sure you'll master the work, and I mean to give you the chance. Come in the morning."

The quick little man whose eyes looked straight through one left me standing in a daze. I watched him turn the corner, thinking of Governor Hauser. Then I began to sail up into the clouds. I wished above all things to be an assayer, to know metallurgy, and to excel in the mining, milling, and smelting of ore. But how, with this running start, could I hope to win? I'd be like a grizzly bear in a china closet. The thought of the laboratory, with its delicate glassware, stampeded me. I needed this opportunity, and now, fearing failure, I wanted to run away from it. I forgot my supper, digging into my books on assaying and chemistry until my nerves were like the quills on a tormented porcupine. The more I read the less I seemed to understand. "I can at least go back to the wilderness and live, even make a good home there," I thought, after putting out my lamp to go to bed, with meaningless masses of figures dancing jigs in my mind. Always, when tormented, I have found a kind of comfort in the thought that I could at any time go back to the wilderness and live happily.

Next morning Mr. Allen went with me to the Butte & Boston assay office and laboratory, and there introduced me to its chief,

Mr. Thomas, a Welshman, who asked me if I'd had long experience in laboratories.

"None at all," I told him. Nevertheless, he gave me the schemes that he wished me to use, and while he watched and guided me, I went earnestly to work. Two or three days later I heard Mr. Allen ask Mr. Thomas how I was getting along.

"Fine," said the Welshman. "He told me that he had had no previous experience, but the moment he picked up a graduate and a bottle I knew he had often handled them before he came here. He's doing fine."

I had never before handled a graduate, however. It was my duty to make all the coppers, silvers, golds, irons, sulphurs, silicas, etc. In fact, all the work, both in the laboratory and furnace room, fell to the first assistant, excepting only the "controls," determinations of the values in purchased ores, and in our own furnace products. Often complete analyses of ores and slags were required. For a time these gave me trouble. Even the giant powder used in the company's mines had sometimes to be analyzed, and this, when first offered, embarrassed both Mr. Thomas and me. I remember that both of us hurried away to find some man who knew a scheme for the analysis of dynamite, and that after consulting several reputable assayers who could not help us, I happened to think of a man who, because of his love for liquor, had never been given a very responsible position. In a last effort I climbed the hill to see this man. "Why, yes," he replied, glad to do me a favor, glibly reciting a perfect scheme for the analysis of giant powder which I jotted down in my notebook. This saved the day for both Mr. Thomas and me, since after its introduction four samples of giant powder were sent to our laboratory every morning for more than a year.

The Butte & Boston laboratory was then in the old Jim Talbot house. The rooms were small and the ventilation miserable. Day in and day out I could scarcely see across the laboratory because of fumes that quickly rendered even the old-fashioned cut-nails driven into the wall so brittle that they might easily be broken with one's fingers.

Sometimes, especially in damp weather, the whole of Butte City was hidden by sulphurous smoke and acrid fumes so completely that it was not uncommon for men on their way to work to lose their direction. We have had them call at our house at all hours and ask its location, so that they might get their bearings. Trolley cars spluttered green flashes of sulphurous light; and funeral processions were all too common in the days of Butte's "stink-piles."

In those days funeral processions were real affairs. If the dead man had been popular, a brass band always led the plumed hearse down Butte's main street, even though the procession found it necessary to go by devious ways to reach it. Here stirring dirges, played with deep feeling on shining silver horns, cast a shivering solemnity upon everybody within hearing, even upon the occasional drunks asleep in their rented carriages far back toward the processions' tail end. But returning from the cemetery out on the flat these fickle processions always fell to pieces, often becoming horse races in which buggies were smashed and painful injuries sustained by both the men and their animals. Before convenient saloons along the way back from the flat one saw many panting horses, hitched to well-cared-for buggies waiting while their drivers revived their spirits by toasting the departed, whom they had so lately, and so gloriously, laid away. Brass bands were kept busy in Butte City then; and they were good bands, too. Cornish, Welsh, and Italians are musical; and the big mining camp had them to spare.

The Frau joined me in Butte as soon as I found employment. We moved our household goods into a decent-looking house at once. But the place was uninhabitable. Not only was it generally out of repair, but it was infested with bedbugs in such numbers that we hurriedly moved into another dwelling, not far from my work. This was a double house. A miner and his wife occupied half of it, and they kept roomers. We did not get acquainted with these neighbors, however. I scarcely ever saw them myself.

One night about a week before our first baby was born we were awakened by a woman's screaming on the other side of the thin

partition that separated us from our neighbors. Getting up, I lit
the lamp. Somebody was coming downstairs pell-mell in the
neighbor's apartment. Then two shots rang out in quick succession. I got the Frau out of her bed, and, lifting the mattress, stood
it up against the wall back of the bed's headboard, hoping to thus
stop stray bullets that might come through the wall. The thud of
bare running feet continued, going upstairs and then down again,
as though somebody were being chased. I stepped out on the front
porch that served both apartments. A white figure flew past me,
then turned to go back. Reaching, I grabbed, and held a woman's
arm that was slippery with blood.

"Help me! He'll kill me; he'll kill me!" she whimpered, trem-
bling in the cold night.

I dared not take her into the Frau's presence. "I'll help you," I
said.

Just then her husband appeared. Seeing me, his warlike attitude
vanished instantly. He became gentle with the shivering woman
who, clad in a nightdress, was clinging to me.

He was a Welshman. "We've 'ad a bit of a row, me an' me
'ooman," he explained. "We'll 'ave no more. Come into the 'ouse,
Nell. I'll not lay a 'and to ye. Come, Nell, gel."

The war was over. They were quiet as mice next door when I
finally blew out the light. Nevertheless, we were glad to move
into another, and this time a brand new, house.

The first baby is a lovely, fearsome thing, its expected arrival
a hope haunted by shadows. Frankly, I was frightened when in the
night the Frau called me, saying that I had better go for the
doctor. Telephones were then few in Butte. I had borrowed a
barber's bicycle for this event, and now I rode like a racer through
the windy March night.

The streets were deserted. Their strange emptiness, the darkened
houses, the vacant lots strewn with rubbish, and the silent,
sparkling lights in shaft houses high up on the hill contributed
something eerie and foreboding to my errand. It was as though
humanity had quietly removed itself from the Frau and me.

On my way back, going downhill at a mad clip, I thought to save time by cutting across a vacant lot at a corner. Blinded by an old-fashioned arc light that sputtered fitfully, I rode, head first, into a newly excavated basement that was ten feet deep. The fall stunned me. I do not know how long I was unconscious; anyhow, I reached the Frau before the doctor arrived. I well remember that when I chided him upon his lack of speed, he said, "Keep cool. Everything would have been all right here if I hadn't come at all."

For me the outstanding feature of the following day was holding the baby. The designing nurse said, imperiously, "Take her for a moment." Before I realized what was happening I had the baby, and the nurse had slipped into another room. I shall never forget how much I feared injuring the fragile bundle in my arms, nor how hopelessly awkward I felt. I would rather have tackled a grizzly bear with a broken jackknife than have tried to hold that baby—and, of course, the baby cried, yelled her best. The scornful look given me by the nurse upon her return for the child didn't register. I willingly gave up my charge and slipped quietly out of the back door to split wood.

I have said that times were hard in Butte. Work, especially in all the mining camps that had been affected by the demonetization of silver, was scarce. Miners drifted into Butte from every point, and with them were many dissolute characters. Burglaries became common. Holdups occurred every night. Sometimes only the lunch buckets of workmen were demanded, showing that men were desperately hungry, willing to do almost anything for bread. This condition fostered political filth, and politically Butte was filthy.

There was to be a second battle for the state capitalship.[3] Helena, Bozeman, and Anaconda had already tried conclusions. Now the race was to be between Helena, the established capital city, and Anaconda, Marcus Daly's town. Daly and Clark, Butte's big men, had quarreled (over a water flume it was said) and

[3] Under the state's constitution, the people were to choose their state's capital by ballot. In 1875, after months of controversy over the result of the election, the capital went to Helena from Virginia City. In 1892 Marcus Daly tried to get it moved to Anaconda, but Helena won the election. In 1894, backed by W. A. Clark, Helena again won.

their quarrel, by devious ways, led first Butte and then all Montana into the greatest corporation battle ever known in the Northwest. Marcus Daly's town was boomed to the echo. Its smelter would "relieve Butte." Daly's railroad, the Butte Anaconda & Pacific, would "go on to the coast," as its name suggested. Daly owned Anaconda and wanted the capital built there.

Clark was for Helena. His interests were large, and his opinion of Daly low. All through the summer and fall the battle raged, the hard times contributing to its bitterness. I do not believe that any man who is thoroughly conversant with any question can be truly neutral toward its final settlement. He may believe that he is neutral and yet have somewhere in his stifled conscience a decided opinion waiting for expression. But our bread and butter "doth make cowards of us all."

Men lined up in this capital fight like soldiers for battle, opportunity to work for either Clark or Daly too often controlling their votes. I believe that this was the summer Coxey's Army, on its way to the nation's capital to protest against the lack of employment, reached Butte.[4] I remember a train of boxcars loaded with men wearing every imaginable kind of clothing that emptied itself in Butte. Spreading over the mining camp, these men begged food and clothing, even bed coverings. The Frau and I gave two rather decent-looking young fellows of Coxey's Army a bed quilt that we really needed ourselves. Most of this tatterdemalion "army" went on, believing in its mission, perhaps. Others remained in Butte, and, securing work from the contending chiefs of the camp, voted for the state's capital, even though they were citizens of some other state. Such acts were easily accomplished then.

Besides the Clark and Daly interests there were other large operators in Butte. The Butte & Boston, the Boston-Montana, and the Parrot Company were the most important of these; and they, too, entered the fight for the state's capital. The Butte & Boston Company that employed me was strongly for Helena. This

---

[4] In 1894 Jacob S. Coxey led an army of unemployed, some of whom had come from as far as the Pacific Coast, on Washington to publicize and present his proposals for public works to aid the jobless.

was pleasing to me, since in the former battle, while in the Curlew camp, I had cut up a pair of bed sheets to make banners, "Helena for the Capital." I had never visited Anaconda. Helena was already the capital city; anyhow I could not, by my vote, consent to moving the established capital from Helena to Mr. Daly's one-man town. As the deciding day drew near there were lengthy torchlight processions led by massed bands. Banners bearing various devices, some of them insulting to those espousing the other side of the question from that represented by the procession, were liberally displayed by marching men. These were the last great torchlight parades that I ever saw. To witness one of them and keep silent was to invite a fight with some obstreperous fellow who differed with you in opinion, expressed or implied or even imagined by him. Men are sometimes strangely loyal to a cause they have hastily espoused for bread and butter. And yet in all the bitterness engendered by this campaign there were laughs for those who had not lost all sense of fun. I remember that one night I was greatly shocked to discover one of our Butte & Boston men in an "Anaconda for the Capital" procession. The fellow was at the very tail end of the noisy throng, a conspicuous place; and he carried a banner, besides.

"What were you doing in that Anaconda procession last night?" I asked him next morning, suspiciously.

"Me? Why, I was getting myself a new suit of clothes for the price of a little walking with a fool banner," he laughed. "And I'll wear that suit when I go to the polls to vote for Helena, and don't you forget it," he added.

A five-dollar gold piece was the price usually paid marchers who were known to belong to the other party; but as the campaign advanced the price went up and up, until a traitor, or a make-believe traitor, got big pay for a little "four-flushing." Of course, not every man voted as he marched, since Montana had already adopted a decent system of balloting. However, a man who could neither read nor write might have a judge mark his ballot for him; but the judges were not always honest. In an election booth on election day I heard an Irishman tell a judge, whom I knew intimately, "I don't give a damn how I votes, so long as I votes for Pat Sullivan for Treasurer, and Anaconda for the capital."

"That was duck soup," said the judge to me, afterward. "That Mick voted for Helena for the capital, and Johnson for Assessor!"

I might add that Helena won easily, and that Johnson, as Silver Bow County's treasurer, skipped out with the public's funds and has never been heard of since.

After this election there was a sharp slump, especially in the disgruntled Daly camp. Voters in both Butte and Anaconda had been given work and colonized for the coming contest. Now many of them were let out, with winter coming on. Men wearing good clothes often followed loads of wood to their destinations and asked to saw and split the wood for food. And yet the big mining camp was a busy place. Scores of whistles, the tone of each well known to its tribe of workers, blew regularly for noon and changing shifts of miners, mill employees, and smeltermen. Their number proclaimed to the world that Butte had many independent employers of labor, that the big camp was wide open to all who wished to play at the game of copper mining.

The miners then in Butte were mostly Cornishmen and Irish. The latter were employed almost exclusively in the Daly mines where Cornishmen were few. And it was generally understood that in the other mines "no Irish need apply." Butte's smeltermen were mostly Welsh. The Cornish and Welsh were all Protestants and nearly all Republicans. The Irish were Roman Catholics and strong Democrats. Most of the Irish belonged to the Ancient Order of Hibernians. The "Cousin-Jacks" were loyal Sons of Saint George. On each twelfth day of July the latter commemorated the Battle of the Boyne with a grand parade; and on each seventeenth of March the Hibernians, with plumed chapeaus and uniforms gleaming with green, shimmering swords, and religious banners, walked in honor of Saint Patrick. On these great days both factions were "on the peck." There were always many fights, some of them extremely brutal. I remember one Fourth of July when the proprietor of the old Sasarac saloon put up tiny

American flags so as to form the letters "A.P.A."[5] Some Irishmen attempted to tear the letters down. In the melee that followed instantly five men were killed, all Irish, I believe. The state militia was called out, and for a day or two Butte was under martial law, while everybody tiptoed about as though open war were imminent. Nevertheless, the old Sasarac saloon that had brought on the trouble by displaying the offending letters continued to do business and on the next Fourth of July put up the letters again. This time nobody molested them; and it is well that they did not, since the Sasarac was ready for trouble now, and a red page might have been added to Butte's history. All this is now changed. The Cornish in Butte are comparatively few, and there is only one whistle—the deep, reverberating blasts of the old Parrot whistle summons hordes of workers to the mines of the Anaconda Copper Mining Company. The rest have been scrapped.

About this time I was somehow elected delegate to a Silver Bow County Republican convention. I got a day off and attended, feeling quite important. In Butte nothing of a public nature had the least bit of significance without a brass band. A band was playing patriotic airs on the street before the convention hall when, dressed in my best, I entered the spacious place that was profusely decorated with red, white, and blue bunting. I had a thrill in my heart and a lump in my throat when I took my seat beside one of the camp's important citizens who greeted me like a brother. The buzz of conversation became a loud babble of voices when the band outside suddenly ceased playing to file into the hall, taking seats on the platform beneath an immense American flag. When this commotion rested, a thin little man whom I had not noticed until now arose from his chair directly in front of the band and began a speech. He had not uttered two hundred words when the man beside me, the important citizen, stirred impatiently, and then somebody hissed. Pandemonium burst upon us. Furniture was broken, the water pitcher on the speaker's table smashed, and

[5] The American Protective Association was a secret anti-Catholic society organized in 1887. It is said to have had a million members by 1896, but in that year split over McKinley's candidacy for the Presidency and died out by 1911.

the speaker ejected, thrown out—and so was the temporary secretary, all in jig time. The place was a wreck. And whether I deserved it or not I got a punch on the nose that made my face feel as large as a stock saddle. I scarcely knew what it was all about, and yet I felt hostile enough.

At last, quiet was restored. The lost dignity that I had so much respected returned to the convention. Speakers promptly cleared away the clouds of ignorance that surrounded such delegates as I. Clark and Daly, both Democrats, "had had their representatives here in our Republican convention, and they had *dared*, etc.!" My indignation was as deep as the Atlantic. I felt proud of my injured nose.

Purged of disturbing elements, the convention held on until nearly morning. There were speeches and yet more speeches. How men did love oratory then! At last, tired out, I went home believing that I had been of service to my country; and I had unwittingly been bitten, inoculated with the virus of political activity that was to keep me in hot water for many a year. But with all my enthusiasm I never learned to successfully play the game of politics with professional politicians. In the years that were to come I grew so used to losing political battles that I should not have known what to do with a victory.

We began to hear a little about F. Augustus Heinze now.[6] He was building a smelter between the Butte & Boston plant and Meaderville. One Sunday, there being little work in our laboratory on this day, I went to see the new smelter. It did not impress me deeply; a one-horse outfit, I thought it then. But just across the valley near the foothills I saw four Indian lodges, looking white against the brown background. The sight of them thrilled me more than anything I had lately seen. The day was fine. The mountain-tops laid shadows upon the four lodges that seemed to belong to

---

[6] Heinze came to Butte in 1891 at the age of twenty. He became one of the three giants in Butte mining, with W. A. Clark and Marcus Daly. J. K. Howard, in *Montana, High, Wide and Handsome*, p. 69, describes him as a "gay, handsome industrial desperado and demagogue"; and Glasscock, in *The War of the Copper King* (New York: Bobbs-Merrill Co., 1935), pp. 235–240, testifies to his ability as an orator.

another world altogether. I walked to the camp, not guessing what Indians were there. Imagine my delight when I was greeted by my old friend, Muskegon, the Cree, who had told me so many tribal folk tales in the Flathead.

Times were growing hard for the Crees, he told me. Game in the open country was scarce. They had been gathering buffalo bones and selling polished buffalo horns in towns. They were now working their way back to the Flathead country, where there were yet many deer and elk in the forest. Muskegon looked dejected. His clothes, ragged portions of white men's apparel, seemed to have lowered both his morale and personal appearance. He was a changed man. Yellow-face, another Cree friend who was in this camp, was more cheerful. However, he was a much younger man, and still wore leggings and breechclout. We visited for hours. They could not understand why I, a hunter, came to be in Butte. And by the same token, I was at a loss to explain their presence so near to the big mining camp. I did not then suspect that the wandering band of Crees and Chippewas, numbering about three hundred men, women, and children, to which these four lodges belonged, would someday become a charge of mine.[7] However, when I went to work the next morning I saw that the four lodges were gone. Several years were to pass before I again saw a Cree.

The Parrot Company, that had been erecting a large smelter near Whitehall, many miles from Butte, suddenly ceased its operations there. The new plant, although nearly completed, never blew in a furnace or turned a wheel. The great merger, or taking over, of all the mines, mills, and smelters in Butte, excepting the properties of W. A. Clark and the tiny smelter of F. Augustus Heinze, had been consummated by a new concern, the Anaconda Copper Mining Company.

Now, one by one, great changes came to the big mining camp. The new company, reaching out, absorbed the lumber industry,

[7] They were, at least in part, Indians who had taken part in the Riel Rebellion in Saskatchewan in 1884 and had been wandering in poverty and distress since. A good account of the Riel Rebellion is in J. K. Howard's *Strange Empire, A Narrative of the Northwest* (New York: Morrow and Co., 1952).

and finally, under another name, the water power of the state. Today in Montana its interests are widespread, its capable representatives everywhere. It owns the state, controls its press, and dictates its politics and its policies as absolutely as though the commonwealth of Montana were a mesmerized nonentity.

For a time we scarcely felt the hand of the new master at the Butte & Boston. The following spring I was given the chief's position in the laboratory, Mr. Thomas having gone to visit his old home in Wales. I felt my responsibility and worked hard to keep things in shipshape. One night, while I was in charge, a fire broke out in the furnace room of the assay office. The smelter whistle goaded me out of sound sleep at about eleven o'clock. Racing for the works, I discovered on the way that the assay office was afire. My heart tumbled into my shoes when I thought of the havoc the fire crew would be sure to make in my laboratory. And what a mess they made of it! Its equipment was tossed about, nearly all the finer glassware smashed, many articles missing. Water and plaster from the walls and ceiling made the place almost uninhabitable the next day; and yet somehow the work must go on there.

Among the "controls" that day there were two lots of ore which the company had purchased from leasers. One lot ran fifty-six ounces of silver per ton. I shall never forget these figures. The other lot, belonging to the same Cornish leasers, carried but three ounces per ton. These returns were sent to the uptown office of the company, as usual. Next morning two wild Cornishmen were waiting for me at the laboratory door. They declared, in positive language, that the two lots had been turned around, that is, that the fifty-six-ounce lot was the larger shipment, and the three-ounce lot the smaller one, it having been shipped to us in order for them to learn if the ore would pay to mine, etc. I explained that the tickets placed in all samples of ore reaching me were made at the sampler, and that I had nothing to do with their descriptions of lots. "I do not believe your lots have been turned around," I told them, "but you had better see Mr. Allen, the superintendent, about it, before it is too late."

In half an hour Mr. Allen came into my office. "I've no doubt whatever that these Cousin-Jacks are wrong in their contention," he said, "but this fire, and the mess it has made here may have made you nervous. I'd run those two controls again, Frank," he advised.

I did run them again. When they were ready to pour I told the furnace man, who had been working there for years, to pour the crucibles. Later on, when I had cupeled the silver, I saw at once that, as far as I was concerned, there had been no mistake, and should have gone no farther. But, being a bit skittish now, I weighed the larger silver bead, simply to check my former figures; and my head began to swim. The silver bead weighed exactly forty-six, instead of fifty-six ounces, a difference of ten ounces to the ton from the returns I had sent to the uptown office. Now, what ought I to do? One thousand ounces of silver at one dollar per ounce was a sizable mistake. I felt giddy as a dizzy duck. Calling in my assistant, I told him what I had done and asked his advice.

"Say nothing," he counseled. "If these Cousin-Jacks get a thousand dollars too much, you may bet your life they'll keep as still as dead kittens."

"Yes, perhaps; but what about the end of the month? I shall then be short a thousand ounces of silver, you see."

"Hell, we can pinch that much before the end of the month," he declared. "Why, with all the lots that are coming in now, a little here and a little there will do the trick, and nobody'll be the wiser. Say nothing, and I will not," he promised, going back to his work in the laboratory.

I sat at the balances, looking out at the ore teams straining at their heavy loads. Only two days before, one of the drivers had beaten his wheelers, two fine horses, with a pick until one of them, catching his shoe in the railroad track, had pulled his hoof off. Running outside, I remonstrated rather violently and the bully had chased me into the laboratory with the pick. I had stopped him at the door with a two-pound bottle of sulphuric acid that I had hurriedly secured and uncorked, with a warning to the horse-killer. I began to hate the place. I'd resign. I'd go straight to Mr. Allen and tell him this at once.

Rising, I took off my apron and got my hat. At the door I saw Mr. Allen on his way to dinner. I called to him. "I've resigned," I said, telling the whole story so rapidly that he laughed at my haste.

"No, no," he smiled, when I had finished. "The fire and too much work have unsteadied you. I don't believe you've made any mistake. Did you pour those crucibles yourself?" he asked, knowing that sometimes when work pressed we let the furnace man pour crucibles.

"No, sir," I said, "but—."

"Well," he interrupted, "run those samples again, and you'll find that your first figures are correct. And, Frank, did you ever notice a black spot on the platform of your fine balances?" he asked, with a hand on my shoulder.

"Yes, sir, and it will not come off," I assured him, wondering what the black spot had to do with all this.

"That black spot used to be a white gum label," he smiled. "On it were once the letters 'B. C.'; and they didn't mean 'Before Christ,' either. They meant 'Be Careful.' I put that label there when I held your job myself, because I made a greater mistake than this one is, even if it proves to be a mistake. Mine was never rectified. Yours may still be taken care of, if it turns out to be a mistake. Anyway, it will make a better man of you. I haven't lost any confidence in you, even though you have yourself."

Later that afternoon when I placed on the scale's pan a new silver bead obtained from the troublesome lot of ore, I'm sure I held my breath until the swinging needle showed exactly fifty-six ounces per ton. I couldn't wait to tell Mr. Allen. Down the hill I raced without hat or coat, my apron flying in the wind. "It's all right, it's all right!" I shouted through his office door.

"Of course it's all right," he smiled, his eyes twinkling, the good little man.

Years afterward, when I was a member of the legislature, he asked me to change my vote on an important measure, but I could

103

not do this, even for him. However, when I told him that I would not change my vote, he said, "I didn't expect you would, Frank. I'm sorry that I felt obliged to ask you to." The last time I saw him he was so nearly blind that he could not leave his house alone.

Toward fall Mr. Thomas returned from Wales, and I again became first assistant in the Butte & Boston laboratory. One day Mr. Allen told me that the Basin & Bay State outfit at Basin, Montana, wanted me to take charge of their assay office. "It will pay you better than your present position as first assistant here," he said, "and much as I hate to see you go, I want you to do the best you can for yourself and family."

I left the Frau and our little daughter in Butte and went to Basin. Within a week I knew that my move had been a mistake. By the values I found in the company's ore and concentrates I knew the outfit could not long survive. To move the Frau and the baby to Basin was now out of the question. All I could do was to wait for the smash that I knew was coming and make the best of it.

The winter was bitterly cold. I slept in a tiny room in the office building, the heat from my furnace fire so warming the bricks that they kept the room quite comfortable. I had but one companion in the camp, James Buskett, the assayer at the Hope mine, nearby. Both Buskett and I were in the same boat. His outfit, like my own, was about to go under. Nobody knows as much about the pay in a mining property as its assayer, and neither the Hope nor the Katy was producing "pay." Buskett, however, was a single man, a fact that he greatly appreciated—and more than once mentioned when we discussed our situations. The camp was small, the Hope and the Katy being the only properties at work. Its tiny business and residence section was strung along the railroad's right of way in a narrow flat shut in by steep hills that rose abruptly. Snow was deep that winter, so that whenever Buskett and I took walks for exercize we used the railroad grade, feeling completely cut off from the rest of the world. Our conversations were not always joyful. Often when we walked we spoke not at all, having tired of each other's company, as men do, without either forgetting that the other was all the company there was. We ate our breakfasts together and then separated for the day, or until one or the other finished working. Whichever of us finished first went directly to the other's office to sit and wait until the time came for us to go for our walk. One extremely cold morning, when the windows were so frosted that they resembled thick, white blankets, I entered the chilly dining room to find everybody painfully quiet, even the generally boisterous waitress. Buskett, who usually pretended morning cheer, at least, merely nodded. "Awful, isn't it?" he said in a tone of voice that gripped me.

I shook off the dread his words awoke in me. "What's the matter, Jim? Has the old Hope shut down?" I asked.

"My God, don't you *know*; haven't you *heard*?" he asked, leaning across the oilcloth-covered table, a case knife held like a dagger in his hand. "Butte's blown up, blown plumb to hell. Nobody knows how many were killed, but hundreds, hundreds!"[8]

I left the table, a dozen useless questions in my mind. Outside in the biting air I stood staring blankly at the snow-covered mountains. Butte blown up—and there would be no train out of Basin until evening. Running to the station, I telegraphed the Frau, wondering if she, or anybody else, would answer. Then I walked the railroad track up and down for half a mile each way until I got a reply. The Frau and baby were all right.

Relieved, I began now to learn a little about the explosion that had wrecked the city of Butte. A warehouse containing many tons of dynamite had exploded in the night, blowing men to bits, wrecking buildings, and sending thousands of steel rabbleheads and unexploded sticks of dynamite all over the city. If the dynamite had not been mostly frozen, the whole camp would have been destroyed. Our house, two miles from the explosion, had had its

---

[8] In a pamphlet entitled "The Great Dynamite Explosions, Butte, 1895," J. F. Davies states that the blast was said to have been heard in Willow Creek, fifty-eight miles away. Glass was shattered at a distance of two miles. The coroner's jury listed fifty-seven persons killed. Describing the destruction, he wrote, in the rhetoric of the day: "Then indeed was there devastation and death! An awful Charybdis escaped only to be cast upon Scylla. Dead bodies by the score were lying everywhere about . . . . Alas! Alas! What woe is wrought!"

transoms blown open. The house shook like a leaf. Lights went out all over the city. The Frau, alone with the baby, believing the explosion to be an earthquake and fearing another, made ready to leave the house.

Wild stories that professed to account for the terrible explosion went the rounds. One was that the dynamite had been intentionally set off by a fuse timed to blow up the "Chippy," a passenger train that was due in Butte at the very moment of the explosion. This train was crowded with members of the A. P. A. who had gone to Helena, where the legislature was in session, to protest against the election of Thomas H. Carter to the United States Senate.[9] They were returning a little late, fortunately. The railroad station and the warehouse were close together, so that if the dynamite had exploded while the train was at the station every soul within a quarter of a mile would have been blown into eternity.

Early in March the Basin & Bay State gave up the struggle for existence. Being now obliged to find employment, I returned to Butte, where work was yet very scarce. I helped dismantle the old Silver Bow mill, a landmark in Butte; I cleaned more brick, and finally wheeled ashes for eighteen months. This work was for the Butte & Boston, where I had been assayer. But Mr. Allen was gone now and was raising apples in the Bitterroot valley. A stranger was in charge of the old works, so that I was a rank outsider.

Another daughter, Verne, had been born to the Frau and me. We both wished to get away from Butte, where there were no trees, not even a blade of grass. Besides this, our neighborhood was not satisfying. English was scarcely ever heard there. Across the street from our home there was an Austrian saloon where beer-guzzling Austrians made the nights merry for themselves, some-

[9] Carter, a young Catholic Republican lawyer, had come to Helena in 1882. In the 1894 election for a congressional seat he defeated W. A. Clark, with the help of Daly forces. He had been territorial delegate from March 4 to November 7, 1889, and was a senator from 1895 to 1901, and from 1905 to 1911. He held several federal offices, and worked especially for government support of land reclamation, once staging a fourteen-hour filibuster against a river and harbor bill.

times foregathering beneath our bedroom window to sing, and even to quarrel violently. To add to our dissatisfaction with our surroundings, our eldest daughter, Wilda, suffered an attack of typhoid fever and nearly left us. My ears were open for an opportunity to leave Butte. At last it came, the merest gamble with success, and yet we took it gladly.

CHAPTER V

Assayer and Legislator

In July, 1896, a man whom I knew leased the old Toledo mine and concentrator at Brandon, near Sheridan, in Madison County.[1] He told me that he intended to install a blast furnace there and smelt his own ore on the ground. I suspected that he was dreaming of boring an auger-hole with a gimlet, but nevertheless, in my anxiety to get out of Butte, I accepted his offer and became his assayer.

The Frau and I looked upon this move as an adventure that would at least give our babies an acquaintance with grass, trees, and flowers—things they had never seen. Our rent was paid in advance. We decided to leave our household goods in the house for a time. Perhaps when another month's rent became due we should know more about our future. These things settled, I went, light-heartedly, to the stage office and arranged to have the coach call for us in the morning.

Never before had our yard looked so forbidding. Its yellowish-brown surface of decomposed granite, without even a weed to grace it, fairly glinted in the summer sunlight. I promised myself that I would never come back to it, that our children should have grass to play upon beneath leafy trees, even though I had again to become a trapper. My ash-wheeling job had not been difficult. It was what was known as a "band job." The company maintained a brass band, a really fine musical organization that became quite famous. To hold its musicians, it kept them employed at easy tasks about the works. Ours was really the Boston-Montana Band, well known as such to this day. Most of its musicians were Europeans. I

[1] The town of Brandon no longer exists.

109

remember one huge fellow who blew a horn nearly as large as himself. His face was absolutely blank, his head misshapen, and his arms like those of an ape, reaching far below his knees. This fellow was given the job of driving old Billy, a fine gray horse that had more brains than his driver. Old Billy had handled his car on the dangerous tramway for years without accident, shunning the yawning ore bins with uncanny cleverness. We all loved Billy, and old Billy loved us all. One day this clownish hornblower, who did not know which end of a horse goes ahead, was the cause of our pet falling into the deep ore bins, where he was slowly smothered. From that day "Joe-joe, the dog-faced one," as we called the fellow, was a hated man. I might be sorry that I left my ash-wheeling job to gamble with uncertainty, and yet I was happy over the prospect ahead.

The coach called at our house very early. Nevertheless, the Frau and our children were ready and waiting, our eldest daughter filled with suppressed excitement over the coming ride. Away we went, the cracking whiplash of the driver startling the children, out over the valley, ravaged by Butte's smoke, and finally over the mountains southward, our wide-eyed little ones not once disturbing the peace of the other passengers. One of these, Rod Leggett, white-haired, and nippy as a collie, was a mine owner whom I knew quite well. Rod and his brother, J. A. Leggett, owned the Leon Gambetti mine in Butte. Rod was a red-hot Democrat, J. A., his brother, an equally warm Republican. Both were quick-tempered and outspoken; both swore like proverbial pirates at the least provocation and both had hosts of friends. Neither forebore loud condemnation of the other's political affiliations whenever opportunity offered, so that there were always new Leggett stories going the rounds. Once, when I was attending a Republican convention in Butte, somebody arose and said, "Mr. Chairman, I nominate Mr. Leggett for the legislature."

He had scarcely spoken the words when up jumped another delagate, who evidently did not know that there were two Leggetts. "Mr. Chairman," he said, sarcastically, "Mr. Leggett is a well-known Democrat and—."

J. A. sprang to his feet, his clenched fist brandishing above his white head. "You're a damned liar, sir; that's old Rod!" he shouted belligerently.

Our coach stopped at noon to change horses. And here we had dinner at the stage station, with lemon pie that I shall never forget. Walking out of the dining room with Rod Leggett, who in filling his corncob was spilling half his tobacco, the gruff old fellow said: "By God, Frank, when I saw those youngsters of yours get aboard the coach this morning I said good-by to peace. I want to take it all back. I've never before seen such good-natured babies. I'm head over heels in love with them." For several years after this trip in the stagecoach, whenever he was in our vicinity Rod Leggett called to pay his respects to our children, never forgetting to mention the long drive on the dusty coach, and always commenting on their neat appearance.

Sheridan, where we disembarked, was a picture to us, a dream come true. There were grass, trees, and flowers without end; and sweet air for the children. Wilda, our eldest, lifted from the dusty coach to the soft grass, cried, sobbed in terror, thinking that she was walking on flowers. Hurriedly Mr. Schultz, the hotel proprietor, brought her a large bouquet of bright blossoms, while everybody anxiously assured her that she was not walking on flowers, but only upon "grass that the cows eat to make milk for little girls." That night, delighted by all this, I declared to the Frau that we should never go back to Butte. "I'll turn highwayman first," I said.

After a few days at the hospitable hotel we moved up to Brandon to be near the Toledo concentrator and the blast furnace that was being built there. But my employer's money did not last long enough to even give him a start, and finally he could not pay me. When he suspended operations the sheriff had levied upon everything he possessed. I did not have a dollar, and another baby was coming along, and so was the winter. We could not pay board bills now. We had to have a house of our own, and quickly.

I borrowed an axe and team of horses, went into the mountains up Mill Creek, and cut a set of house logs. These I hauled to Brandon, the old mining camp that once came within one vote of being capital of Montana Territory. Now there were but three or four

cabins in Brandon, besides our own. All the others were occupied
by bachelors who mined or prospected in the surrounding hills. My
rifle furnished us with plenty of meat, mostly rabbits and blue
grouse, with sometimes a deer for variety. There were trout in the
creek not twenty yards from our cabin door, and duck and geese in
the sloughs down by the Ruby River in the valley. Many a time
while the Frau was dressing the children I caught enough trout for
our breakfasts out of the sparkling water of Mill Creek within sight
of our cabin. Our root house that I had dug into the bank just
below our wood pile kept meat fresh for a long time, even in warm
weather, so that millionaires could have fared no better, as far as
meat was concerned.

Our youngest daughter, Norma, was born in this cabin in Brandon soon after its roof was finished, so that now there were five
Lindermans facing an uncertain future. My mention of the cabin's
roof has reminded me of a battle that it had with a gale of wind.
The roof was the conventional one, being dirt-covered. Heavy rains
came, causing every other roof in Brandon to leak badly. Ours, as
though out of respect to the babies, stubbornly held out the water
until a week had gone, then the fun began with us. One day I came
home from Sheridan, where I had gone to get samples of ore for
assaying, to find pots and pans set everywhere to catch dripping
mud-colored water that kept up a lively drumming whose tones
were tuned by the size of the pot or pan catching the drops. The
carpet was soaking wet, the beds a sight to behold, and the top of
the cookstove sizzled spitefully with dripping water that left muddy
stains on its surface. The Frau, wearing my slicker and overshoes,
was busily attending the numerous receptacles set about the cabin.
Wilda, wearing a coat and rubbers, glided about beneath her tiny
red parasol, her little feet splashing delightedly in puddles on the
floor. Verne, our second daughter, who was not yet steady on her
feet, was seated in the highchair beneath the ridgepole where as yet
no leak had shown up. Baby Norma, not caring a rap for leaking
roofs, was sleeping soundly in the bed that was covered with a
wagon sheet. Our cabin wasn't a pleasant place just then. However,
I managed to get some lumber and cover the dirt on the roof's top

with it, so that we should never again have to worry about rainy weather. One day, soon after the protecting boards had been placed upon our roof, a high wind blew down the gulch. It snatched the boards away, carrying some of them fifty yards from the cabin. It even took the stovepipe, lifting it off the stove and dragging it out through the hole in the pole roof and its dirt cover more handily than human hands could have removed it. The Frau was cooking on the stove when the stovepipe was carried away, filling the cabin with smoke and the household with consternation.

Looking back to the Brandon days I think only of their happiness; and yet, because of worry, I had a bad case of nightmare there. The cabin was partitioned, the front end being sitting room, dining room and kitchen, combined. The other portion was a bedroom, containing two beds. The walls of both rooms were the uncovered logs, except in the bedroom where a large American flag covered the end wall from top to bottom back of the beds. Our eldest child slept with me. One night in a distracting dream I thought that a terrible-looking man whose eyes burned like live coals was reaching across me to get Wilda. I felt his arm touch my stomach, slide stealthily across me toward the sleeping child. Its touch paralyzed me. I struggled to move my body and could not stir. Exerting every ounce of strength I could command, I sprang from the bed, seized a chair, and struck blindly at the demonlike thing that was now standing on the bed. The chair, swung with all my strength, smashed to splinters against the log wall; and the flag fell down, waking Wilda. I had somehow missed the thing! Running into the other room, I snatched my rifle from its pegs and loaded it. Then I lit the lamp, and placed it upon the floor so that its light would shine under the bed.

"What is it! Frank! Frank! You must be dreaming." I heard the Frau's voice, and Wilda, crying in fright, but so dimly that they were unreal. "Frank!"

"Shut up, damn it," I whispered savagely, getting down on my belly to crawl under the bed after the thing that by now had hidden there.

I came out of that dream with a bad chill. My teeth chattered,

113

and I was quite ill for more than an hour, and yet I felt so glad that the whole thing had been but a dream that we laughed over it.

During my tantrums, which were awful to me, the Frau had called to me many times, but I did not waken until I got down to crawl under the bed. I remembered everything that I did, even to my saying "shut up" to the Frau, for which I felt sorry. Next morning I hid my cartridges and took my rifle to pieces, so that to use it I should first have to put it together again—and then find my ammunition. But never afterward did nightmare trouble me.

The assay outfit had been left behind by my late employer. This I appropriated, intending to do custom assaying for the prospectors and miners of the district. I walked three or four miles to Sheridan every other day to get any samples of ore that might have been left for me at the store of H. D. Rossiter. During the first month I earned thirteen dollars. Later, I somehow got a horse and a rickety cart and set up an office in Sheridan, use of a small building being donated for the purpose by Winthrop Raymond. The old mare that drew my cart was well bred and yet mean as a magpie. She ran away with me twice within a week, all but wrecking my ancient cart. I wished to get rid of her, letting this fact become known.

One morning the young son of one of my best patrons met me on my way to Sheridan. This boy was riding a good-looking cayuse. Stopping me, he asked, "How will you trade horses?"

"Son," I said, "this mare isn't to be trusted."

"Neither's this one," grinned the boy.

"Your father would never forgive me if I traded you this mare," I went on. "She will run away at the drop of the hat, and she can kick a chew of tobacco out of a man's mouth."

"I bet she ain't a darn bit worse'n this here one. And Dad said I might trade, if you was willin'."

"All right," I agreed, thinking that if the boy's father should object to our arrangement I could trade back again, that there would be no great harm done.

I was taking my old saddle with me to Sheridan that morning, having promised to loan it for a few days. Now I should need it myself. The boy quickly removed his own saddle from the cayuse, and

I now discovered that the animal was a sway-back. However, this blemish did not show under a saddle, and I was heartily sick of the old mare.

Pitching his saddle into the cart, the boy drove away in a hurry. "His name's Boxer, Mr. Linderman," he called to me through a cloud of dust.

I saddled Boxer, wishing that I had not hampered myself with rifle and lunch bucket this morning. The horse knew that I was not afraid of him, and yet as soon as I was in the saddle he went after me. I had to let the lunch bucket go by the board, but kept my rifle until he had finished bucking. Then I got down, picked up whatever I could find of my scattered lunch, and led Boxer the rest of the way to Sheridan, determined to show him who was chief as soon as I could rid myself of my hampering rifle and lunch bucket. Borrowing a pair of spurs from Rossiter's store, I rode Boxer until I thought that he had quit, but he hadn't. He never did quit. I owned him for many years and never saddled him but what he bucked. He was the best saddle horse I ever owned, at that. We got along famously, and yet Boxer never loved me, nor any other man. He was unique in one way at least, nobody ever wanted to borrow him.

Each morning when I left Brandon for Sheridan everybody was out to see me off. Boxer and I were Brandon's greatest attractions. I remember one morning especially when we put on a good show there. I had some partners in a quartz mine up Mill Creek and wished to take a few heads of cabbage up to them. Putting the cabbages into a sack, I tied it behind my saddle. Boxer bucked it off as fast as I could tie it on. The cabbages were suffering damage by the frozen ground. Besides, the onlookers began offering advice and banter. Thinking that I would take all the buck out of him and then tie on my sack of cabbages, I prepared to mount when—.

"Hey—hey! Mr. Linderman, please, *please*, do'n' git hon dat dam son-of-a-gon. She ha'nt no good Cat'lick, dat wan," called old Alfred Ledeau, a Frenchman, from his cabin door.

My assay business was so poor that I could not meet my grocery bills—and we had no others. I began to sink a shaft on a prospect that I owned near Brandon, working alone, and climbing out to windlass the gob. At grassroots I had earlier taken out half a ton of high-grade gold ore. The small pay shoot had pinched to a thin knife-blade stringer that I believed might lead to another pocket of rich ore, as they often do in lime formations.

One morning Charley Dorsey, an old Kentuckian who gophered a little in the surrounding hills and had a cabin in Brandon, came to my shaft. Looking down, he asked, "Got a turkey for Thanksgiving yet?"

"Nope," I said, "nary turkey."

"There's a turkey shoot down in Sheridan today," he went on. "I'm going down. Better come along. I reckon I can win us both a turkey."

Old Charley was a fine fellow and a good shot. A turkey would be both a surprise and a change. "All right," I agreed, climbing out. "Let's go first to my cabin," I proposed. "I want to get my rifle."

We trudged to the turkey shoot, where we found fifteen men. My rifle, an ancient Sharps that had seen hard service on the buffalo range before I owned it, excited considerable curiosity, and a little ridicule, one fellow advising me to "throw it away and get some rocks." However, the old weapon was dead center, and I knew it like a book.

The mark was a black dot, one inch in diameter in a six-inch circle, at seventy-five yards. The first round displayed no exceptional marksmanship, the turkey going to a man who, I felt sure, had taken too many drinks to repeat his success. Four successive rounds failed to give my generous partner a single turkey, let alone two. There had been no good shooting done so far; our chances of eating turkey on Thanksgiving appeared to grow slimmer each round. I entered the fifth and sixth myself and won two turkeys, giving one to Charley, of course. But I was now broke. I had spent all I had on the two shots—four bits. I was ready to start back up the gulch now, but my old Sharps had won so much fame, in spite of its worn appearance, that I had to loan it to the man who had advised me to "throw it away and get some rocks," so that he might win a Thanksgiving turkey.

I had been at work in my shaft for several months, interrupted often by my assaying, when I struck a large vein of rotten white quartz. I cleaned up the shaft's bottom, dug up a good specimen of my new strike, and climbed out of the shaft to have a better look at it in daylight. It didn't impress me. It looked dead and poverty-stricken. Nevertheless, I thought that I had better assay it, and started for our cabin with the chunk of quartz under my arm.

Old Tom Branham's cabin was just below ours on Mill Creek. As I approached it I saw old Tom standing in his open doorway. "What ye got thar?" he called, coming out to the trail to inspect my strike. He was a typical prospector who had come from Missouri to the gold diggings in the sixties and had been in Brandon ever since.

"I'll bet she'll prospect," he declared, after examining my quartz critically. "Let's us pan some of it right now," he proposed. I readily agreed.

Pulverizing a piece of my specimen on a bed stone from an arastra, old Tom carefully brushed the powdered ore into a gold pan. I followed him to the creek a few yards distant, not expecting to see a "color" of gold. I nearly shouted for joy when an unbelievably long string of gold showed up before the process of panning was half finished.

"She's rich, boy," grunted old Tom, his mouth so full of tobacco juice that he could scarcely speak. "I knowed she'd pungle good."

"Whoopee!" I hurried home with the good news. The Frau had just finished a large washing; she looked weary. "You'll never have to wash another darned thing, anywhere, Frau," I chortled. "Look! Just take a good look at this!" I proudly showed her the gold from old Tom's pan that I had carefully saved in an envelope.

My shaft's bottom was floored with this quartz. Even though it proved to be only a pocket in the lime, there would be a decent stake there. I could scarcely wait for morning. Lying awake that night I built a fine house, even laid out its grounds, while impatiently waiting for daylight to come again. I hurriedly cooked breakfast, as I have always done and do to this day, bolting the food in my anxiety to look again at the bottom of my shaft. And I hired a miner on my way to my mine. I could afford this luxury now.

117

Together we walked to the bonanza, where we worked until nearly noon, he in the shaft and I at the windlass. Glancing up at the sun, I called down to my miner, "Come up, Herb. We'll call it a shift. I want to assay this quartz before I get into debt," I said.

The stuff was as barren of value as a cuckoo clock is of real bird-song. Old Tom had willfully salted me, later on admitting the truth.

"I'll get even with him," I promised myself. "I'll make him break his old back digging barren quartz. I'll teach him that salting is a dirty trick." And of course my opportunity to even things with Tom came quickly enough. But when I had made out a lying certificate of assay of ore that old Tom had brought me, I could not sign it. Instead, I tore it up and made out a reliable one. One day soon after this the old fellow was missing. We found him dead on his waste dump, with a round hole blown in his chest. He had capped and fused a plug of giant powder, lighted the sputtering fuse, and held the deadly thing tight to his breast, waiting for death—or so it seemed to us who knew him best.

My awakening from this golden dream was good for me. I need-ed it. In all my mining experiences I never again permitted my imagination to handle a situation for even a minute. I abandoned my mine, that I had named the Wildaverne for our two older daugh-ters, believing that I now should have to go back to Butte for em-ployment. But, as though to prevent this move, opportunity in the strangest garb imaginable presented itself.

Admitting the egotism that an expressed belief in fatalism seems to imply, and without professing faith in any particular thing, excepting a good rifle (which of course means oneself) I declare that I have, more than once, been turned from my intention and even from my avowed determination, by circumstances that were not of my own making. Grope as I have for a more satisfying term for this influence that has so often arbitrarily decided my affairs, I can find none better than "fate." Anyhow, it covers all the others, and is equally vague.

To go to Butte I should have to borrow money. With this in mind, I went to Mr. Rossiter's store in Sheridan. Great flakes of soggy snow were falling so thickly that one could not see through the store's windows. Mr. Rossiter was not in. The clerk and one or two others were seated upon the counters. "How's Brandon these days?" they asked through habit.

"Not booming. The Wildaverne has shut down," I replied, laughingly. "I'm leaving for Butte, if I can borrow the stage fare," I added, more seriously.

"Gosh, that's bad," said one. "We sure need an assayer in this district. There ought to be plenty for one assayer to do here, I should think."

"There isn't," I told him. "Besides this, there are few who have the money to pay for assaying. I never have refused to determine the value of any man's ore, pay or no pay. I've been glad to help whenever I could. But one cannot feed a family on promises. I've got to get out."

The fellow who had spoken closed his jackknife with a snap. "Say, why don't you buy out our newspaper man? He's sick of us and we're plumb disgusted with him. I bet you he'd sell out for a song."

"The trouble is that I can't sing," I laughed. "I'm broke."

"Here," said the fellow, handing me a five-dollar bill, "go on over there and bluff our newspaper man into selling you the plant. Offer him a payment of five dollars down. I bet you he'll take it."

"I dare you," chuckled another, between the bites he took from an apple filched from a box beside him on the counter. "Go on; play the game out. We all dare you."

Perhaps it was only the dare that led me to the front door with the five-dollar bill in my hand. I had never in my life been inside a newspaper office, had never written anything longer than a location notice for a mining claim. I knew nothing whatever about a newspaper plant, large or small. I did not even know the newspaper man, had never seen him. And yet, with the borrowed five dollars I was going to try to buy him out. The absurdity of the situation suddenly halted me in the middle of the snowy street. Not a soul was in sight; and yet I knew that the men in the store were watching me, probably chuckling over the joke they'd played. But perhaps it was not a joke, after all. I had nothing to lose. The fellow might kick me out, but I'd go on, I decided. Considering my bank roll, how ought I, a stranger, to open so delicate a proposition as the purchase of a newspaper plant with five dollars? I could think of no way.

"Here I go, anyhow," I thought, crossing the rest of the street, to stop again, this time beneath the snow-blurred sign of *The Sheridan Paper*. I tried to peep through the grimy window, could see nobody, and finally opened the door without one backward glance toward the store. Something fell to the floor in another room, where I heard a man's voice swear gruffly. "Not a good beginning," I thought, walking straight into the proprietor's lair, where near a potbellied stove fed with unwrapped exchanges I saw my man seated upon a high stool. He wore a green eyeshade, and was thin and tall.

First spitting at a grimy cuspidor that he missed widely, he asked, "How's Brandon?" evidently knowing me. Then, without waiting for my reply, he opened up, damning the weather and the country, once in a while pausing in his typesetting to glance out of the dirty window at the thickly falling snow. "Shove some more of those papers into that stove, will you? It's cold as hell in here."

"Which ones?" I asked, glad of a chance to speak.

"Oh, any of 'em, all of 'em," he said fretfully. "I wish I was out of this damned town."

"Are you a married man?" I asked, remembering how easily I had moved about when I was single.

"I should s-a-y not," he sniffed. "I can't feed myself, let alone a woman and a raft of kids."

"Then why don't you get out of this town if you don't like it?" I asked, guessing his answer.

Within ten minutes I had actually bought *The Sheridan Paper* [on March 3, 1899] (and a five-hundred-dollar mortgage that I didn't know about) for $150.00, paying the borrowed five-dollar bill down to bind the bargain. I soon managed the rest, at least enough to let the fellow get out of town, and later I paid the balance, mortgage and all.

The alacrity with which the man got down from his high stool and removed his green eyeshade and apron startled me. "Come on," he said briskly, "I'll buy a drink on this transaction."

"Wait," I countered, a little worried now. "You'll have to help me for a few days, show me a lot of things. I know less about this publishing business than a billy goat knows about side whiskers."

"Aint you a printer?" he asked, evidently shocked.

"No, not yet. But if you will show me a little about it, I will be."

"Well, I'll be damned!" The fellow leaned back against the type-cases, looking me up and down. "Hell, man, you can't learn the printer's trade in a few days. What are you going to do with this paper?" he asked suspiciously.

"Publish it," I declared, walking to the imposing-stone to have my first look at forms in chases.

He burst out laughing. "You've got a gall as big as a church," he said. "Anyhow, let's get that drink while I've got this five-dollar bill."

After we had returned to the print shop he explained that he bought the paper's "guts" (patent inside) from a Spokane house, that this came by mail each week, so that there were but sixteen columns to be set, including ads. "Six galleys of type does it, generally. Most of the ads are changed once a month," he went on, while we leaned over the forms of *The Sheridan Paper*.

Seeing that I was in earnest, he first placed 36-point caps in the type boxes, moved another high stool to the rack, handed me a stick and rule, and I began my first lesson, my fingers seemingly all toes. I weighed about 136 pounds. My movements are yet quick, and with a little practice fairly accurate. I was then young, and determined to run that newspaper. Three days later we got out the issue on time. Then the fellow left me. I had learned to set type, even to "make up," after a fashion. Fortunately for me, there was then no job press in the office, so that I believed I could stagger along. Nevertheless, I sent to Butte for a friend who was a printer-man, and a good one. He had worked on many a newspaper, and was smart and bright as a weasel. He came, with his family, and became chief of the newspaper, which I supported with my assaying, since the thing did not pay its own way.

We at once changed the paper's name to *The Sheridan Chinook*. During my partner's time, at least, the paper was a credit to the little town. I was sorry to see him leave, but there was seemingly no future there in his line so that at last he went away, leaving me alone with the newspaper, and the assay office, with no part of the mortgage paid. Even while times were pinching us hardest my partner and I never quarreled. One day, however, he came into the office feeling his liquor a little. Climbing upon his stool beside me, he began to talk loudly, using language that I feared might be heard beyond the thin partition where some women had a millinery store. My remonstrance angered him. Deliberately placing his stick of type on the cases he got down from his stool. "Get down, damn you, and I'll lick you for that," he said, his fine eyes blazing.

He was heavier than I, and, I believed, an abler man. Nevertheless, I too got down and faced him, waiting for his attack.

"Hell," he blurted, proffering his hand, "you're too good a fellow to fight with. Shake!" And we shook hands. May his moccasins make tracks in a hundred snows.

Business began quite suddenly to pick up after he was gone. I sold the Toledo mine, making a tidy commission, paid off my mortgage on the newspaper plant, bought a job press, purchased the only furniture store in town, was elected to the legislature,[2] and became police judge, all within a year.

I refused to qualify for the judgeship, however; but not until I had had a 'case'. An hour after the mayor had notified me of my appointment, the city marshal brought in a man whom he had arrested. I've forgotten the offense now, but it was a finable one; and, being busy, I fined the fellow quite promptly. He as promptly refused to pay; and I, not once thinking of the jail, told him to pay up or take a licking. After the fellow had gone the marshal asked me why I had not ordered the culprit jailed. My answer, "Why, I forgot all about the confounded jail," furnished the foundation of a story about my court that went the rounds until at last a real artist made it fairly bristle with high lights.

[2] Linderman served in the state legislature in 1903 and again in 1905.

I was as busy as a man could be, and yet could make only enough to pay the expenses that seemed to keep two or three jumps ahead of my earnings. We had, of course, moved to Sheridan where our eldest daughter, Wilda, was attending school. My election to the legislature was a surprise to everybody, including myself. I had beaten a good man, Mr. Winthrop Raymond, one of the outstanding citizens of Madison County and of the state. What was I to do with my newspaper and assay office when I went to Helena, the state's capital? My salary as a lawmaker would be six dollars per day. I might be able to employ a good assayer for five dollars per day, but poor as printers were, generally, I could not hope to employ one for a dollar a day.

But good luck came along just in time. I let an assayer whom I knew use my outfit for whatever he might earn with it during the winter, and at the last moment a printerman took over my newspaper on nearly the same basis. My father and mother had come to live in Sheridan. We helped them to build a home there. Now we gave them the furniture business, so that when I came to leave for Helena I believed I had cleared my deck for action. But the confounded newspaper man to whom I had turned over my plant proved to be a Democrat in disguise. He began, almost at once, to roast me as a lawmaker. I could not return from Helena and turn him out, because I might not be able to find another man to take his place. The paper had to be published, since I had a few "legals," and these had to appear in a certain number of issues. I felt obliged to do as the little boy did when a jackass kicked him—to consider the source, and try to forget the incident. I am sure, however, that no regular subscriber to *The Sheridan Chinook* read that paper more carefully than I did during the winter.

Ours, the eighth legislative assembly, was the first to sit in the new capitol. So young and uninformed were its members at the beginning of the session that they found it necessary to employ an instructor in parliamentary law before they could even pass their own salary bill. But at last they worked well, and, in spite of the bitter struggles over Butte's corporation differences, formed an association, of which I was elected secretary "for forty years."[3] This association met biennially until six years ago, when, there having been so many deaths among its membership, I did not call its meeting.

The Clark senatorial battle in the preceding legislature, famed the country over, his subsequent appointment to the United States Senate by bold chicanery, and many other political squabbles where tactics were disgusting, had given Montana a bad name.[4] Grover Cleveland, President of the United States, said, "Montana is a rotten borough"; and it then was rotten politically. Politically it is yet rotten, and it will remain rotten politically for many years to come. One of the contributing factors to this condition is our present primary law, framed to "give every citizen political opportunity," and to "get everybody to vote." In the first, it has succeeded, even beyond the expectations of its framers. In the second, and most important, of its aims, it has failed dismally, since Americans cannot be made to vote. It is true that our old system of nominating conventions had grown corrupt, and that reform was needed. But ours is, and it seems to me that it must remain, a government by parties, or fail. Our Montana primary law has disorganized both political parties. Under our old system a Democrat could not cast his vote in the selection of a Republican nominee for any office on the Republican ticket, nor could a Republican have any say in the party affairs of Democrats. Under our new system a voter may cast his primary ballot for a candidate, or for all candidates, on either ticket, so long as he does not divide his political patronage. This permits of skulduggery, since among the many candidates for nomination on both tickets the partisans of *one* party may succeed in nominating a weakling in *another* party, and then easily defeat their primary choice at the polls in the general election.

[3] It was known as the Eighth Legislative Assembly Association, and the members met every year or two for a banquet, with Linderman often presiding.

[4] W. A. Clark was sent to Congress in 1899 as a senator from Montana, but resigned his seat after charges of vote-buying were brought against him and before the investigating committee could report. He was returned to Congress in 1901. C. B. Glascock, *The War of the Copper Kings*, devotes a full chapter (VIII) to the affair. J. K. Howard also discusses it in *Montana, High, Wide and Handsome*, pp. 58–68.

Besides this, instead of having one campaign by candidates backed by organized political parties, we now have two campaigns by self-selected men or women sponsored by their own egotism, and the expense to the state is great.

I was a member of the legislature that passed this primary law, and voted for it, believing at the time that it might work wonders, and it has. Not many years ago I might have truthfully declared that I knew every man of any importance in the state of Montana. And yet, since our primary law has been in effect, I have had to cast my vote for a candidate for the United States senatorship whom I had never even heard of until he had been nominated. Incidentally, I have heard nothing of him since his election. He did not even return to the state that elected him to the United States Senate, that I ever heard of. A few years prior, four I seem to remember, to his election, he rolled into Montana like a tumbleweed, and when, under our primary law, political preferment rolled him out again, he remained out. Amen.

Our old system of political preferment failed only because so few Americans took part in public affairs. Its framers, in the light of their own zeal for public service, could not visualize our present ponderous, and careless, majority submitting tamely to government by a tiny, organized minority. Smug apathy and ignorance of public affairs are becoming more and more dangerous to Americans. Skimming only the cream from the world's greatest natural resources, we have grown so fat, and so vain, that we do not care what our neighbor does, what crimes he commits against the skim milk generation that must follow ours, or the cream skimmers, so long as he does not drop his baited hook into our private fishing hole. The older I grow the more strongly I am convinced that our present regime cannot last, that reforms must come, and that only energetic, and general, participation by citizens in our public affairs can temper them, perhaps preventing a vicious political upheaval. But I will get on with my story.

F. Augustus Heinze, the brilliant young man whose beginning in Butte had not been ushered in by brass bands, had prospered. Keen, cunning, capable, and aggressive, he had acquired control of

several good mines in Butte, besides his smelter, that had been en-
larged. By the time I had been nominated, in Madison County, for
the legislature, Mr. Heinze and his able lieutenants were battling
the Anaconda Copper Mining Company for supremacy, not only
over Butte itself, but over the state of Montana as well. The old
Clark-Daly feud that had already given the state a bad name was
now eclipsed by the struggle between these new masters, whose tactics were the devil's own. Neither had any politics. Both were ably
represented in both political parties, so that nearly every political
convention was dominated by one faction or the other, even in
counties where mining was unknown.

When one knows every man by his first name, on both sides of
such a contest, as I did, he often finds himself in difficult positions,
no matter how carefully he tries to keep clear of the mess. I made
my campaign with a team and buckboard, as was then necessary.
Twice, in out-of-the-way places, I met representatives of Mr.
Heinze who generously offered me "campaign money," which I
declined to accept. Nevertheless, toward the campaign's end Mr.
Heinze's newspapers endorsed my candidacy, his last-moment
literature appealing to his friends for my election. Whether this
increased my majority I do not know. I do know, however, that I
would have been elected without it, and that now I began to hear
"Heinze-man" whispered to me.

I went to Helena alone, where the Frau joined me a week or
ten days later. We had planned to live in Kenwood, a suburb
of Helena, during the session, because of expenses in Sheridan
and the state of my finances. This information had somehow
reached the capital ahead of me. Old Butte friends who, for
reasons that I was soon to learn, were plentiful in the lobbies of the
city's hotels, were genuinely glad to see me. "Where are you
stopping for the session, Frank?" asked one whom I had known
for years.

"At the Helena," I replied, "But when Mrs. Linderman joins me
we shall live in Kenwood," I added.

"Too far out, Frank," he said in a warning tone. "You can't
afford to be so far from your seat in the House this session."

I noticed the emphasis that he had placed on "this" session. "Well," I said, "I cannot afford to stay at the Helena!"

He led me to a corner. "What's the matter with the Grandon?" he asked, the cigar in his mouth cocked rakishly. "The whole bunch is up there, you know—everybody."

"The rates are the same there," I told him, "and anyway, I've made arrangements to—"

He stopped me. "There's a nice suite of rooms for you and your whole family, all paid for, meals and everything, at the Grandon where the gang is," he whispered. "It's just like a bottle of beer that's been opened, Frank. If you don't drink it up it'll spoil, go flat. Let's us take a look at those rooms right now."

"——," I said, good-naturedly, although inside I was boiling angry, "whenever any other man buys food for Mrs. Linderman he will be head of the house and I'll be gone."

"Ain't sore, are you?" he asked quickly.

"Oh, no," I assured him. We remained friends until he crossed into the Shadow-hills.

I found it difficult to meet and fraternize with more than one man whom I had known in old Butte days, because they were no longer their own masters, good fellows though most of them were. As the legislative session progressed the influence of the warring factions of Butte grew bolder, often intruding itself in matters inimical to mining. To vote for or against a bill sometimes branded a member a "Heinze-man" or an "Amalgamated hireling" when he was neither one nor the other. This situation brought forth a story that, whether true or false, shows the conditions that existed in Montana during the Heinze-Amalgamated squabbles. A member of the House of Representatives declared that he had been offered a price to vote against a certain bill in which his constituents could have no interest. He declined, thinking that now he would vote in favor of the bill. The next day, however, he was again approached and offered the same amount for voting in favor of the measure. Again he declined, deciding to absent himself and not vote on the bill at all. But even this course was not without its complications, since the now befuddled member was offered double the amount previously tendered him if he would dodge roll call and neglect to vote altogether.

These skirmishes over legislation that seemingly could affect neither of the warring interests were but tests of factional strength. A real battle that stirred the state was brought on. One bitterly cold night when the Frau and I had been long asleep, the doorbell rang. Hastily getting into some clothes, I went downstairs to learn what was wanted, fearing bad news from Sheridan, where our children were with their grandparents. I opened the door to four old Butte friends, who filed in to group themselves about a hot-air register that had been cold for hours, a look of deep mystery on their faces. They implored me to accompany them into the city four miles distant, without saying why my presence was necessary. To my repeated questions I got only assurances that my aid was needed by friends, and that as soon as the situation was set forth by those who were competent to make a thorough explanation, I would be returned to my bed. Three of my callers were employees of the Anaconda Copper Mining Company, always called "the Amalgamated" in Montana. The other, a merchant of Butte, had always opposed Mr. Heinze. Nevertheless, all were warm friends of mine, especially the merchant. I returned to my room, finished dressing, and accompanied them into the city. I shall never forget the knowing look that the cab driver gave me as he opened the door to permit me to enter his horse-drawn hack. If the cabbies of those days had chosen to talk, there would have been the very devil to pay; but wise as hop-toads, they held their peace and collected fat fares. I had not noticed the hour until the horses turned into Main Street, when the clock in the courthouse tower boomed two o'clock.

The lobby of the Helena Hotel was strangely quiet when we entered it. Most of the lights had been turned out. The chairs were in disorderly piles, the night clerk was dozing behind his desk, and old Judd, a negro, was industriously mopping the tile floor near the elevator that ignored our repeated ringing, seeming to have lost life. At last, however, it came grudgingly down and took us up to the top floor, where I learned that, being neither a "Heinze-man" nor an Amalgamated supporter, I had been selected to father a resolution demanding the impeachment of Judge Harney, of Butte, of "high crimes, and malfeasance in office."

No sooner had the proposition been made me than a dozen men, all old friends who had been waiting there for my arrival, gathered round to impress me with the importance of the proposed resolution, the iniquities of the judge being forcefully presented. They pointed out the prominence that the introduction of this resolution would bring me, mentioned my future welfare, even hinting of party leadership in Montana. This whirlwind raised so suddenly by friends whom I trusted was baffling indeed. If Judge Harney were guilty of one-half the crimes that these friends of mine declared he had committed, even hanging was too good for him. However, I did not know Judge Harney. I did know that Mr. Heinze had lately won several lawsuits involving mining property in Butte and that the Anaconda Copper Mining Company, or its agents, had been the loser, and that charges of fraud had been loudly made. Nevertheless, I was not conversant with these suits, knew almost nothing about them. I could not introduce a resolution charging a judge on the bench with "high crimes and malfeasance in office," demanding his impeachment, when I did not even know the judge, let alone his judicial record. "No," I said, finally, "and now I wish to go back to my bed."[5]

This resolution was introduced in the morning by a member who is no longer living. And what a storm it raised all over the state! Instantly the Amalgamated newspapers praised it to the

[5] Harney, a member of the Heinze group, was a judge in the Second Judicial District from 1901 to 1905. Among the Linderman papers is a letter to him from Allen J. Bennett, of Virginia City, dated February 1, 1903: "It is the nearly universal opinion of the republicans of this county that the impeachment of Judge Harney is not, and is not intended to be a wise measure of public policy." Another letter under the same date, from Judge Lew Callaway, reads: ". . . my fear all the way through has been that this would degenerate into an Amalgamated-Heinze scrap. It was first put to us as a high-minded, above-partisanship effort to purify the judiciary of the state, which would work good to the republican party. We saw through the transparent scheme at once, but thought possibly it might be well for the republican party to place itself on record as in favor of having our public morals decent. The resolution was going to be introduced anyhow; I am indeed more than glad now that you did not father it, by request or otherwise."

skies, while Heinze sheets condemned it and its sponsor to eternal perdition. After a hard-fought battle the House, by one vote, I believe, referred the resolution to a committee with instructions to thoroughly investigate the charges and report its findings.

I voted to refer the offending resolution to the committee, because serious charges had been made against a judge on the bench. I felt that without investigation such charges ought not to be dropped. My vote did not express either condemnation or commendation of Judge Harney. If the committee found that he was innocent of the charges made against him, his name would be speedily cleared. If, on the other hand, the committee should find him guilty, I would, without hesitation, vote for his impeachment. My vote had scarcely been recorded when a prominent member of the Heinze organization, the leading Democrat of the House, rushed to my desk, his face ashen with rage. I liked the man then and like him to this day, but his conversation was exceedingly short on this occasion.

It was now that my newspaper began backbiting me severely. Men, good friends of mine, came to Helena trying to persuade me to change my vote on the Harney resolution. Some of them went very far in their efforts, proving insistent and difficult; but I did not change my vote. I was notified that a contract for assaying I held in Madison County had been cancelled. This was the big item of income that kept my assayer in Sheridan satisfied. I was troubled. The contracting concern was composed of easterners. I had sold the Toledo mine to it only a little time before this. Its representatives in Montana had been extremely friendly toward me. Now, because of my vote on the Harney resolution, these men, strangers in the state, had suddenly become my enemies. Both my newspaper and my assay office seemed now to have lined up with unfriendly spirits against me, so that thoughts of my home-going brought me no pleasant thrills. The Harney affair dragged on like a crippled turtle, the committee seeming to be fearful of making any recommendation whatever. This situation fostered further efforts to induce me to change my vote, which, by now, would have certainly quashed the resolution. Although the Harney resolution was not mentioned, what I believe to be one of these last efforts to get me to change my vote is worth recording.

A page handed me a note requesting my presence in the lobby of the House. I went out to meet a mining engineer who was then in Mr. Heinze's employ. He said that he had heard I owned a mine in Jefferson County, that the property had interested him because of the nature of the iron contained in its ore, besides its gold content, which he had been told was sufficient to pay mining, and freight charges to Butte. I told him that the property was not yet a mine, but that it appeared to be a good prospect, and that the figures he had quoted as to the ore's value were correct.

"We'll buy it," he said, "if you will name a fair price. I'll take your word for its value, too—that is, unless you are out of reason," he added, smiling.

His statement made me believe that all was not quite straight, that there was a mouse in the syrup keg. "I'll see you tomorrow," I told him, going back to my seat in the House.

That afternoon I gave a friend who now lives in White Plains, New York, a bill of sale of the property, telling him to sell it to the mining man, who had rooms at the Grandon. But upon offering the mining claim for sale, the "interested" man would not even listen to its new owner, who was prepared to sell it cheap enough and to keep half the money.

At last the committee reported that it had found no good grounds for the impeachment of Judge Harney of "high crimes, and malfeasance in office," and soon after this the legislative session ended. But another was called immediately, and then yet another, the last to pass the famous "fair trial bill," so that the warring interests in Butte might take their legal cases out of Silver Bow County, or in other ways disqualify judges to the number of three, I believe, if this became necessary in order for them to receive "justice."[6] This measure was bitterly opposed by the Heinze faction, so bitterly that there were even fistic encounters among

[6] The bill provided that a litigant could charge a judge with prejudice and force him to disqualify himself and call in another judge. He was not required to prove prejudice.

lobbyists. Nevertheless, it became a law; and when in the next legislative session the Amalgamated tried to have it repealed, the Heinze faction fought as hard for its retention as it had earlier battled to prevent its passage.

My legislative experiences had not been pleasing. I was ill when I finally reached home, feeling that I had had enough of the game of politics. Nevertheless, two years afterward [1905] I was again nominated for a seat in the House. This time the legislature must elect a United States senator. Madison County Republicans, in convention in Virginia City, formally instructed its legislative nominees not to vote for Thomas H. Carter, who was a candidate for senatorial honors. I was glad of these instructions, since I did not approve of Mr. Carter, who had already served Montana in the United States Senate. Since beginning this story I found, among my papers, two sets of resolutions commending me for my opposition to the election of Mr. Carter to the Senate.[7] These resolutions, drawn up and signed by many of my Madison County constituents, were forwarded to me in Helena, together with a personal letter from the chairman saying, "We sent you to the legislature to fight and we are not being disappointed."

The campaign was a warm one. This time Mr. Heinze's supporters in Madison County opposed my election, in one case that I know of posting notices that anybody electioneering for me would be discharged. Mr. Heinze himself came into Madison County to work against me, spending money freely. In the mining camp of Rochester he addressed the miners, saying that I had "sold out to the Amalgamated crowd." He was billed to speak in Twin Bridges, where I determined to be present. The day was windy and cold, so that when I entered the hall I wore a long coonskin overcoat. Mr. Heinze arrived in the first automobile that I had ever seen, a large, brilliantly red car, carrying, besides himself and chauffeur, a quar-

[7] Among the Linderman papers is a letter from Twin Bridges, in Madison County, signed by nineteen men: "... Believing as we do that Mr. Carter's election to office would mean the disruption of the republican party in Montana and be a calamity to the state we urge you to use every honorable means within your power to defeat that end, pledging you our earnest support in your action." There are also several letters from individuals commending Linderman for his stand against Carter.

tet of negro singers with banjos. Mr. Heinze saw and spoke to me, so that there can be no doubt about his knowing of my presence. He talked for nearly forty minutes. I thought him a little flustered, that he was not saying exactly what he had intended to say. Finally, however, as though he had at last screwed his courage to the sticking-point he said, "Two years ago the Republican nominees for the legislature in this county came to me, personally, and pledged me their support. Then, after their election, they went to Helena and sold out to the Amalgamated Copper Company."

"You lie!" I shouted, letting my coonskin coat fall to the floor as I started for the platform. They threw me out. I waited outside for Mr. Heinze, but when he finally appeared he was so hemmed in by heelers that I could not get near him without being wrecked. Later on, in Helena, he told me, "I'm sorry I said what I did in Madison County, Frank. I was drunk that day in Twin Bridges."

I had been elected by less than fifty votes over my competitor. There had been so many harsh words spoken, so much underhand work done during the campaign, that I felt as full of fight as a badger. I felt vengeful, wanted to play even, a proof that I am neither a good politician nor, in office, a fair representative of the people. I began at once to organize the Tom Carter opposition in the House and Senate.

"The Indians," as we were called, on account of my earlier associates, dared not sit in any party caucus of the House and Senate that did not exclude from its proposed business the election of a United States senator. If we had permitted ourselves to do otherwise we should have been whipped into line by the Carter men, who were in the majority. A good deal of pressure was brought to bear upon the "Indians." The tribe lost four of its members before it had fairly taken the warpath. All of the political patronage of a United States senator was peddled, jobs being offered to the tribesmen with fancy promises for trimmings. Day after day the vote for the senatorship resulted in "no election," until Democrats from Silver Bow County began voting for Tom Carter. Then, like a bubble, my tribe went to pieces. For every imaginable reason, flimsy ones and some that I believe were substantial, my "Indians" laid down their arms, leaving me alone.

I shall never forget the final vote. Word quickly went abroad that the Indians had weakened. The galleries of the House were jammed with Carter enthusiasts when the gavel fell. Instantly a silence that was electric in its suddenness held everybody spellbound until the clerk of the House, calling the roll of the House and Senate in joint assembly, named the first "Indian." He voted for Carter. The capitol shook with the cheers and uproar of the onlookers. So great was the demonstration staged to strengthen the weaklings that the sergeant at arms was ordered to restore quiet in the galleries. Nevertheless, whenever an "Indian" voted for Mr. Carter his admirers burst out anew. Finally my name was called. A breathless silence, even in the galleries, seemed to dare me. I voted for Col. Wilbur F. Sanders,[8] whose bronze statue now stands in the capitol's rotunda, and at once began to dodge trash thrown at me from the galleries, while some in the throng hissed themselves dizzy.[9]

Now ostracism, the subtle weapon of bossism, was quite generally used against me. I began to be shunned by nearly all of Mr. Carter's supporters, excepting the Senator himself. Suave, able, and delightfully entertaining, Senator Carter was never lacking in his attention to me in any gathering. I liked him immensely, and did not believe in him at any time. When, later, I became state agent for a life insurance company, he offered me business, but I refused it, because I did not feel that I ought to accept it. Once, however, he did me a favor. I mention this because it perfectly illustrates his tact and character, which would win him high station anywhere.

An old Indian friend of mine wished to travel outside Montana

[8] Wilbur F. Sanders was the prosecuting attorney in the public trial of George Ives, the first of the Plummer gang of highwaymen and outlaws to be convicted and hanged. The trial was held outside in winter at Nevada City in Alder Gulch. Sanders was a staunch fighter for right to the end of his days.

[9] According to a daughter, Mrs. Linderman saved a clipping that read: "Linderman will go down in Montana's political history as the only Indian who escaped the Carter Massacre of 1905." A cartoon among the Linderman papers shows the "Indians" flailed and laid out by Senator Carter, with Linderman bumped on the head but rising.

with quite a following of his people. Being fearful that white settlers might object to his passing through their sections on his way westward, he asked me for a letter telling inquiring ones who he was, etc. I knew that outside this state my name would count for little, and yet I wished to help my old friend, a chief. I asked the United States marshal for a suitable letter, but he began at once to hum and haw so squeamishly that I left him to find the county sheriff, who I felt would accommodate me with the required letter. The sheriff not being in his office, I set out to find him. A political campaign was on, the sheriff himself being up for re-election. I thought I might find him in Doctor Lanstrum's office, the doctor being then the Republican chairman.[10] I found the Doctor busy, and rapped on his private door. "What do you want?" he asked, standing in his doorway.

I hastily explained.

"Come right in, Frank. I'll fix you out in a jiffy," said the pleasing voice of Tom Carter, out of sight in the Doctor's sanctum.

I did not feel that he owed me any consideration, and yet I could not refuse so gracious an offer.

"Put a United States Senate letterhead in the machine," he told the stenographer, and then began his letter. "To Whom It May Concern. The bearer of this letter—What's his name, Frank?" turning to me.

"Full-of-dew," I told him.

"Full-of-dew," went on the Senator. "What tribe does he belong to, Frank?"

"Chippewa," I said.

"A Chippewa Indian, has been known to my good friend, the honorable Frank B. Linderman, for—How long, Frank?"

"For twenty years, Senator."

[10] Dr. Oscar Monroe Lanstrum was titular head of the state Republican organization and owner of the Helena *Record-Herald*. In 1918 he defeated Jeannette Rankin in the primary for the senatorship; but she ran in the election, against Thomas J. Walsh and Dr. Lanstrum, on the ticket of the National Party, the front for the Non-Partisan League, splitting the vote. Walsh was elected. See Merrill G. Burlingame and K. Ross Toole, *A History of Montana* (New York: Lewis Historical Publishing Co., 1957), I, 253 ff.

"For twenty years, etc."

This letter, carried over the country by the Indian, did two things: it was magic in making friends for its bearer, and it proclaimed to its readers that its writer and I had made political peace, that we were now the best of *tillicums*.[11] More than once Tom Carter's proffered favors proved a little embarrassing to me, since I never learned to fly a flag under which I could not consistently fight.

[11] *Tillicum* is the Chinook Jargon word for "friend."

CHAPTER VI

Insurance Agent and Friend of the Indian

THE campaign that, by a narrow margin, had given me a seat in the House of Representatives had made A. N. Yoder, of Butte, Secretary of State. Mr. Yoder was a warm friend of mine; being incensed by the open hostility toward me, he asked if I would become his assistant. The offer tempted me for two reasons: first, our daughters would have greater advantages in Helena, and second, my acceptance of the office of Assistant Secretary of State would prove to be a sandbur under the saddle blankets of my political enemies. However, there were two good reasons why I ought to decline the appointment: Mr. Yoder would quite naturally incur the enmity of those who so bitterly opposed me, and there was a law forbidding a member of the legislature to hold any other state office. I declined Mr. Yoder's offer, going home to Sheridan determined now to let politics alone. But Mr. Yoder was insistent, and at last we packed up and moved to Helena, where I became Assistant Secretary of State.[1]

To clean up, I had hastily leased my newspaper plant, which by now had increased a little in value, and sold my assay outfit. But I had been unable to get much money from either transaction. A little time before this the Frau's father and mother had come to live in Sheridan and we had helped them buy a home there, so that when we moved to Helena we were again broke.

The Frau and our daughters, having spent the winter in the capital during the legislative session, had made many acquaint-

[1] He served in that capacity from 1905 to 1907.

ances there. We placed the girls in school, settling ourselves a few blocks from the capitol, which permitted me to walk to my work.

Mr. Yoder was not in good health. At times he was obliged to quit the state for sea level, thus leaving me to handle the affairs of the office. I enjoyed it all, but my salary of $1800 per year would not reach far enough. I saw that I should have to make a change; and how I did dread telling Mr. Yoder that I must resign! There had been some talk of invoking the state law to oust me from the office I held, and how I did wish that my political enemies would start this ball rolling! But nobody did. I remember that once when I sat down beside Mr. Yoder, intending to explain my situation and resign, a man who for many years had held a very responsible appointive position entered the private office. Seeing us together, the man excused himself, turning to tiptoe out.

"What is it, —?" asked Mr. Yoder.

"Why, I can come in again," stammered the man, hesitating.

"No, no. What is it you want? There is nothing important going on here."

"I am seeking reappointment. A word from you to our new Governor would go a long way, and—"

"No!" interrupted Mr. Yoder, half rising from his chair. "There are hundreds of men in this state that think you are as crooked as hell, and I'm *one* of them."

How could I leave such a man? I went back into the business office, trying to forget my need of a new suit of clothes, sticking it out for another whole year. Then, while Mr. Yoder was out of the state, I wrote him that upon his return I wished to resign as soon as he could comfortably replace me. He offered to increase my salary out of his own pocket, but this I could not permit. Mr. Yoder passed away while Secretary of State. A more honorable, upright man had never graced our state government.

I bought out a custom assayer on Main Street in Helena, taking up my old work of blasting the dreams of prospectors and miners. My assay office was next door to the Cruse Savings Bank. Old Tommy Cruse was a famous character who often spent hours with me in my office.[2] In earlier days, clinging like a bulldog to his mine, the Drumlummon, named for his birthplace in Ireland, Tommy had often found it difficult to obtain even a sack of flour on credit. Nobody believed in his mine, and yet Tommy asked a million and a quarter for it, gophering on the property in the firm belief that it would make him wealthy. At last an English syndicate bought the Drumlummon and made it famous, paying old Tommy his price. Tommy demanded the money on the spot, and the representative of the English syndicate had difficulty in proving that he did not have that amount of money with him. At last it was agreed between them that a half-million be paid within a week or so, with other stipulated payments following monthly until the million and a quarter was fully paid. One month, [after] Tommy had already received over a million dollars on account, a payment was delayed somehow. Tommy went straight to the English company's office in Marysville. "I'm damned tired of gittin' me money in dhribs an' dhrabs," he said vehemently. However, when he finally got it, Tommy took very good care of it. His bank next door to my assay office was unique in the Northwest, if not in the whole world. It was Tommy's plaything, the hiding place for his money; in its vault there were heavy bars of gold. Its statements showed almost no loans, while its deposits were exceptionally large. Every old miner and prospector who had a little stake turned it over, for safekeeping, to Tommy Cruse, who could scarcely read or write. When, in 1893, the silver panic forced several banks in Helena to close their doors, Tommy piled his bank's windows with golden bars and bushels of gold coins. And when, in the stress of disastrous runs, the other financial institutions appealed to him for aid, Tommy seemed to remember the days when bankers had refused him a grubstake. "I didn't help to git yez into this scrape, an' I'll not help to git yez out," he told them shortly.

[2] Thomas Cruse, born in Ireland, came to Montana Territory in 1866. He prospected in Alder Gulch, in Idaho, and around Marysville, Montana, a town of about three thousand inhabitants in its heyday. Cruse and his heirs contributed heavily to the construction of the St. Helena Roman Catholic Cathedral in Helena.

I timed my lighting the furnace fire in my assay office by Tommy's arrival at his bank each morning. Always he came in a phaeton drawn by two old brown, and overly fed, horses, and always a negro coachman aided him to reach the bank's door. Old Tommy put on considerable style, and yet his money brought him a lot of misery—but that is another story.

The Crees and Chippewas had been camped near Helena for more than a year now. Of course I had become their arbiter. Their condition was pitiable indeed. Living upon offal garnered from the stingy slaughterhouses on the city's outskirts and whatever else they could find in Helena's garbage cans, they were in a state of health that was deplorable. Instead of the old-fashioned lodges (tepees) these Indians were hovering in tattered tents and shelters made with old gunny sacks and bits of rotten canvas. Wood, mostly green willow brush, was difficult to obtain, so that comfortable campfires were luxuries. To save fuel and yet contrive to warm their miserable shelters, they converted old iron wash tubs, salvaged from garbage dumps, into heating stoves. Their tiny tents, heated by these ingenious contraptions, were dangerously foul. I insisted upon openings being made in their tops, often making them myself; but as soon as my back was turned the Indians would plug the holes I had made.

Often hunted from the alleys by police, desperately hungry, clothed in filthy rags, I could scarcely recognize these old friends of other days, when there were few fences and plenty of game. I begged clothes for them, carried ads in the city newspapers soliciting cast-off garments, even begging funds with which to buy them food until people hid away when they saw me coming. Every morning the chief, Little-bear, and an interpreter would be standing by my office door, waiting to ask me some difficult question or to offer some dispute for settlement. They were always hungry as wolves, and many a needed dollar was thus lost to my family. The community looked upon these Indians as renegades. In a sense they were just that, since they had no home, no reservation, no place where they might make a living. Besides this, the Crees of the band belonged across the line in Canada. However, more than half the band of some three hundred were Chippewas (Ojibwas) of the United States, who had a right to remain in the state. Claiming kinship with the Crees, and knowing nothing about the white man's line that divided the United States from Canada, these Chippewas had fought with the Crees in the Riel Rebellion against Canadian troops, so that, in a sense, they were outlaws with the Crees themselves. Both had adopted Montana as their home after the fighting across the line, neither doubting that they had as much right to remain here as anybody else. The history of the band, garbled to suit unfriendly white men, began to spread, making my task of bettering its condition more difficult. One or two miserably petty things were done. I secured work from the city for one of these Indians, Young-boy by name. After working two days he came to me, saying that the white men would not permit him to go on because he did not belong to the union. I gave him five dollars, the price of membership in the union; he was rejected because he was an Indian.

Young-boy was a good worker. Once I got him employment from a friend of mine. A week later his employer called me on the phone to say that my Indian had charged him ten cents an hour more than a white man would have demanded for the same work. "I haven't yet paid him," he said. "I thought it best to tell you about it first."

I found Young-boy and told him what my friend had said.

"Yeah, dat's right, Prank. Me, Hi'm do hit more work dan de w'ite man, me," he declared frankly.

Within an hour I got his employer on the telephone, wondering if we should now have an argument, since I proposed to back Young-boy. Repeating what the Indian had told me, I waited for it to sink in.

"I guess he's right, Frank. Yes, I know he's right; and by George, I'll pay him. Send him up," said my friend.

Telling of the suffering of these Indians has reminded me of an incident that occurred near Great Falls. A Cree and his woman were camped on the plains within sight of the city during most of a severe winter, living as best they could on whatever they managed to find in the way of food. One day a government official connected with the Department of Indian Affairs asked this man to go with him to Box Elder to do some interpreting. All Indians respect officials, and the man believed he had to go; besides, he would be paid for his services. Leaving his woman alone in their tattered tent on the plains, he accompanied the officer to Box Elder, where he remained several days. The night he left his woman a blizzard came out of the north. During the raging gale the woman gave birth to a baby. There was no wood in the camp, nor any food. Covering her baby, the woman went out into the blizzard to a patch of green willows and began to cut the brush for fuel. Seven days later the man found her frozen to death in the willow patch, and the baby frozen in the ragged blanket—all this within sight of the twinkling lights of a white man's city. I can tell many more, and much worse, stories of the sufferings of these people.

I now began appealing to Washington for substantial help for these Indians, asking that a reservation be set aside for them. One winter while Congress quibbled, I managed to get President Taft to order them fed by the soldiers at Fort Harrison, just outside the city of Helena. I felt relieved for the time. They waxed fat, and yet all the clothes they received were the cast-off garments that I solicited. And here I will admit that the old saw "give an Indian a foot, and he'll want a yard" is largely true. No matter how much one does for an Indian, the recipient feels that it is the Almighty alone who deserves thanks, since He put the hospitable mortal on the earth.

One morning Little-bear presented himself to tell me that Rocky-boy, who was at Browning with a following of Chippewas, was starving. I had received this message the day before, however, and had managed to get a joint resolution through both the House and Senate of the State Legislature, then sitting, asking for permanent aid for both the Crees and Chippewas, and had had it signed by the Governor, all within two hours, a record for our legislature, I'm sure. Besides this, I had, the night before, delivered an address to three lodges of Masons in joint meeting where I had told about the suffering of these red men. A collection of one hundred dollars had been given me by these Masons. This money I had at once sent to Rocky-boy, whose name was Stone-child, so that I could now assure Little-bear that Rocky-boy and his people had food for the time being. The old fellow smiled happily. Then he said, "I want three dollars."

"What do you want three dollars for?" I asked, determined not to give him the money.

"I promised Rocky-boy that when the soldiers at the fort butchered a steer I would send him the guts and the head and the shanks, if the soldiers did not want them; and they killed a steer at the fort yesterday."

"But Rocky-boy and his people have good food now," I reminded him. "He doesn't need the things you mention."

He took off his hat with its eagle coup feather. "Look, Co-skee-see-co-cot," he said, pointing to his graying locks, "my hair is growing white because I have never spoken to my friends with a forked tongue (never lied). I promised to send Rocky-boy the guts and the head and the shanks that were left when the soldiers killed a steer. They have slaughtered a steer, and I have the things I said that I would send. The railroad man says he will take the guts and the head and the shanks of the steer the soldiers killed yesterday to Fort Browning for three dollars. I want three dollars, Co-skee-see-co-cot," he said decisively.

I did not have three dollars in my pocket, but wrote a check while the old fellow watched wonderingly. Taking my check into the bank next door, I brought Little-bear the money.

"If I could do that thing, making writing on paper and get money with it, I would do it for you all day, brother," declared the old Cree, going out to ship the offal to his friend at Fort Browning.

Late that afternoon he came again, this time presenting me with a black stone pipe that he told me had belonged to his grandfather, his father, and himself. "I give you this because you are the only white man I have ever known who does not lie," he said. However, the old fellow had misjudged me in this.

An assayer who deals with miners and prospectors is himself

always dabbling with mines and prospects. Prospects and Indians kept me flat broke, even though I was doing rather well in my business. Our daughters were growing up and my expenses were growing with them, so that when the Germania Life Insurance Company, of New York, (Guardian Life since the War) offered me its state agency I accepted, selling my assay office and laboratory to Goodall Brothers.

We had bought and paid for a home in Helena, and now with my new business I began to make considerable money. Up to the moment when I so suddenly became the Germania's state agent in Montana I had never seen a rate book and knew less about life insurance than a kingfisher. Nevertheless, I was successful from the beginning. During my first year I sold more insurance for my company than any other individual in the United States, or so the agency inspector told me. But I was never a good organizer. I had no agents, and was therefore obliged to maintain my contract with the company by selling the necessary amount of insurance each year myself. This kept me travelling over the state for nine years. I was seldom at home for more than a week at a time, so that when our daughters were ready for college I began to realize that I was losing acquaintance with my family and its home life.

I had long dreamed of someday going back to Flathead Lake and settling down there to write some books. I had set $35,000 as the amount of money necessary to carry me from a beginning to literary success. Now I had nearly this amount in renewals alone. Why wait longer? For years I had picked up and saved every little scrap of iron, bolts, and whatnot that might come handy in tinkering around a cabin in the timber. When finally we came to leave the city I had the most amazing collection of scrap stuff ever gathered, I'm sure. And even to this day it serves me. I find almost anything in those boxes, filled so long ago. I enjoyed storing these odds and ends more than any hoarding I have ever practiced.

Our going to Goose Bay [in 1917] was a great adventure for our daughters. The deep forest and blue lake fascinated them. We built a large log house, with modern conveniences, even installing a lighting plant, at the head of the bay, towing the necessary lumber down the lake from the Somers sawmill. Winter had come before the house was finished, and yet we moved in, bag and baggage. For a time Hudson's Bay blankets served as partitions, the deep fireplace furnishing heat for the whole household until the furnace was finally installed. We had great fun getting things done.

The girls began now to know the timberlands in winter, and the "forest-folk" as well. Each morning when fresh snow had fallen, deer and sometimes mountain lions left records of their night visit to the beach near the house. Always there was something new at Goose Bay, something to remember. For a time we had a pet flying squirrel that came every evening for his dish of condensed milk and bread until an owl got him. I found his beautiful tail a little way from the shed one morning; and this truly was the end of Jimmie. He was the only pet flying squirrel I have ever known, and even Jimmie was not exactly a pet. He was more nearly a star boarder, never missing a meal after his first reception, until he met his fate not far from his dish of bread and milk. Night noises in the surrounding forest were a joy to the girls. The whistle of a deer or the yelping of coyotes was sure to set them calling out to each other. But the pygmy owl, who begins his monotonous whistling toots in February when generally the snow lies deep in these northern woods, was never appreciated by the Frau. More than once I have had to go out in the night and drive a tormenting pygmy out of a fir tree near her bedroom window. Christmas times, and on all holidays, we had great fun. Our house is large, and yet sometimes when our company exceeded our expectations we have had to make beds on the floor near the fireplace for youngsters just old enough to feed the fire and forget to go to sleep. Our first winter at Goose Bay was so busy that I did no writing.

The second summer was hot, and so dry that at last careless campers set the forests afire. For weeks the sun and moon were red balls in the sky, both being finally obscured by smoke from burning timber. Ashes fell about the house, deadening the grass and leaves. Smoke, especially at night, nearly choked us. Deer and bears, hunted out of their forest haunts by flames, sought the water of the big lake; birds filled the trees and bushes near the house, all being so quiet, and seemingly so much afraid, that their coming added to our anxiety. Each day a letter went to Wilda, our eldest daughter, who was attending summer school at the University of Montana, telling of the fire in the forest about Goose Bay, and yet carefully avoiding too colorful details. On the night of the sixteenth of August the fire seemed to have skipped us, to have traveled around us. But there was so-called backfiring by people who had little thought for others than themselves. When morning came, shifting, squally winds warned me that the time had come to get the women safely away from the house. I told them I did not expect to save the place, to get into the boat and row to Miller's point, two miles below us, warning them not to go too far out on the water for fear they might not again find the land in the dense smoke that by now was smothering us.

"What shall I take with me?" asked the Frau, glancing hastily round the living room as though she might never see it again.

"Take old Rain-in-the-face's pipe, a shirt, and a pair of shoes for my part of saved plunder," I told her, helping to gather needed articles and carry them to the boat. I did not know it then, but they somehow lost the stem of the prized pipe on the beach, where I afterward found it, unburned.

No sooner had the rowboat, carrying the Frau, Verne, and Norma, left the shore than she was completely hidden by the smoke. I called good-by and ran back to the house, where my father, who was eighty years old, was stringing hose. First driving the car out of the basement into the lake until only its top stuck out of the water, I started the machinery in the pump house, got hose onto the roof, and began alone to fight the flames that roared like trains running over long, deep trestles. The heat, coming in great puffs with red balls of fire that rolled over the house, was so great that the roof caught fire eight times. So dense was the smoke that I feared stepping off the roof into space as I dragged the hose about. I knew that prized possessions were burning. My painted lodge on the point was going up in smoke, together with its

146

contents, fine old Hudson's Bay blankets and camp equipage. But I dared not leave the roof, wondering all the time at the faithfulness of the usually fickle engine that was driving the pump like mad, without a drop of oil. I could not take the time to get down and look after the toiling machinery that must have been nearly red-hot. I thought that I should have to let it run as long as it would, and then get along without it.

But, learning that Goose Bay was doomed, Ted Miller, a young friend of mine, came through the smoke to the assistance of the suffering machinery. He fed it, stuffed it, coddled it, while it raced on like a mad thing wishing to make up for past cussedness. Twice the flames swooped so low that they burned my clothes, singed my hair and eyebrows, and forced me to lie flat, clutching the steep roof with blistered fingers. The fire, chased by mad winds in all directions, raced down the hill from the highway, came across the point, and along the beach, all at once, as though the devil himself were trying what tricks might be played with flames. Even the driftwood on the gravelly beach burned to white ashes.

I had just launched a sailboat that I had built. The fire burned her anchoring lines. She went adrift to sail the lake like a phantom thing in the dense smoke for two weeks before I recovered her. Once, when I choked down and was lying with my face buried in the charred grass near the house, I gave up the struggle. Getting to my feet, I called my father, who was greatly excited, took a last look at the living room and my collection of Indian curios and old Kentuckys, intending to wade out as far as I could into the Bay and wait for the end, whatever it might be. Ted Miller, fearing that his father's place might now be burning, had gone, so that together my father and I started for the water. But just then two men, who had been up the lake fighting fire came running along the shore. I hailed them, and after much begging and many promises of reward got them to help me try again.

Asking my father to sit on the porch where I might quickly find him if a retreat had to be made, I climbed back onto the roof with the strangers. One of them proved to be crazy as a March hare. After a particularly desperate struggle with the flames, he

147

raised himself up to his hands and knees to peer dazedly through the smoke at me. "They got my brother," he husked; his eyes, dripping tears, were crazed, wild, his words wilder. I saw that I had now to deal with a crazy man in a crazy situation. I dared not turn my back to him. My father, forgetting my request that he remain on the porch, entered the house to get his pet rifle, which he carried to the beach. The crazy man saw this and wanted to get the gun, talking of nothing else, until I wished him a thousand miles from Goose Bay. My throat and lungs were sore, my head dizzy.

At last the worst of the flames swept over us, and I was glad to dismiss the wild man. His disappearance in the smoke was a relief that I shall never forget. Sitting down, I took stock of myself. My shirt was without a back, my hat without a crown, and I had no more eyebrows than an old Indian. I had left off my shoes so that my stockinged feet might cling to the steep roof covered with forty-eight thousand shingles. Now my socks had no bottoms, and my blistered feet were full of slivers. And how thankful I felt that a tiny grove of fir trees near the house had been spared. Once, during my first battle, I had left the roof to look for my axe, intending to cut these trees for safety's sake. But some firefighter had stolen it. This was the only favor the hired fire-fighters did for me. I give them no thanks, dallying with the forest fires as they did that year. They ran away from me as though I were a leper, one or two pausing long enough to advise me to run while I could. After the worst was over one man, named Shroeder, a neighbor living eight miles up the lake, came to help me. This man remained at Goose Bay overnight, accepting no pay for his services. The steamboat, on its regular trip, steering entirely by compass, did enter the bay, but seeing nothing of our house in the dense smoke, reported that we were burned up.

What a relief it was to learn that the women were safe at Miller's point! And what a wreck the flames had made of beautiful Goose Bay! It was a rather sad homecoming for the Frau and the girls. All this was in August, 1918. Today the young trees are growing everywhere, and Goose Bay is again pretty. But I shall have been camped on some showery cloud for many a year before these young trees look as beautiful as the old ones did. Goose Bay will never again be the same to me.[3]

At the beginning of these memoirs I told of witnessing the workings of the so-called moccasin telegraph, saying that the Frau had been deeply impressed by her own experiences with the forecasting of events by Indians. Several times when I suddenly returned to Helena from some point in far eastern Montana I learned upon arrival that the Frau knew I would come home that day. Indians had told her. One day, after having called at our Helena home and not finding me there, Full-of-dew, one of my favorites, told the Frau that I would be home very soon, before the sun set, and that he wished to see me at my office in the morning.

He came early, with an interpreter. Sometimes my private office was piled with old clothing that Miss Kenyon, the cashier, had accepted during my absence, and always there was a black line along the wall that had been made by Indians who had leaned against it with their hands held behind them. This morning I had not only a large supply of cast-off clothes, but found a piece of highly medicated gauze tied over the receiver of my telephone. How Miss Kenyon dreaded old clothing and my Indian visitors!

"What is wrong?" I asked my dignified caller.

"What is sickness?" he asked, a puzzled look in his fine eyes. "When I was a young man," he went on, "warriors died of wounds, of starvation sometimes, and of cold, but nobody laid down on his blanket and did not get up again, as they do now."

I thought I saw opportunity here if only I could grasp it. Picking up my telephone I called a number, saying some trivial thing when a friend answered me. Then, turning to Full-of-dew, I asked, "Do you believe that I talked to a man with this thing?"

"Yes," he replied simply. And then as though guessing what was in my mind, he said, "I will believe anything you tell me."

---

[3] Linderman exhausted himself fighting the fire, and his health was permanently weakened as a result.

"Would your father have believed that I could talk with a man in Great Falls with this telephone?" I asked.

"No," he said, shortly, adding, "I will believe whatever you tell me."

"Wait and see," I countered. "What I am going to tell you, and show you, will be more difficult for you to believe than it would have been for your father to have believed that I could talk with this 'phone to a man who was five-days' ride from this place. Come with me."

I led him, with Roasting-stick, Fine-bow, Big-sky, and the interpreter, to the laboratory of Dr. Emil Starz, who is a master chemist, and there quickly explained the conditions in the Indian camp. Dr. Starz was delighted at this opportunity to help these people to know that cleanliness is the first attribute of health, and that sickness comes with unsanitary conditions and filth. Under powerful microscopes whose polished surfaces gleamed with deep importance he showed my friends, one by one, many kinds of germs, even taking saliva from the tongue of Full-of-dew in his demonstrations. One look at the hideous forms was enough for Big-sky; two or three looks cut down the kind Doctor's Indian audience to Full-of-dew and the interpreter, who remained until Doctor Starz could show them no more.

During all this exposition, that must have been a terrible revelation to him, Full-of-dew uttered no word. Looking at his highly intelligent face, I saw not only deep bewilderment there, but awe, as he, in his turn, looked down through the shining tube at the strangely formed, many-legged mites in the light below. Returning to my office with me, he sat for a long time smoking, taking deep draughts from his stone pipe. I did not disturb his thoughts. Finally he put his pipe away and stood up. "Ho!" he said abruptly, and went out, his moccasins making not the slightest sound in the hall. I wondered if I had offended him.

Next morning I saw Raspberry, the interpreter, on the street. "What did the old man think of the things that Dr. Starz showed him?" I asked.

"God! De hol' man she hant sleep las' night. Dis mornin' she's call hit hall de peep; mak' hit clean de camp, clean de camp. Sacre Bleu! Everybody now dat speet mus' speet hin de *tin*-can. Yes, sir, oui, by gar!"

Full-of-dew, with all his gentle traits, could be cunning. Years before this he came to my camp in the Flathead country with a silver dollar. Being anxious to increase his capital, he offered to bet the dollar, against a like amount, that he could beat me running. "No," I said, "but I will bet you a good blanket against your dollar that I can beat you shooting at a mark."

"No, no," he signed, sitting down by the fire, where my partner placed a camp kettle of boiled venison and a bannock before him. He ate prodigiously. When the Indian could hold no more my partner, who had purposely stuffed him, said to me in English, "Let's us try him out. You run a hundred yards with him. If you beat him, or hold him pretty well, I'll take him on myself. I can beat you running, and we need that dollar."

Full-of-dew, like ourselves, was then young and readily agreed to a race with me, believing that my partner and I had bet a plug of smoking tobacco on the outcome. There was a crust on the snow that would bear the weight of a horse. After making the scratch [mark] my plotting partner stepped off the one hundred yards and drew his six-shooter.

We were off with the shot; I beat the Indian by a few inches, which surprised me not a little.

"Now," confided my resourceful partner, "we'll git that there dollar." Going to our bedroll, he drew out a red blanket that belonged to me.

"Wait," I objected. "I don't want to lose that blanket. I'm no runner. *Anybody* can beat me running."

"Wasn't I watchin'," he grinned wisely. "That Injin was doin' his damndest; an' this is the only *single* blanket in the camp."

"Well, go ahead," I agreed reluctantly.

This time I made the scratch myself, stepped off the hundred yards and fired the starting shot—and then slept cold the rest of the winter.

Full-of-dew did not know English. He either sensed my partner's trickery and played to beat him, or, because of his friendship for me, threw the first race so that I might win my partner's tobacco. Just here I will tell what befell Full-of-dew.

One winter two United States Army officers came to see me. They said, "We have been ordered to move the Indians who are camped in the Prickly Pear valley to Browning. The chief says that he will not go there. We can do nothing with him by talking and do not wish to use force. However, we must obey our orders. Can you help us out, and so save real trouble?"

I told them that I would try. We drove out to the camp; and what a sight was there! Pinched by hunger, and driven inside by the bitter cold, men, women, and children were huddled in every miserable shelter. Full-of-dew's tent was quite neat, however. He received us there like the prince that he was. He listened, as all old Indians will, until I had finished speaking. Then he said, simply, "I will go wherever these soldiers take me, if you tell me that you wish me to go. But if I go to Browning I shall die there within ten days."

"No, no," I assured him. "You will be fed at Browning. There will be no sickness there. These soldiers will take care of you and your people, so that you will all be warm; and they will take you on the train, too," I added, to make him happier.

He smiled. "No, Co-skee-see-co-cot," he said, with finality, "I will not ride on a train. Someday one of those things will fall over and kill many people. I will ride my horse to Browning. (A distance of at least 300 miles.)

This was the last time that I saw Full-of-dew. He died, as he had predicted, within ten days after reaching his destination. The following summer I visited the reservation of the Blackfeet at Browning, and there saw Full-of-dew's brother, Rocky-boy, who, in a formal meeting with thirty old warriors present, gave me my old friend's dying message. "Tell Co-skee-see-co-cot that it is my wish that he take my brother (Rocky-boy) into his heart, as he took me." This was all. There was no rebuke, no sting in the message for me, and yet I felt that I had sent him to his death. Perhaps he is better off in the Shadow-hills. I know that he was miserable here.

On the occasion of my meeting Rocky-boy and getting the message, I had come to the reservation because of an invitation from the Piegans (Pecunnies) themselves.[4] The tribe was holding a big dance and ceremonial, and had induced their kin, the Bloods, and other Indians to join them, so that there must have been in the village more than three hundred lodges, besides less attractive shelters, when I arrived. On my way to the Indian village I stopped in Great Falls, where I invited my old friend Charley Russell, the cowboy artist, Theodore Gibson, Charley Elliott, and Percy Raban, to go with me to the powwow. Our train was late. It was near midnight before we reached the ancient buffalo-skin lodge that the tribe had set up for my use in the very center of the great circle of lodges that formed the village. Serenaders began at once to entertain us, the huge drums of the Piegans being used to accompany the singers. Two o'clock came before our little lodge was vacated by the host of visitors who had been coming and going ever since our arrival. Only one now remained, a half-breed, who perhaps believed that we had liquor in our baggage and would give him a drink. I was unrolling my blanket when Russell held up his hand in the light of the tiny fire we had kindled for light. "Listen!" he said, standing up, with a hand on a lodge-pole. An Indian drum was beating monotonously.

"Dat's de Crees," offered the half-breed. "Dat's de sun-dance. Tomorrow's de las' day."

"I sure would like to see them in the firelight," Russell mused wistfully, going to the lodge door to look out.

"You can't go in dere. Dey won't let nobody in dere, nobody but a Cree, mebby," declared the breed discouragingly.

"Crees?" I asked him.

"Yeah. No damn good, dem Cree; mean lak hell."

"I believe that I can take you in, Charley," I said. "Anyhow I'll try. Come on, all of you white men."

[4] The following story is also told in Linderman's *Recollections of Charley Russell* (Norman: University of Oklahoma Press, 1963).

A hurried walk of nearly two miles brought us to an immense brush lodge with bright spears of firelight darting through the already wilted leaves on the young saplings that thatched its top and wall. Red sparks from the fire within were going straight up, clinging to life that the still, early summer night seemed not to wish to foster. The drums, several of them, beating in unison, sounded savagely forbidding. Nevertheless, I lifted the canvas door and entered, followed by the others.

The drums ceased, heads turned, angry eyes glared. In a jiffy Little-bear, the Cree chief, clad only in a breechclout, sprang toward us, speaking rapidly in Cree. But he stopped as suddenly as he had started, a broad, happy smile lighting his powerful face.

"How! How!" he greeted; then, turning to his people, "My brother has come to us. My heart sings," he said, going on with a long speech of welcome. Finishing, he strode majestically to the center pole of the sun lodge where two or three pieces of finery, "medicine," were hanging, lifted down an adorned otter skin, and handed it to me. "This," he said, "was my grandfathers'. It is big medicine. Brother, I now give it to you forever."

I accepted the rare gift from his hands, held it up in the firelight, and then said, "Brother, my heart is made glad by this gift. I will keep it as long as I live. But that it may be with you and your people until the end of this dance I ask you to keep it for me until day after tomorrow, and to then bring it to my lodge."

Little-bear gladly, and with reverence, replaced the precious otter skin on the lodge's center pole; and then instantly the drums began again, and the dancing in the firelight, making Charley Russell very happy.

Charley Russell was the most lovable man I have ever known. My remembrances of our days and nights together, alone in camps, and of his frequent visits in our home at Goose Bay are highlights that brighten with passing years. His paintings and bronzes have done more to depict the life of the old Northwest than the combined work of all other painters, sculptors, or writers. I am glad that it was I who induced the Montana Club in Helena to purchase the large Russell hanging in its reading room, as well as the De-

Camp painting in its club room. Both are fine examples of the work of these Montana artists, and both have grown considerably in value since their purchase by the club. When I hung the Russell, lighting it as best I could so that the board of governors might view it to advantage, Colonel Tatem and others appeared to have a look at the picture. The Colonel sniffed, "That's a miserable buffalo bull in the foreground," he said, leaving the room.

My interest in the canvas was not mercenary. Except in a friendly way I was neither Russell's agent nor the club's. Colonel Tatem's speech stung me deeply, especially when I remembered having seen Charley paint this same buffalo over and over again. The huge beast would one day be seemingly perfect; the next he'd be gone, painted out entirely. "I've fought that bull for six months," Charley told me, when finally the painting was finished and turned over to me. And yet, after all this, after the master himself (and in painting buffalo he was a master) had worked so long with the bull in the foreground, Col. Tatem pronounced it a miserable figure. I told Charley what the Colonel had said and shall never forget his reply. "Well, mebby it *is* a bum bull, but it's the best damned buffalo bull that *I* ever painted," he said evenly. This canvas brought him more money than any he had previously sold, except the immense painting in the state capitol—and I had a hand even in that. Besides, it was I who caused the bronze tablet commemorating the bravery of James Williams, captain of the vigilantes, to be placed in the capitol. I proposed the measure, drew the bill, and inscribed the tablet. I have mentioned this because there is nothing to show how the tablet came to be in the capitol, except the history of the bill making the appropriation.

The buffalo-skin lodge that had been pitched for me in the Piegan village was the only one left in the tribe. It belonged to Joe Kipp, a half-breed Mandan who had spent his life among the Piegans. Joe's father, James Kipp, built Fort Piegan at the mouth of the Marias in 1832 for the American Fur Company. Joe, whose life was full of adventure, nearly lost the friendship of the Piegans because of the Baker massacre in 1870. His part in the disgraceful affair came about in this way.

155

A band of Bloods, another tribe of the Blackfeet like the Piegans, had committed depredations, making a killing or two among white settlers, so that General Baker was looking for them. The soldiers were camped at Fort Conrad,[5] where, in January, Joe Kipp went on some errand of his own. Baker asked Joe if he had seen the Bloods. Joe told that he had, that the Bloods were camped on the Marias. The General (then a major, I believe) engaged Joe to lead him to the Indian camp, the whole command setting out at once. Joe, not knowing that the offending Bloods had moved their lodges, had gone out of the country since he passed that way, led the soldiers to the Marias, where, on the same ground lately occupied by the Bloods, there were an equal number of Piegan lodges in which innocent Indians were sleeping peacefully. Here was the camp. In the dim light of the cold January dawn Joe Kipp saw nothing to warn him of his mistake; and Baker, anxious to win fame, opened fire. The slaughter was awful, the soldiers even killing the wounded Indians. One of the women, whose ankle had been shattered by a bullet, showed me how her mother had supported her in a standing position while the soldiers [were] dispatching the wounded, so they might not learn that she had been shot. One little boy of four years was made to climb high up on the poles of his father's lodge by his sorely wounded parent, while bullets cut the lodge to ribbons. This boy, raised by Joe Kipp, grew to be a man of gigantic size, and more than once, when he had been drinking, made Joe hide out until his ward grew sober again.[6]

Kipp's life story would have made interesting reading. Being a good friend of mine, I once tried to get it. "Nope," he smiled,

[5] Linderman's memory must have slipped here, for the Baker or Piegan, Massacre took place in January, 1870, and the soldiers came from Fort Ellis, near Bozeman and Fort Shaw on Sun River. Fort Conrad, constructed in 1875 on the south side of the Marias River, was an important Blackfoot fur-trading post and stopover for travelers from Fort Benton to Forts Whoop-up and McLeod in Alberta, Canada.

[6] Major E. M. Baker of the Second Cavalry at Fort Ellis was in command of the four companies. In the attack on the wrong camp, 120 men and 53 women and children were killed, and 100 women were "turned out on the snow-covered plains on foot with scant attire and no food or equipment, a number of them infected with smallpox." See Burlingame, *The Montana Frontier*, pp. 224–225.

his half-closed eyes shining in the candlelight; "Nope, Frank. By God, if I'd tell de truth dey'd hang me yit, sure's hell, you know."

When automobiles were new Joe bought one. The salesman taught him how to operate it, but the next morning, under Joe's handling, the car tore first the back and then the front out of the barn before piling itself up in a deep ditch. Joe, viewing the wreck, swore strange oaths. "She's got too many triggers, de damned t'ing," he said, disgustedly.

About this time I began to get inquiries from Washington respecting my tribe, as many people called the Crees and Chippewas. The government was preparing to abandon Fort Assinniboine, near Havre, Montana, and some time before this I had asked that a portion of this old military reservation be given these Indians. Politicians objected; through its newspapers the city of Havre protested. I well remember the *Havre Plain Dealer* saying editorially that in all my work for the "renegade Indians" I was constantly "hiding under a mantle of Charity," that all I really wanted was to become Indian agent on the reservation I proposed to establish, that I gave no consideration to the rights of white settlers, etc. These charges went the rounds, and yet I am certain that few people believed them. My business brought me more money in a single year than an Indian agent could earn in half a dozen.

Franklin Lane was then Secretary of the Interior, may his name live forever. He was coming to Montana. I easily arranged to have him meet not only me but Little-bear, the Cree Chief, in Helena. Our meeting was not particularly successful, owing largely to the old Chief's attitude. He insisted upon telling Mr. Lane what he thought of white men, and in spite of my stepping repeatedly upon his moccasined foot he kept pouring out his venom. However, I managed to signal the interpreter often enough so that he tempered the Chief's sentences a little. Nevertheless, Mr. Lane was angered. "I don't like his attitude, Mr. Linderman," he declared, "but I will hear your story when you come to Washington."

I was in the nation's capital almost as soon as Mr. Lane reached his office there.[7] Within two hours after my arrival, Saturday afternoon, the Secretary had told me that he would see me at ten o'clock Monday morning. Former United States Senator Paris Gibson, of Great Falls, Theodore, his son, and Mr. Boles of the *Great Falls Tribune*, all staunch Democrats, prominent in their party, had helped me greatly, especially Mr. Boles, who made a trip to Washington in behalf of my tribe. Few others had given me the least bit of aid in my efforts to secure a home for the help-less Crees and Chippewas. Some who called themselves my friends even dealt me crooked cards while pretending to play fairly. But now I found myself in Washington with an opportunity to tell my tale to the only man who could give us a reservation. I could scarcely wait for Monday morning.

Doctor Lanstrum, the leading Republican in Montana then, having business in Washington, had accompanied me. We stopped at the Willard, where Mr Sam Blythe[8] came to see us. Blythe was quite fond of the Doctor, and spent the evening in our rooms. After he had gone Doctor Lanstrum said to me, "Frank, ask Sam to give you a letter to Lane. It would help you a lot, I think."

"But I don't need his letter," I told him. "I have already arranged a meeting with Secretary Lane, and besides, I know Mr. Lane personally."

"Oh, ask him anyway. It will hot-air him a little, and he likes that stuff," urged the Doctor, who wished to play up to Blythe.

"All right," I agreed, "I'll ask him." I was perfectly willing to put a little dry wood on the Doctor's political fire at any time.

Sunday morning I went down to breakfast before the Doctor was ready. I had but seated myself in the dining room when in came Samuel G. Blythe and at about the same time an Assistant Attorney General of my acquaintance, as well. Both these gentle-men sat down at my table. Upon getting their assurances that they

[7] Linderman paid his own expenses for the Washington trip, according to his daughter.

[8] Newspaperman, mazazine editor, and writer, best known in his day perhaps for his book *The Making of a Newspaper* (Philadelphia: Henry Altemus Co., 1912).

had already breakfasted, I turned to Mr. Blythe and said, "Sam, I'm here in behalf of some distressed Indians in Montana and must have a talk with the Secretary of the Interior. Would you mind giving me a letter to Mr. Lane, assuring him that I'm not a horse-thief?"

I can see him expand even now. "I should say I *would* mind. I'm besieged—."

I felt humiliated. "I don't want your letter, don't need it, never *did*. I asked you for it because Lanstrum thought it would hot-air you," I told him.

He hastened to assure me that there was nothing personal in his refusal; but I didn't care to listen.

Promptly at ten o'clock Monday morning I was shown into Mr. Lane's private office, where he greeted me in a most friendly manner. On his desk I saw a copy of the *Havre Plain Dealer*, the issue containing the nasty editorial I have mentioned. Pointing to the newspaper that was spread out as though it had recently been read, I said, "Mr. Secretary, I see that you are a subscriber to the *Havre Plain Dealer*."

Mr. Lane laughed merrily, then brushed the newspaper into his waste basket. "Please sit down, Mr. Linderman. I want to hear your story, all of it," he said briskly.

In an hour Mr. Lane arose. "Thank you," he said, offering his hand. "We'll get this reservation, or know why. You may go home to Montana feeling that I am behind you in this affair. I'll keep you informed as to progress here."

At least two more years dragged by before we finally got two fractional townships at the southern end of the old Fort Assinniboine Military Reservation for a Chee-Chippewa home. It was mostly high and dry, and confined to narrow limits; and yet these Indians are now expected to raise bananas where white men would have difficulty in raising a wall tent.[9]

Our accomplishment was not much. For a time we believed that

[9] Much of the Linderman Collection in the Museum of the Plains Indian at Browning, Montana, deals with Linderman's efforts to obtain a reservation for his Indians. He played a much larger part in securing the reservation than is generally attributed to him.

a reservation of size might be obtained in northeastern Montana. But nothing came of our dream, mostly because the Great Northern Railroad Company opposed the measure. An excursion train of protesters, kept merry on the way with "Rocky-boy" cocktails, sped to Washington, and the proposition was dropped. Then a large sign that might easily be read from its moving trains appeared on the railroad company's right of way. It was on the edge of the proposed reservation, and appealed to white settlers with these or similar words: "ROCKY BOY LANDS. GET A FREE HOME HERE." [When I was] talking with Mr. Kinney, who, I believe, was then the Great Northern's president, he said, "We don't want a lot of ragged Indians along our right of way." But now that Glacier National Park has been established, and virtually turned over to the Great Northern Railroad, the company *advertises* Indians, and Indian dancing, *features* Indians who would themselves be ragged if the railroad company did not pay them to wear feathers for its tourists.

Many of the finer characters that made the Cree-Chippewa band interesting to me had gone to the Shadow-hills before our little reservation came true. Full-of-dew and Rocky-boy were both gone. Little-bear soon followed them, so that when finally the Crees and Chippewas were given a stingy strip of poor land they were without their old leaders.

Full-of-dew was a silent man, always anxious to learn, a profound mystic. Once on a day in winter I met him. "Are you hungry?" I asked, because he shivered.

"Yes," he answered.

"Come, and we will eat," I said, turning my horse toward my camp.

"No," he said, firmly. "My woman is sick. I have promised Manitou that I will not eat for four days and four nights."

"Who *is* Manitou?" I asked, as always when opportunity offered.

He looked about, his eyes settling for a moment on the far mountains white with snow. "The mountains, the lowlands, the rivers, the birds, my fire, the people, the big trees," he said slowly.

Then he added, "I believe that the big trees speak to you, Co-skee-see-co-cot, but not to many other white men."

Rocky-boy was fine of feature, without the least visible animosity towards the white race, and gentle as a woman. Little-bear was a born fighting man. His face was like a Roman senator's, and yet lurking in his eyes there was an easily awakened expression of keen humor. He laughed readily, but was decidedly moody, his mouth suggesting a pouter. These men, and many others of the band, had counted coup in battle, and always wore an eagle's feather as a mark of distinction. Perhaps they were the first men to face a hostile Gatling gun in action, and before it they gave an excellent account of themselves as fighters, as the Canadian history of the Northwest will show. Telling me of this battle, Little-bear described the unexpected and rapid firing of the Gatling by slapping his palms together. "No good," he exclaimed in signs, his wide lips set in a straight line, his eyes sullen. "If the Big White Chief in Washington will give me plenty of ammunition I will take Canada and give it all to him," he once told me.

At another time in a more detailed story of the fighting across the line he described his own position in thick brush. "The year was young," he said, "the nights cool, and the middle of the days hot. A creek ran along near my hiding-place. The soldiers were just across it in the bushes, like myself. I saw a red coat. It was moving carefully toward the water in the creek. At last a soldier stuck his head out of the bushes right across from me. He was thirsty. He looked at the water. Then he looked all about, up and down the stream, and even up into some trees. I might have killed him, but I didn't. He was very thirsty. I let him creep to the creek, and drink all the water he wanted; then I shot him."

Invest an old Indian with authority and he will carry out the orders of his superior to the letter. Little-bear loved authority, and yet I once knew him to turn against it. When the Department of Indian Affairs, under Mr. Cato Sells, first sent food to the Crees and Chippewas at Box Elder, government red tape temporarily prevented its distribution. A Cree of Little-bear's band was commissioned by the government's agent to guard the food

161

stored in a cabin near the Indian camp. The band was starving. The Cree guard would listen to nobody, not even to his old mother. Little-bear, torn between his respect for the guard's orders and thoughts of his people's plight, came to see me.

"What shall I do?" he asked, his eyes on the ground. "The children are crying."

I possessed no authority. However, the silliness of the situation stung me into assuming that I had. "Go back and take that grub," I told him.

He was gone almost as soon as I had spoken the words. I expected scareheads in the newspapers, to see my name and record riddled. But, fortunately for me, and the heroic Cree guard, the food had been distributed by government orders before Little-bear reached the camp.

And I remember the action of Big-thunder, an Indian policeman, wearing a uniform on the Fort Belknap Reservation. Sent with orders to bring in his own brother, dead or alive, Big-thunder brought the law-breaker in, dead; and then went alone to the tribal burial place and shot himself.

Another man of the Cree-Chippewa band that interested me was Iron-collar. More than six feet tall, straight as a rifle barrel, old Iron-collar wore a wide band of copper laced in two sections about his neck. So wide was this collar that its wearer could scarcely look down at his own moccasins; and yet he never left it off that I know of. I had noticed from the beginning that every member of the tribe looked upon Iron-collar as a distinguished man. At last I learned why. In the fighting across the Canadian line he had counted a most honorable coup. Armed with a bow and arrows, he had managed somehow to pull a cavalryman from his horse, to disarm him, keep the soldier's weapons himself, and then permit the disarmed soldier to go unharmed back to his own lines. Iron-collar was the only Indian I ever knew who stammered a little in his speech. His christened name was "Sitting-horse." I got the secret of making Indian colors fast from him.

By now the reader may believe that I see the old Indian in too warm a light. I do not. I know his shortcomings well enough. He

162

is not a saint. Instead, he has more than once qualified as a nearly perfect devil. Ever since our advent in North America, the red man's misdeeds have had willing heralds. Few have spoken of his finer qualities. And yet it is only the discovered good in man that builds humanity. Napoleon said after reading *The Iliad*, "I am specially struck by the rude manners of the heroes, as compared with their lofty thoughts." The Indian has startled us by the same contrast, and so confounds us in our final estimate of the race we have conquered—from whom we might have learned needed lessons, if we had tried.

Many times while we waited for our reservation I tried to explain Congress to my tribe, drawing a rude map of the nation on the ground, marking off the states, showing them the number of representatives that each sent to Washington, always trying to make these Indians understand and excuse the slowness with which the ponderous body acts, even though I did not myself understand it. One day while I thus was laboring to justify Congress in the minds of my tribesmen I decided to run for a seat in that body myself. The primary law was then in full force, so that besides myself there were several other self-selected candidates for the one seat Montana had in the lower House. However, Miss Jeanette Rankin, the first Congresswoman, was nominated and elected.[10] By the time her political planet had faded into an ordinary star, Montana had been redistricted and would have two representatives in the House of Congress.

Montana is normally Republican in politics, and yet its First Congressional District is strongly Democratic. I tried a second time, winning the nomination easily. The World War was on. Many questionable devices for Democratic success were used. Our governor opened the campaign for the Democrats with a widely advertised meeting or two, and then proclaimed that no further political meetings be held in the state because an epidemic

[10] She served in the House of Representatives from 1917 to 1919, distinguishing herself by voting, alone, against declaring war on Germany. She had been a social worker in Washington, California, and Montana, and had been field secretary of the National American Woman Suffrage Association.

of flu was on its way westward. Besides this, large handbills and posters bearing the pictures of President Wilson and Montana's congressman were displayed everywhere. Over the glorified heads of the pair were the words "A vote for a Republican Congressman is a vote for the Hun." There was no opportunity to speak against such declarations as these, no chance to even meet the people during all the campaign.

Republican newspapers in Montana are as scarce as freckles on an Indian's nose. Most of those that called themselves Republican sheets listened carefully to dictation from the Hennessy Building[11] in Butte, so that there was nothing to do but wait for the end. My friend, Honorable John M. Evans, was declared elected, and today I am glad that he got the seat instead of me. Nevertheless, many people believed that I received more votes than he did, and that I was counted out in the efficient county of Silver Bow. Senator Lodge interested himself in the charges of fraud that were made at the time. Little was done about them, however; nothing at all by me.[12]

When it finally became evident that "He kept us out of war" only until after his election, Congress busied itself. On the evening of our declaration of war against Germany I made three speeches, one each in Glasgow, Malta, and Dodson. Next day I tendered my services to the War Department, but my age was against me. However, there was talk of raising several regiments of Indians for service on the Mexican border, where trouble was feared by many people. Here, I thought, was my opportunity. I

[11] The Hennessy Building in Butte housed the offices of the Anaconda Copper Mining Company.

[12] Lee Hawley, secretary of the Republican County Committee in Butte, wrote Linderman immediately after the election: "The democrats voted between the hours of five and six o'clock seventeen hundred ballots, all absent voter's [*sic*] ballots. The Clerk and Recorder of the County delivered between forty and sixty of these ballots to the larger precincts in Butte just before the polls closed, giving the election judges no opportunity to examine affidavits printed on the outside of the envelopes, and permitting no comparison of signatures with the 'Application for Ballots'. . . ." Linderman wrote to Senator Henry Cabot Lodge about this irregularity on December 28, 1918, and to Will Hays, the Republican National Committee chairman, on January 18, 1919. Hays replied, "I think we are going into this matter thoroughly." An investigation was made, but too late to be of any advantage to Linderman.

offered to raise a regiment of Indians in Montana. My offer was declined. Nevertheless, the Indians heard of my intention, and many old warriors offered to enlist with me. Besides the Indians, there were white men who wished to go with me to the border—doctors, dentists, and veterinarians, high in their professions, the best of fellows. I should have like to have served in such company. But the Mexican border gave us no trouble during the World War. Perhaps, after all, it is ourselves who stir up most of the squabbles there, when we are not too busily engaged elsewhere.

CHAPTER VII

Writer at Goose Bay

I NOW settled down to write the books that I had planned. *Indian Why Stories* was already published by Scribner [1915]. *On a Passing Frontier* [1920], a collection of sketches and short stories of early life in the Northwest, followed; and then *Bunch-Grass and Blue-Joint* [1921] a tiny book of verse, by the same publisher. I expected little from the last, but hoped the sketches would do something worth while. Reviewers were enthusiastic, and yet my royalties were jokes. Nevertheless, I believed that I could yet beat the game. I wrote *Indian Old-Man Stories* [1920], and finally a novel, *Lige Mounts; Free-Trapper* [1922], thinking that now a little success would come to us. But Scribner's continued to send me such modest royalty checks that I began to feel thin ice beneath my literary moccasins. What I ought to do about it was a question that kept my mind in a turmoil. Our three daughters were yet in college. The conditions brought on by the World War had reduced the purchasing power of money, so that my savings were dwindling rapidly. Besides this, neither the Frau nor I was in good health. "Let's get away from it all. Let's go south for the winter," I proposed, determined to "let the tail go with the hide."

The Frau and daughters had already spent several winters in southern California while I was in the life insurance business. They had enjoyed life there. On October 1, 1922, we headed our car for Santa Barbara,[1] leaving my old trapping partner Lincoln Lee to

[1] An interesting account of this visit when the Charley Russells lived next door is in Linderman's *Recollections of Charley Russell* (Norman: University of Oklahoma Press, 1963), pp. 72–85.

take care of our home at Goose Bay. I had written Link asking him to take charge of the place on October first. He had replied that he would do as I asked. But up to the evening of September 30 he had not made his appearance. We were worried. The car was all packed, ready for an early start next morning, and yet Link had not shown himself. Just at dusk I saw him coming afoot along the beach, a rifle over his shoulder and a small bundle in his hand.

"I thought you'd forgotten all about us," I said, shaking hands, since I hadn't seen him for years.

"Nope," he replied slowly, shifting his rifle to the other shoulder, "Tomorrow's the first, ain't it?"

Somehow, on the Flathead Reservation, I turned into a wrong road that led us into deep sand where I stripped the car's drive pinion. Disgusted with my clumsiness, I looked about for help. I needed a team of horses to pull the car out of the sand, and there was no ranch or house in sight. Taking the back trail, I finally reached a house that we had noticed an hour earlier. A half-breed stood by a wobbly gate leading into a small orchard where the trees were heavy with apples, pears, and plums. Green leaves rustled in the evening breeze. The rich odor of ripe fruit was pleasing, but I felt peevish. No sign had warned me of the deep sand ahead. I blamed somebody, anybody, everybody, for this carelessness, and felt a little "on the peck."

"Where can I get a team to pull my car out of the sand about three miles from here?" I asked the breed, without any other greeting.

He was true to type. "I donno, me. You ask dat man dare," he answered, pointing to an old fellow standing by a bubbling spring, with a tin cup in his hand.

I hurried to the man's presence. "Partner," I said, a little impatiently, "can you stake me to a team to pull my car out of the sand that this unmarked road led me into?"

He drained the tin cup, and then refilled it from an earthen jug of cider out of the cold, gurgling spring. "What's your name!" he asked, sipping again, as though time meant nothing, even to me, who was stuck in the sand.

"Linderman," I told him, thinking of the Frau and daughters grouped about the crippled car.

"Name ain't *Frank*, is it?", he asked between sips.

"Yes, it's Frank."

"They ain't *two* Franks, are they? Have some o' this here cider, Frank. Don't you know me? I'm Al Sloan."

A feeling of immense relief came to me instantly. Al Sloan had hauled me and my two companions into the Flathead country in 1885. I hadn't seen him since. "Al, you old coyote, get out a team and make their tails pop around corners. My wife and daughters are up yonder in the sand."

He spoke to the half-breed, who now came to life. "Harness Bess an' old Blue," he said. Then turning to me, "Have some cider, Frank, while I go over to the shack an' tell the woman to git you folks some supper. I'm damned glad to see you again; nearly forty years! Gosh a'mighty!"

We were there for five days, waiting for repairs to come to us from Spokane. The joke of it was that we were not yet half a day's drive from Goose Bay. But what an experience this proved to be for the girls. Mrs. Sloan was a good cook, and did whatever she could to make them comfortable. Like all Indian women, she was at first reticent. Little by little, however, she and I began to talk of the old days over our meals and after supper. One afternoon while I was putting the finishing touches to the car the girls came to me, chuckling merrily. "Daddy," they said, guarding their mirth, "Mrs. Sloan has been telling us stories of old times, and she said, 'Tst, tst, tst! Your papa he used to run with some bad, bad ones; tst, tst, tst.'"

"I did," I agreed. "I ran with some mighty bad ones. Those were tough days; men were tough as the times. And yet one need not become a horsethief because some of his friends steal horses."

We spent seven months in delightful Santa Barbara where we enjoyed ourselves, meeting people who have remained our friends to this day. My books brought us in touch with congenial folk, and spring came only too quickly. One evening at a dinner in Montecito our hostess introduced a lady who had arrived a little late. "Oh, Mr. Linderman," gushed the tardy one, "I'm so delighted to meet you. I just wondered what you looked like. You see, I'm a teacher of backward children, some of them *very* backward. And do you know you are the only poet I can get them to listen to?"

She stopped, her face reddening. When I laughed she fled. Six years later when we were again wintering in Santa Barbara this lady was once more presented.

"No, no," I objected, "this introduction is quite unnecessary. I already know Miss ——." Then I told the story of our first meeting, much to the lady's relief, I am sure.

"Yes," she added, when I had finished, "and if I hadn't seen a twinkle in his eyes I should have passed out at his feet."

Our journey home was not exciting. The spring in the Northwest was backward, the tamaracks scarcely showing their exquisite green when we finally reached Goose Bay. Link's hair and beard were long. He had not left the place since we went away in the fall, except to kill a deer for fresh meat.

During the spring and summer I wrote another book, which Charles Scribner's Sons rejected. None of my books had been given any advertising, except a notice or two in *Scribner's* magazine, so that when fall came my royalty check would not have furnished a feast for a fox. I had little money left now. My literary efforts had failed.[2] Somehow I must get into business or work for wages, a thing I have seldom done. Our daughters wished to strike out for themselves, but neither the Frau nor myself liked the idea. We had been a tribe so long that thoughts of separation tormented us. Fall came again, then winter. By now I had several manuscripts that had been rejected by Scribner's, and made up my mind to quit writing forever. But writing is a disease.

---

[2] Linderman tormented himself with the thought that he was a failure as a writer, refusing to admit, though knowing, that his writings were successful literarily although not selling widely. Friends tried to console him by telling him that the reading public for Indian materials was limited, but he would not accept that fact as the reason for the small sale of his books. He insisted that if he wrote well enough, people would read in numbers. He was unsuccessful as a writer, however, only in terms of financial return.

Late in December when the weather was extremely cold and the snow unusually deep at Goose Bay I heard that the Hotel Kalispell was for sale. It was the leading hostelry of the little city twenty-two miles from Goose Bay. I managed to buy it, borrowing on my life insurance and from banks, until I somehow had the $16,000 to pay for the hotel's furnishings. I had a partner in the beginning, but we did not get along together. Within three months I had the hotel to myself. When I look back at this venture and think of the opposition, the obstacles that were purposely put in my way, I wonder how I managed to win the game; and yet I did win it. I ran the hotel for three years, paid off my debt, and then sold the furnishings for $21,000.

When I bought the hotel neither my office help nor myself knew anything about the business, and yet we managed to make the reputation of the Hotel Kalispell travel far. Withal, the venture was a pleasurable experience. Besides, it gave me money so that I might write more books. The move from Goose Bay to Kalispell during the cold weather was difficult. One load of our household goods got stuck in the snow on Angel Hill. Without notice to me, this load, containing my collection of Indian relics and trappings, my Kentucky rifles, and other things precious to me, was left there exposed to the elements and possible thieves until I went myself, with another truck, and unloaded it. The house which we were obliged to take in town was badly in need of repairs, cold as Greenland, and unsuited to our requirements. I was very busy at the hotel from the first day in town, so that the Frau and our daughters spent ten disagreeable days getting settled. At first I tried sleeping at home. Two nights settled this scheme of things, however. The first night I was called at one o'clock, and the second at two in the morning. After this I remained in the hotel of nights until I finally sold out. "Please, Mr. Linderman, if you've got to be away nights, leave your hat on your desk here. It helps a lot," said my night clerk, who had found it necessary to call me.

Not long after taking over the hotel I began to receive letters asking me to run for the Republican nomination for United States senator. I answered most of these letters promptly, refusing to even

171

consider such a race. But finally petitions began to reach me, bearing this heading:

> To the Honorable Frank B. Linderman, Kalispell, Montana: We, The undersigned citizens and voters of the State of Montana, believing that in the United States Senate the interests of the Commonwealth can be best served by you, respectfully request that you offer yourself as a candidate for United States Senator on the Republican ticket, at the primary election to be held on August 26th, 1924.

These petitions, signed by many thousands, decided me to toss my hat into the ring. Mr. Wellington D. Rankin, my formidable opponent, was the state's Attorney General. He had a hard-working organization, besides being extensively advertised. I possessed neither advertising nor an organization, and yet I won the nomination at an expense of less than three hundred dollars, which included a short trip down the Yellowstone where I had been told Mr. Rankin was especially strong. I made no other excursion, remaining at my desk at the hotel most of the time until election day.

Now, however, I must make a real campaign, since I owed so much to my petitioners. My opponent was Senator Thomas J. Walsh, of Teapot Dome fame; and he had just set the Teapot boiling, so that sudden interest had settled upon him. I determined to make a clean fight, refusing financial aid that did not come through regular sources. These refusals to personally accept campaign funds contributed much to my defeat.[3] However, there were other causes, and more vital ones. I fumbled my own campaign, made a mess of it, as far as management was concerned, and yet I worked hard enough. Our bitter gubernatorial battle and the La Follette-Wheeler presidential ticket were serious obstacles to my success. Wheeler, being a Montanan, led many railroad employees and others belonging to the labor movement, to support La Follette and himself, so that when Senator Robert La Follette, a supposed Republican, telegraphed messages to Montana asking his friends

[3] Walsh had already served two terms as senator. Linderman lost by only 17,681 votes.

to vote for Senator Walsh I lost thousands of votes. Anyhow, I was beaten, and this time I felt my defeat for several weeks. Nevertheless, I am now heartily glad that I was defeated. I have since finished several manuscripts that I would rather leave behind me than a certificate of election to the United States Senate. The sting of defeat is long gone, and yet every humorous incident of my senatorial campaign remains with me, finding deeper appreciation each year.

At one of my meetings I discussed the tariff, as all good Republicans will. When I had concluded, a man rose in his place in the audience, and said, "Folks, yesterday when I was driving a band of sheep across the river, below here a piece, the leaders jackknifed at the bridge. The dogs couldn't do a damned thing with them, so I ran up ahead to find out the reason why the sheep wouldn't cross the bridge. And there was reason enough, God knows—Senator Walsh's picture was nailed to the bridge's timbers, on both sides. Vote for Linderman."

I shall always remember talking to the Blackfeet Indians. I had been told that Senator Walsh's interests were being fostered there, not only by local Democrats, but by the Roman Catholic missionary priests and nuns who worked among the Indians, and that on the reservation of the Piegans he was very strong. Nevertheless, I was unable to arrange a meeting on the reservation until the end of the campaign. The night was blustery, with half-frozen gumbo that skidded my car in every direction, when I reached the roundhouse on Two Medicine. In the firelight that glanced on dark-skinned faces and feathered finery, five hundred Indians were waiting for me. Curly-bear, the aged chief, who is now gone, spoke first. He said, "I have known Iron-tooth (my Piegan name) for more than forty years. He used to live as we lived. He killed his meat as we killed ours. He is our kind of man, and our friend. He is not afraid to take our hands in his hands, not afraid that our hands will soil his own. And he does not lie. I know Senator Walsh, too. He claims many things that are not rightfully his. He has told us that he did things when we knew it was another who did them, and not the Senator. He makes me remember a young man when I, too, was young. This young man was a poor hunter, and yet he always managed to have meat. And this is the way he got it. He used to follow the buffalo-runners. When he came to a dead buffalo on the plains he got down from his horse, pulled out the arrows that had killed the buffalo, and then stuck his own arrows into the holes, so that by his arrow mark all the people would believe *he* had killed the animal himself. Senator Walsh is much like that young man."

Before I spoke to these Indians in the roundhouse, partly in the sign language, Curly-bear insisted upon my passing the pipe to the five hundred, a most tedious ceremony. To smoke the offered pipe was equivalent to taking an oath that the smoker would vote for me, so that I performed the task at the chief's request. Out of the five hundred Indians in the roundhouse to whom I offered the pipe four men and five women refused to smoke with me. A speech made that night by a Cree, who had ridden a long way to help me, was beautiful. He opened a letter that I had written to his father years before, showing it to the company in support of his statement that his people had known me ever since he could remember. The seams or folds, in the letter paper had been sewed together with sinew, so that the sheets might hold intact. The very manner in which this Cree handled the old letter was eloquence of a kind that is understood best by red men.

This mention of the Cree's speech in the roundhouse of the Piegans has reminded me of the campaigning that Little-bear did in my behalf when I ran for a seat in the House of Representatives. The old fellow managed to secure a few of my campaign cards bearing my likeness. These he would industriously distribute in the towns he visited. But upon leaving, he always went back to every man to whom he had handed a card and demanded its return. Little-bear continued this peculiar campaigning for me for years after I had been beaten, his overworked campaign cards finally becoming quite disreputable. One day I received a letter from an old cowman friend. "Better call off Little-bear. He won't believe the fight's over until you tell him you're licked," it said.

Another amusing incident of my senatorial campaign: returning to the hotel election day, our youngest daughter, who had been managing the business during my absence, said, "Daddy, you must scold the porter. He's been drinking, I think; and he has missed several trains lately."

Two days later, when I knew that Senator Walsh had defeated me, I was working on the hotel books. The porter came softly and leaned against the desk. "Mistah Linderman, sah, could you advance me twenty-five dollahs on my *next* month's salary?" he asked sheepishly.

Now I had him. "Boy," I said, scowling my fiercest, "you've been drinking and missing trains. What have you been doing with your money?"

The negro was uneasy, toying with the handle of a mop. I pressed him. "Speak up! What did you do with your money?" I demanded, pointing my pen at him.

"Why, why, I ain't been heah but two months, sah; an' I done bet one month's salary on you, I shuah did figure you gwine beat dat Mistah Walsh, sah."

I made the check for twenty-five dollars, and forgot to scold him about missing trains.

In Helena, a few days later, I unexpectedly met Senator Walsh and shook hands with him, not once thinking of offering my congratulations. I am never formal, am always a jump or two behind propriety, and forgot this altogether. Nevertheless, the Senator (I believe) lost no time in getting my blunder into print. These things I remember as high spots in a losing fight; these, and another of far greater importance. A young Virginian, out of our overseas army, came to the hotel one day just before I commenced to campaign. I liked him instantly, so much that in talking with him I said, "If there is anything about this hotel that pleases you you may take it."

Returning once during my campaign, this young man walked with me to the train that was to carry me to another political engagement. On the way he said, "Mr. Linderman, you once told me to take anything around your hotel that I wanted. May I have your youngest daughter, Norma?"

175

I didn't hesitate. "If she wants you, I'm content," I told him. Now the Frau and I are grandparents, proud of two sturdy grandsons, James Beale and Richard Linderman Waller.

With the hotel disposed of and no senatorial toga in sight for me, the Frau and I paid a visit to Former Governor McKelvie of Nebraska, who with his lovely lady, was spending the summer in the Black Hills, South Dakota. I had met the Governor during my senatorial campaign. We had become fast friends, so that our visit to the McKelvie summer home in the Hills was a joy to us. The following fall, our daughters being now on their own, Wilda tutoring French, English, and Latin, Verne reporting for a local newspaper, and Norma happily married, the Frau and I went alone to Santa Barbara. I had continued my writing while managing the hotel, so that *Kootenai Why Stories* was just out. Besides this book, I had finished *Old-man Coyote* and *The Crows*, sending the manuscript to Scribner's from Santa Barbara. But Scribner's, for some reason of their own, wished to publish it in a cheap edition that would not go well with my other books, and I withdrew the manuscript, writing nothing else, except an article on Charley Russell, the cowboy artist, who had gone to the Shadow-hills in October. This was published in the *Outlook* in the month of April.[4] My time was not occupied now. I grew fidgety, wanting something to do with my hands. I wanted to tinker at something, anything, and finally thought of modeling clay, a thing I had never touched. Nevertheless, I made a bear that pleased me for a few days, even getting me out of bed at night to look at my creation, that kept growing worse and worse in my eyes. And yet modeling interested me more deeply than any other thing I had ever attempted. Finally, I fashioned a bust of an Indian that I liked well enough to want it cast in bronze; and I wished to do the casting myself. To learn something of this art I took a very short, and inadequate, course of bronze-casting at the School of Arts in Santa Barbara, where we cast a small model I had made. Returning to Goose Bay in the spring, I built a furnace out-of-doors, using a fifty-gallon oil tank

---

[4] Russell died in 1926. The article appeared in *Outlook*, CXLV (April 13, 1927), 466–488.

which I lined with firebrick. By the use of thirty-five feet of stove-pipe for draught, and burning coke, I cast my Indian bust, a genuine bronze, after the lost-wax method of Cellini. Besides this I made my own alloy. I am not now proud of the bust's modeling, but I am yet proud of having cast a genuine bronze piece in the tall timber, without the proper implements. Now whenever I find that I cannot write, I model, generally Indians and wolves. Sometimes I cast my models in plaster; but always, after a little time, I wish that I had not cast them. The work I thought so fine grows less and less attractive until I hide the casts or throw them away. But modeling is work for my hands, nevertheless.

We had not been back at Goose Bay very long when, to my surprise and deep gratification, the University of Montana offered me the honorary degree of Doctor of Letters, for my literary work and my research in the field of Indian customs, beliefs, and traditions. This was the first recognition ever given me in this field by home-folks, and I felt extremely proud of it, receiving the degree on the sixth of June, 1927.

This has reminded me of *The Frontier*, a magazine that Dr. H. G. Merriam, head of the English Department at the State University, began publishing in 1920, its contributions being at first mostly the work of his students.[5] Its excellence attracted quick attention, so much [so] that a few years later its founder told me that he intended enlarging the publication so that he might publish the writings of northwestern authors. I thought the scheme rather ambitious. Nevertheless, Dr. Merriam went ahead, and today *The Frontier* is a credit, not only to him and the University, but to all the Northwest. It ought to have wide support.

This was the summer [1927] that President Coolidge fished so consistently in the Black Hills. Governor McKelvie invited me to his summer home near Mystic, where, besides the President and Mrs. Coolidge, Charles Crary, of Illinois, and myself were the

[5] *Frontier* was a campus literary magazine at Montana State University from 1920 to 1927; in the autumn of 1927 it became "A Magazine of the Northwest," frankly regional in nature. From 1933 to 1939 it was "A Magazine of the West," having taken over the subscription list and name of *Midland* magazine and appearing as *Frontier and Midland*.

only guests over a weekend.[6] The way—one cannot call it a road—from Mystic to Sam McKelvie's place in the Hills is actually up the dry bed of a prehistoric creek littered with boulders as large as camp kettles; and most of the way is straight up. I shall always remember the morning that we went to get the Coolidges. A dead-ax wagon was the only available vehicle.[7] In truth, this is the only kind on earth that might be expected to stand the strain given it by Sam McKelvie's trail. The Coolidges were game, however, so that up the hill we went, tottering, teetering, and grinding over the boulders, followed by a horde of wild newspapermen and wilder camera operators who struggled along afoot. Some of these cameramen carried immense movie cameras that, with the stiff climb and the heat of the day, made the perspiration actually drip from their faces. But on they came, panting like a band of winded cayuses, to take every advantage of position, sometimes grinding their cameras within a few feet of our faces. Once, when the wagon was stopped to give the horses a rest, a fat man, groaning beneath his heavy load, climbed into the wagon and, pointing his camera's lens at Mrs. Coolidge and me, began to grind industriously.

"That man is irrepressible," declared the President; and this was the longest voluntary speech I heard him make, even when the trout refused to strike in Sam McKelvie's creek.

Mrs. Coolidge sat with me in the tottering wagon, holding a chow puppy in her lap. And what a gracious, lovely woman this first lady of the land proved herself to be! I shall always remember her, and feel proud of having ridden beside her up the steep hill from Mystic to Goveror McKelvie's summer home. She was even more than I had dared to anticipate. The President was just as I had imagined him to be,—"safe and sane" sure enough. Here's the real Cal for you.

Charles Crary: "Mr. President, how would you like to see Mr. Linderman and me pan some gold this morning?"

---

[6] Linderman and McKelvie became fast friends, as many letters in Linderman's Estate papers testify. McKelvie wanted Linderman to tell his western tales to President and Mrs. Coolidge. After the visit, Linderman sent them two of his books, which Mrs. Coolidge acknowledged.

[7] A dead-ax wagon is one without springs.

Mr. President: "I'm sure I cannot say until after I have seen you."

This Presidential visitation was a revelation to me. The silent, lonely Hills became suddenly peopled. Telegraph wires were hastily strung over the mountain by important-looking men in overalls, Secret Service officials watched the coming and going of everybody, and newspaper men waited for bits of news as anxiously as frogs wait for chance flies.[8] I had noticed that Mrs. Coolidge wore a long gold chain about her neck, and that attached to it there was a whistle. Knowing that every bush hid a Secret Service man or a newspaperman or a camera fiend, and remembering Mrs. Coolidge's whistle I thought of Sir Walter Scott's "Lady of the Lake." Surely the golden whistle might easily have "garrisoned the glen at once, with full five hundred men."

"Frank," said Mrs. McKelvie, "Grace and I are going across the creek to rock out some gold. We do not want an audience. Please don't permit anybody to cross the creek while we are operating the rocker. Can you manage them, do you think?" she asked, remembering the crowd's persistence.

Could I manage them! "If anybody gets across that creek they'll have to walk on me," I declared, taking my station with a determination that nobody should pass.

The placer miners had long ago left an old rocker just across the creek from the McKelvie place. I had seen it and had noticed that it had lately been used, probably by Mrs. McKelvie, who sometimes rocked out a few colors for the fun of it. Now, after the ladies had crossed the creek, I could not see them at their rocking, and yet I could hear them shoveling gravel into the rocker occasionally. I hoped that nobody else knew what they were doing. But the newspapermen and the camera operators discovered what was going on, so that within a few minutes a big fellow, the one who had climbed into the wagon, came up to me.

"Lemme across!" he snapped.

---

[8] W. J. Bulow, in E. C. Lathem's *Meet Calvin Coolidge* (Brattleboro, Vt.: Stephen Greene Press, 1960), pp. 122–123, states that "at the temporary office in Rapid City the President issued his famous statement that he 'did not choose to run.'"

"No," I said, "You are not wanted over there."

"Get out of my way! I *am* going over there."

"What'll you bet?" I asked, thoroughly enjoying the situation.

Another man came now, and yet another, and another, like wolves to a kill on the plains. I stood them off, however, until Colonel—— (I'm sorry that I've forgotten his name), the President's aide, arrived.

"Mr. Linderman, the President says he wishes that you would permit these men to cross the creek," he said with considerable suppressed amusement.

And over they went, with dark looks at me. The ladies, disturbed now, blamed me not a little, until I explained matters to them; even then I believe they were a little disgusted with their appointed guard. The place was a wreck when the visitation was past, the grass trampled flat, the bushes broken as though a band of wild horses had passed in stampede.

In the deep quiet that now crept back to the McKelvie cabins like a timid kitten, a fall of rain washed away the footprints of many a man who will not be likely to walk in the Black Hills again. About midnight, the telephone (a new thing in the cabin I occupied) began to ring. At last I answered it. It was I who was wanted by a representative of the *New York Herald-Tribune*. After expressing regret that he had not learned who I was during his visit to the McKelvie place, he asked for an interview over the phone.

"What has the President said about running again?" he asked.

"The President has said *nothing* about *anything*," I told him, trying to break away.

"May I say that you are going to run again for the United States Senate?" he asked, adding quickly, "I think I can promise you front-page position in every reputable New York City paper if you will run."

I thanked him for his gracious offer, at the same time telling him that I was afraid New York newspapers, great as they were, would prove to be too far from the political battlefield to do a senatorial candidate much good. Nevertheless, most of the New York papers had something to say about this interview, besides publishing many pictures taken at the McKelvie summer home during the President's visit there. But, as far as I was concerned, Montana's newspapers ignored both.

When Governor McKelvie's invitation reached me to be one of the house party at his summer home in the Black Hills, I was making ready to visit Chief Plenty-coups, of the Crows. For years I had tried to bring this about, so that I might write the story of the Chief's life; and now he had sent for me. To hobnob with the Chief of the Nation I should have to pass through the domain of the Chief of the Crows. I therefore decided to make one trip toward the east answer for both engagements. Under these circumstances I could not hamper myself with camp equipage, but trusted luck to furnish me with accommodations in the land of the Crows, where I stopped first. And, as I had hoped, luck was waiting for me there. Reverend John Frost, an old friend who is a half-blood Indian and proud of his breeding, said that I might sleep in his church on Arrow (Pryor) Creek. John himself lived many miles away, however, and I wondered where I was going to get my meals while I visited the Chief. "I've arranged all that for you," John told me. "The ladies in our mission house will feed you."

I had the little church all to myself. The ladies in the mission house were gracious, besides being splendid cooks. Each morning after breakfast they gave me a lunch to take with me to the Chief's camp, so that I need not make the long journey back to the mission house for the midday meal. Miss Wiggman and Miss Norton, who were stationed there, already had two visitors, ladies from eastern states, when I became their boarder, so that there were five of us at the dining table every evening. These ladies were interested in my work, each evening asking me to relate the particulars of my day with Plenty-coups. I shall never forget telling them the old Chief's medicine-dream, of how, in the most exciting situation, he had suddenly ceased speaking to me to turn aside and whisper, "Oh, Little-people, you who have been my good helpers during a long life, forgive me if I have done wrong in telling Sign-talker these things. I will see you soon and explain why I told them."

My own interest in the Chief's dream may have made my story-telling a little dramatic. Anyhow, the ladies were as deeply impressed as I had been. Silence fell at the table, and it was a weighty silence, the kind that one does not wish to break. At last the lady from Massachusetts said with deep feeling, "Isn't it a great pity that we are unable to give the Indian a better God?"

"I'm not certain that such a thing is possible," I replied. My words just hopped out. I meant no sacrilege, did not mean to offend, and perhaps should not have spoken as I did. But now there was no opportunity to explain. The ladies pitched into me and had their say. I did not try to interrupt them.

"Will you not admit that the Indian's religion is all superstition?" asked the lady from Massachusetts, when the first fierce flurry had subsided.

"No," I replied, "I will not."

"Did you not tell us that Plenty-coups turned aside, while telling his dream, and whispered to 'the Little-people?' " she demanded, leaning a little toward me in her anxiety to be understood.

"Yes," I said, "he did."

"Well! Wasn't that a perfect demonstration of superstition?"

"Yes," I admitted, "it was. And just before I inadvertently turned our conversation into this desperately roily channel didn't I hear you make a declaration that your health is much better since coming to Montana?" I asked, as innocently as I could.

"Yes," she answered, "and it is true!"

"I believe you," I assured her. "Montana is a healthful country. But when you made your declaration did I not see you lift the table-cloth and knock the tabletop with your knuckles?"

"Oh, you surely do not think I *believe* in such things." She blushed.

"No, no; of course not," I said. "But you are a little afraid to leave some of them out, just the same. However, I am not going to declare that knocking on wood is a part of your religion. It isn't; any more than whispering to the Little-people is a part of the religion of old Plenty-coups."

I went to the church, and to my bed, wondering ever so slightly if I had lost my lovely boarding place, for I somehow felt that neither Miss Wiggman nor Miss Norton had taken offense, that they had, in fact, understood me. Both had been among the Indians for some time and knew there were many beautiful beliefs in the religion of red men, that the plains Indian believes in one God. I was quite certain that these bosses of the cupboard would not turn me away in the morning. I went to sleep, hearing the exhaust of the tiny electric-lighting plant in the basement of the mission house, my mind's eye on the face of the old Chief whose medicine dream had led me into hot water.

In the morning everything, the weather, the breakfast, and the ladies were lovelier than ever. "We were awake half the night discussing what you said," they told me. "We decided at last that we had not perfectly understood you."

Good women! I made further explanation, and with an extra fine luncheon set out for the camp of Plenty-coups, going through Pryor, where already there were half a dozen saddle horses standing in front of the trader's store. I became so interested in the old Chief's story that I was sorry to leave him for the visit to the Black Hills. However, after my short visit there I returned to the Crow country, where I finished the life story of Plenty-coups, which was published in April, 1930, by the John Day Company, New York, under the title *American*. The book is dedicated to my grandson, James Beale Waller.

Old Indians have always impressed me. In their presence, especially when they are telling me of old customs, or speaking solemnly of their religious beliefs, I feel nearly as they do, I am quite certain. I have tried to break down that something which separates me from them by thinking as old Indians think, perhaps with only imagined success. And yet I believe that I understand many points in their philosophy of life that I cannot yet express in words. Perhaps I never shall learn; certainly not from the offspring of these warriors, who know next to nothing about their people's ancient ways. Now is too late to learn. The real Indians are gone. I am grateful for the privilege of having intimately known many of the old warriors themselves; may they find peace and plenty in the Shadow-hills.

The story of Plenty-coups proved to be a difficult piece of work for me. I wrote it twice from beginning to end before finally submitting it to Scribner's, or asking if they could use it in their magazine. They were not interested, or at least could not use the story as I suggested. Besides this, they rejected another book, *Beyond Law*, a sequel to *Lige Mounts; Free-Trapper*.

All this was disappointing. I wished to write more books, particularly biographical sketches, to save material that is being lost, if I could do the work and yet carry on. Men, friends of mine who had known life in the Northwest, were passing rapidly. This, and my failure to write successfully, plagued me not a little. I began to count the stories that had been lost to me, not the least being Jack Teal's. Jack's life fascinated me. He was a Texan. Honest, slow-spoken, and deliberate as a turtle, he had in turn been cowpuncher, outlaw, and deputy sheriff, attributing his several mankillings to bad luck. Of his outlaw days he spoke to me sparingly, "I was plumb drove to hit, Frank," he said, "an if you will come an' set whar I kin look at ye I'll shore tell ye all about hit, so's ye kin see fer yerse'f." Now Jack was gone, and I had failed to get his story.

The last time I saw Jack Teale he had lately killed a desperado, and wanted mightily to talk to me about it. "I've had a mess o' bad luck ag'in, Frank," he began, getting out the makings of a cigarette. "The sheriff done told me the feller was plumb bad; said fer me to take some he'p along. But I figured I could take keer o' jest one man myse'f. The snow was nigh eighteen inches deep. A cuttin' wind, whippin' out o' the no'th, was blowin' hit when I picked up a pony's trail that was partly covered up. I knowed hit was the feller's, shore enough; so I follered hit nigh fifteen mile to a cabin. I see whar the feller'd got down thar, an' walked to the cabin door; but I didn't see no hoss nowhar. I reckoned mebby there was a shack someplace whar the hoss was put up. Anyway, I wa'n't particular what become of the hoss; an' I didn't want fer to make no gunplay, so I gits down, an' raps on the door, like a white man ought ter, whar they might be women folks. Shore enough, a woman opens the door; an' right quick I says, 'Lady, is Mister—— in thar, please?'

"Before she kin say a yes or a no the feller hisse'f sticks his head over her shoulder. He didn't have on no coat nor vest, an' I see the strap of a shoulder holster across his breast when the woman moved to one side, like she knowed trouble hed come a-visitin'. Up goes the feller's hand, fer his gun.

" 'Quit!' I says, pokin' my hand down in my coonskin's pocket, so's to be ready, like. 'If ye make another move like that I'll shore as hell *kill* ye,' I says.

" 'You shore as hell will *hev* to,' he says, goin' fer his gun.

" An' I shore as *hell did.*"

At about this time Hermann Hagedorn and his delightful family came to Flathead Lake.[9] I had met Hermann several years before this when he was writing *Roosevelt in the Badlands*. He had called at Goose Bay to see me. Later, in Santa Barbara, we had the good fortune to know his family, who were with him there. His *Rough Riders* was being filmed in Hollywood. I shared his grief over the changes the movie-kind insisted upon making in his story, so that we were now close friends. I showed Hermann Hagedorn the manuscripts of both *Beyond Law*, the sequel to *Lige Mounts*, and the life story of Plenty-coups, the Crow chief. *Lige Mounts* has no greater admirer than Hermann Hagedorn. He liked both of these new manuscripts immensely, as did all the Hagedorns.

"You must go to New York, Frank," declared Hermann. "You must meet and know your publishers."

This became the favorite topic of conversation now, my going to New York. The Hagedorns all and my own family talked of little else. To add to their arguments now came Dr. Ernest Horn, of the University of Iowa, and his family, who joined the others in urging me to visit New York City with my manuscripts.[10]

I had met Doctor Horn the year before. The Montana State Teachers' Association had invited me to speak at Great Falls, where

[9] This was in the summer of 1928. There are many letters to Linderman from Hagedorn in the Estate papers.

[10] Linderman met Dr. Ernest Horn, of the University of Iowa, after one of his lectures. Horn visited at Goose Bay in the summer of 1928. He believed that Linderman's books would have a large sale if presented to schools, and helped promote that sale.

I met Doctor Horn, who delivered an address there. Hearing me talk, he invited me to speak at the University of Iowa, later on arranging a date for me in Davenport, so that the trip might pay me a little above expenses. The Horns had been good friends, so that I listened when the Doctor advised me to send the manuscript of *American* to the World Book Company, at Yonkers, New York, who publish only school books.

Finally, the Hagedorns and the Horns returned to their homes in the East; then Wilda, our eldest daughter, accepted a position to teach in the Santa Barbara Girls' School. Now the Frau and I were alone at Goose Bay. I did not like to think of having her here all winter with no other woman to talk to, and yet I dared not propose a trip south when my financial affairs were so unpromising. At last, after weeks, the World Book Company sent me a publishing contract for *American*, the life story of the Crow chief. I signed it wondering what measure of success awaited the tale in school-book form.

During the winter both Hermann Hagedorn and Dr. Horn wrote several letters reminding me that I ought to go to New York. The months dragged, because I had lost interest in writing. The time had again come when I must get into some other business, one that would at least make a living for the Frau and me. To go to New York would cost more money than I could well afford. Besides, I did not wish to go there. I realized that I was in a rut and was growing stale, and yet I dreaded the necessary struggle to get out of it.

Wilda returned to Goose Bay to spend her vacation, bringing new life to the place. Then, while the summer was yet young, Mr. and Mrs. William F. Scott, of New York, came to visit us. Mr. Scott was an old friend of mine, a born Montanan. Since establishing himself in New York he had many times written that I ought to visit that city and bring my manuscripts. Now, at Goose Bay, both Mr. and Mrs. Scott insisted that this be done. "Come and visit us," they urged; and at last I promised to go east as soon as I could conveniently get away, hoping that something might yet save me from the ordeal of having to peddle my manuscripts.

September was nearly gone when Wilda returned to Santa Barbara to resume her teaching there; and the Frau and Verne went with her, leaving me to go to New York a little later, as we had planned.

No other section of our country is so beautiful as Montana in the fall of the year. Our first light frost is a worker of miracles. Every hillside is quickly transformed into a huge bouquet of blazing colors beneath the bluest of skies; and there is always a silence in the forests that makes one feel reverential toward the mysterious change that is being wrought. Flathead Lake, blue as the oceans, is always a joy; but in the fall it takes even a firmer hold of me. With everybody gone from Goose Bay I wished more than ever to stay here. The woodbine on our porch was a solid mass of crimson, with here and there a single scarlet leaf to complement the deeper shade. Every living thing about the place—pine squirrels and chipmunks and all—were busy making their caches of winter supplies, a work that I have always enjoyed myself.

I began to wish that I had not sent the Plenty-coups manuscript to the World Book Company. I believed now that it ought first to have been published by a general publisher. This belief grew so steadily that I finally wrote to Mr. Hodgson, the president of the company, setting forth my reasons why the manuscript ought first to go to a general publisher. I asked him to cancel my contract. His reply was so fine, showing so much good-fellowship, that I felt ashamed of my request. "Go ahead," I telegraphed; "I'll let the tail go with the hide."

The day I sent my telegram that forever ended my hope of getting back my manuscript I received letters from two New York publishers asking for the Plenty-coups story. Hermann Hagedorn, despairing of my ever coming to New York, had interested publishers in the Chief's tale, so that now they were asking for it. But the manuscript was tied up. There seemed to be no way that I might again get hold of it. Nevertheless I telegraphed Mr. Hodgson to hold my manuscript without publication until I arrived in New York on October 1. He answered, promising to do this, and I began getting ready for the trip.

I had bruised my right index finger, as usual giving it no attention. My whole hand was quite sore when on September 25, [1929], my sixtieth birthday, I packed my bags for the journey. But I got no farther than Kalispell. Our daughter, Mrs. Waller, noticing my wounded finger, that by now was badly swollen, insisted that I go to a physician. I followed her advice, and then kept to my bed for two weeks with a bad case of infection.

On the fifteenth of October I again set out, with my hand looking as though it had been through a threshing machine. For two whole days on the train I held my hand in hot water, so that by the time I reached Washington, where I visited with my old friend Gilman Bullard and his wife, I could button my own collars.

Washington was very beautiful now. In its parks the oaks and bushes flamed with high color, and yet the air was balmy and quite bracing. We visited the Smithsonian Institution, the Corcoran Art Gallery, saw the sights, all, as one does on such occasions, and I had an enjoyable time in the nation's capital. And how I did dislike the idea of leaving Washington for New York City! I should not get along with the editors there, a bunch of self-constituted authorities on western life. But I'd go on now, and have it over with, once for all time, and then forever quit writing my time away. This state of mind, instead of abating, grew with every day spent with my friends in Washington until I could wait no longer. I'd have it over with, and then join the Frau in Santa Barbara in jig time.

The magnificent Pennsylvania Station gave me two things when I went there to board my train for New York—a thrill and a lesson that kept me thinking all the way to my destination. It was inscribed over the building's main entrance and read: "He that would bring home the wealth of the Indies must carry the wealth of the Indies with him." So it is in traveling: a man must carry knowledge with him, if he would bring home knowledge.

Reading this inscription over and over, I was conscious of a change in my attitude toward my destination. I took myself in my lap and talked to me: "This going to New York City is not a habit with you," I said. "It's an adventure, Don't hobble yourself with prejudice on a new range. And what have you got in your baggage

188

to exchange for the wealth of the Indies, anyhow?" Altogether, I had quite an understanding with myself on the train, so that when it finally pulled into the Grand Central Station in New York City I'd willingly have bought a dinner for a book publisher.

Bill Scott was to meet me, but he was not at the station, and there was no use looking for him that night. I went to the Hotel Pennsylvania, and to bed. Next morning my telephone called me early. Within an hour I was in the Scott home bag and baggage, expecting to remain there ten days at most.

The first thing I did was to go to Yonkers to see Mr. Caspar Hodgson of the World Book Company. I dreaded this, because I well knew that my business with him was not according to the rules of the game; besides, Caspar Hodgson was a stranger to me. The lights were already on in the company's offices when I reached Yonkers. Luckily for me, Mr. and Mrs. Elmer Green were still there. I had had some correspondence with the Greens, so that they knew who I was when I told them my errand. Mr. Green led me to Mr. Hodgson, and after an introduction left me with the man I had come to see. I waded in; "Mr. Hodgson," I said, "my book, *American*, will not make you any money as a school book; and therefore will do nothing for me. Will you not permit me to find a general publisher for the manuscript?"

He looked straight at me a moment and then smiled. No doubt my impertinence amused him. "Linderman," he said slowly, "anybody who had read that story of yours, and your letters dealing with it is a friend of yours. He'd *have* to be. You may disregard our contract. You'll have no trouble finding a general publisher for your manuscript, and when you find one that suits you I want you to make it known to him that I wish to publish this story as a school book after its general publication. And say," he added, "tell your publisher, when you find him, that I will pay one-half the cost of making the plates, with the understanding that I may use them. Now let's go over to my house. It's just across the yard here. I want you to meet my wife and daughter. The rest of the family are away from home just now."

"And this is hard-boiled New York," I thought, following this

189

man, whom I quickly learned to like immensely, across the beautiful grounds to his palatial home, where afterward, he gave two dinners in my honor. I spent many a pleasant hour with Mr. Caspar Hodgson, and number him among my warmest friends. And Mr. and Mrs. Elmer Green! The world would be better if there were more people like them. I had my manuscript again. Now, what should I do with it? Whom ought I to see? Arriving at the Scott home on East 87th Street, I learned that Hermann Hagedorn had called, that he had arranged a luncheon for me at the Century Club the next day at twelve-thirty.

My room at the Scott's was excellent. Its tall French windows opened upon the street. By leaning out, I could catch glimpses of the lights on shipping passing up and down East River where tugs and steamships continually whistled signals I had learned when a small boy. However, the noises outside, and finally the peculiar odor of fog that had settled over the city, kept me awake. As the fog thickened the whistles on tugs and steamships grew louder and more frequent, their tones ranging from high falsettos to deep, shivering blasts that seemed to make the whole island of Manhattan tremble. Sleep would not come, even when finally the fog lifted and the ceiling showed reflections of the dawn. I watched the gray light grow, wishing that it were time to get up; and then suddenly I heard familiar sounds. Horses' hoofs! And horse bells! In New York! The bells sounded as though a band of horses might be going up 87th on a fast trot. With a thrill of pleasure I hopped out of bed and ran to the window. Just beneath me, on my side of the street, an ice wagon, drawn by *one* fat horse, was jogging merrily by, the animal's shod hoofs clattering on the pavement; and across the street, close to the curb, I saw a flat-footed Hebrew pushing a two-wheeled cart bearing four horse bells strung on a jiggling wire, so that the bells jingled exactly as though they were on the necks of trotting horses. Chagrined, I glanced at the glass door that opened into the hall to see if anybody was there to laugh at my mistake; but nobody was yet stirring. I got back into bed to wait. Long before anybody in the Scott home was up, the city was wide awake and busy. Later on I learned that it never sleeps.

Writer at Goose Bay

I found Hermann Hagedorn waiting for me at the Century Club, where he had assembled an interesting company of men to meet me—all of them publishers or editors, excepting Mr. Arthur Guiterman, the poet, whom I especially liked. The luncheon, with the visiting that followed, held on until after two o'clock, when one by one most of these busy men left the club. Mr. Pringle and Mr. Guiterman remained to talk longer with Hermann Hagedorn and me. Finally, Richard J. Walsh, the one man who had been unable to accept Mr. Hagedorn's invitation, joined us. I liked Dick Walsh on sight. The afternoon was nearly gone when we five—Hagedorn, Guiterman, Pringle, Walsh and myself—finally separated. I knew now what to do with my manuscript. I would give it to Dick Walsh, of the John Day Publishing Company.

I have often known the feeling of loneliness, and yet I have never been lonesome. Outside, in the jammed streets, I suddenly felt myself alone. The feeling let me down considerably. I knew that it was neither the noise nor the traffic that affected me. My eyes are always to be trusted, and I'm quick on my feet as a cat, so that traffic has no terrors for me, nor did the city's roar disconcert me greatly. I wondered why, among so many humans, I felt so completely alone. And I felt timid besides. Even a newsboy might have bluffed me into Hudson River. I could not understand this.

Down in a subway station that was choked with determined humanity I found myself shunted to one side, like a cottonwood chip in an eddy of a swift-running stream. A train roared into the station, packed with passengers. "No chance here," I thought, and then wonderingly watched a hundred men and women get off the train, and double their number get on it, to be whirled away underground. A second, and then a third train stopped, each disgorging a battalion and taking on a brigade; and yet the station was as full as before. Not once did I see a man or woman greet or even recognize another. The fourth train was a sight, worse than the others. Its doors opened petulantly, spat out the equivalent of a village's population—and this time, in the rush that followed, I was first to pass through the nearest door, squeezed flat against a woman holding a baby. The guard shoved and actually held a tall negro against

191

us both, so that the train's door might close; and away we went.
I began to feel my spirits rise a little. When the train reached 86th
Street I got off, pushing my way without once stopping, until I was
on the sidewalk in the open air. "Paddle your own dugout or sink,
is this town's motto," I thought, turning to walk to the Scott home.
This was the same challenge the wilderness had presented to me so
long before, and the feeling of loneliness had, at first, been the same
—only the air had been better. I had managed to make my way in
the wilderness; I could make it here. After this, New York City and
I became fast friends. Instead of staying in the city ten days, I remained nearly seven months, and had the time of my life.

The Scott home was a jolly one. The butcher, the baker, and
candlestick-maker vied with each other for the privilege of doing
it a special favor. Much as I liked to be there, I began to have so
many engagements that I was absent most of the time. Instead of
abating, my opportunites to attend dinners, week-end house parties,
and luncheons increased until I began to get my dates badly mixed.
This continued during all my stay in New York. At last I began to
hide out a little. I felt obliged to do this, since I was unable to keep
up and be forever on the go day and night.

Within a week the John Day Company had accepted the Plenty-
coups manuscript, and I had signed a contract for its publication
under the title *American*, not forgetting Mr. Hodgson, with whom
I quickly signed a contract for the story's publication as a school
book. Dick Walsh was enthusiastic, declaring the old Chief's story
to be the most important manuscript the John Day had ever published. He was anxious to have the book illustrated by a first-class
artist. "I've got a man in mind. Unless you object, I'll call him up,"
he said.

"Go ahead," I agreed.

"He's a busy man," he continued, before calling a number.

Then, while we waited, he told me that he had already let the artist read a small portion of my manuscript. "He may not be able to
illustrate it," he added. "He's mighty busy."

Now I was introduced to Herbert M. Stoops, a wiry man who
sized me up as a cowman would a beef, and then turned to Mr.

Walsh; "I'll illustrate this book. I'll be glad to," he said earnestly.

"Good!" Dick Walsh was evidently pleased. "We'll pay you five hundred dollars for four full-page illustrations."

"The money matters not at all in this case. I *want* to illustrate this book. I'd do it for nothing rather than not do it at all."

I felt a thrill. "And this is hard-boiled New York," I thought again.

Herb Stoops and I left the publishing house together. At the building's entrance, where we stopped to talk a little, the artist asked, "Can you afford to stay in New York until your book is out? If you cannot, I'll let you have what money you need."

Remember that this man was a stranger, and that this was New York City. "I can afford it," I smiled, with a lump in my throat.

This, just as I have told it, was my introduction to Herbert M. Stoops, the man who so beautifully illustrated my book, *American*. How much I wished to call on him the next day; but I realized that he was too busy. I did not go near him for many days, wondering when chance might bring us together again. Finally he called me. I believe that by this time he knew the old Chief's story by heart. I found him to be the best literary critic I have ever known, and haunted his studio to talk to him, even dodging dates to be with him and his wonderful wife. I wrote in his studio, and modeled there, besides spending several weekends at his summer home on Masons Island, near Mystic, Connecticut. At last, when he had finished his illustrations, I found that instead of *four*, as ordered, he had made *forty-two*. "What will they say at the publishing house?" I wondered.

When finally the illustrations for *American* were ranged along the walls in the John Day offices they created a sensation. "Blossoms of the text," Hermann Hagedorn called them. They are, indeed; they are more than this. They give the old Chief's story essential background that no words of mine could depict. And when the John Day Publishing Company offered to pay for the illustrations—forty-two of them, instead of four—Herbert Stoops said, "I wish to donate whatever you owe me toward advertising

193

this book." Then, while yet we were speechless with surprise, he amended this; "Wait," he said, "give me a check for five hundred dollars. I'll do my *own* advertising."

When the book was out Herbert Stoops ran the following full-page advertisement in the *Saturday Review of Literature*, and in two other publications, paying the bills himself:

I am paying for this advertisement myself because HERE IS THE FIRST EPIC OF THE NATIVE AMERICAN. Not because I illustrated Frank Linderman's "AMERICAN" but only because I want this voice of a vanishing American to be heard in every school, in every library, in every home, wherever books are read, I contribute this advertisement.

I was raised in Idaho. As a boy there I learned the look and feel of Indian country. I saw many Indians and knew a few. I saw also some of the last chapters of the shameful history the white man has written in his dealings with that unspoiled race and their transformation almost overnight into what Frank Linderman calls "Montgomery-Ward Indians."

Time made me an illustrator and led me to New York. One day last autumn, a publisher who knew my origin called up and asked, "Do you want to illustrate an Indian book?" I was interested but skeptical. I had read too many Indian books that were spurious—synthetic.

Then I read the manuscript of "AMERICAN." Under the influence of its rhythm, as insistent as the beat of an Indian drum, I knew that I would illustrate it. It had stirred me more deeply than any book I had found in ten years. I went through it six times. The making of these pictures became an exercise in humility.

This is perhaps the one period of all time in which such a book as "AMERICAN" could be written and widely read.

We have only now shaken off the spell of the dime novelist and of the land grabber whose vicious slogan was "the only good Indian is a dead Indian."

And a few years hence there will be no man left of those few who knew the Indian as he really was.

In 1885, Frank Linderman went out to Montana to become cowboy, trapper and hunter. For more than forty years he has been a friend of the Indian tribes in that territory.

Linderman has got under the skin of the Indian. His is the first voice—I fear that it may be the last voice—that will ever be heard to speak with conviction about that whole civilization that is nearly gone, now.

Linderman has published several good books before "AMERICAN." But this is an epic. It is not only his book; it is also the book of Plenty-Coups, Chief of the Crow Nation, a chief great in war and in peace. Plenty-Coups is now eighty-three years old. Out in Montana they say that he is clinging to life only that he may see this book—hold it in his hands, for he cannot read it—before he goes where he may "live again as men were intended to live."

For many weeks Linderman went day after day to see Plenty-Coups and draw out of him the story of his life. Mostly they spoke through interpreters; verified by sign language.

And when the tale was all told, Plenty-Coups said to him: "I am glad I have told you these things, Sign-Talker. You have felt my heart, and I have felt yours. I know you will tell only what I have said, that your writing will be straight like your tongue, and I sign your paper with my thumb so that your people and mine will know I told you the things you have written down."

> H. M. STOOPS
>
> *New York, March 30, 1930*

As soon as the John Day Company accepted *American*, I offered them *Old-man Coyote and the Crows*, and *Beyond Law*, the sequel to *Lige Mounts; Free-Trapper*. They accepted both manuscripts. *Lige Mounts*, under Scribner's management had done nothing. I determined to buy the plates and rights from that publishing house and turn them over to the John Day Company, if they would accept them. They did not hesitate, publishing the story under the title, *Morning Light*.

I had now placed every manuscript I had brought to New York and had called upon only one publishing house. *American*, besides being published by the John Day Company and the World Book Company of Yonkers, as a school book, is also out in England, published by Faber and Faber, of London, so that from even a business standpoint my visit to New York City was successful.

195

Socially, it proved a little too much for me, but someday I shall go there again.[11]

I know that many people may smile at my credulity, and yet if I were asked what most attracted me in New York City I should answer, "Its kindness!"

One has only to look about him to see this everywhere in New York. The fat horses and pampered dogs, the latter possessing greater street privileges than Jimmy Walker, attest that New York is kindly. Let a nose bag fall off a feeding horse by the curb and a dozen men will rush to replace it. They may replace it upside down, but they will do the office out of kindness. I have seen horses drawing milk wagons stand for half an hour crosswise of busy sidewalks while their drivers were flirting with housemaids. Hundreds of men and women willingly walk around these sidewalk-obstructing horses without protest, some even pausing to caress the obstructors as though they were personal pets. Horses in New York City? Yes, indeed; there are more horses in use in New York today than there are in all the state of Montana.

If asked "Do you like New Yorkers?" I should say, "Yes, but just what is a New Yorker?" If one were to ask each of the first hundred men he met in New York City where he was born, every state in the Union might be named, besides a foreign country or two. I like New York. It is a city of superlatives. The best brains in civilization went there for company or a market. The best and worst of everything is there.

In its clanging streets one sees even the primitive struggling for expression. The makings of plainsmen and mountaineers are there, if only opportunity could use them. Small boys kindle fires in the gutters to huddle about them, pretending that they are in deep wilderness. Looking down East 87th Street of an evening, one may see a dozen of these fires, kept burning with broken boxes and old newspapers. Grouped about each are small boys who talk mysteriously of "the West" as though it were yet a country filled with grave dangers, and was just around the corner. I have slipped up in the shadows and heard them talk. It was good for me. It made me

[11] However, Linderman did not visit New York again.

know that, East and West, real boys are much alike, that the old spirit of the pioneer is not dead by a long shot. Nevertheless, I could not help feeling sorry for these little campfire-builders in New York City. And yet I do hope that they will dream on. Anticipation is often finer than realization, anyhow.

APPENDIX A

The Life and Work of Frank B. Linderman[1]

I

THE Linderman family in the United States was of German origin. The first ancestors came to America in the early eighteenth century and settled in New York and Pennsylvania. Frank Linderman's grandfather was a farmer in New York State, and his father, James Bird Linderman, a merchant there and, later, in Ohio and Chicago. His mother, Mary Ann Brannan Linderman, was of Irish stock. In about 1905 he brought his parents to Sheridan, Montana, and turned over to his father the furniture business he had purchased there. His mother, a spirited woman, organized amateur theatrical performances in Sheridan in which Frank, who had a flair for acting, played. He had one brother, Percy, nicknamed Pip, who became a successful businessman, buying jewelry for a Chicago firm. Percy died at the age of forty-five. Born in Cleveland on September 25, 1869, Frank attended schools in Lorain and Elyria, Ohio, and a business school in Oberlin (1884–1885), as well as public school in Chicago. At the age of sixteen he headed west to Montana and lived there the rest of his life.

Frank was not a large man—five feet eight and one-half inches tall, slender, weighing around 155 pounds, with brown hair that

[1] This account is based on information supplied me by Linderman's three daughters, on papers and letters in the Linderman Estate, on my article "Sign-Talker with Straight Tongue" in *Montana*, XII (Summer 1962), and on my friendship of eighteen years and my reading of his writings. For a very few dates I have had to rely on the memory of the Linderman daughters and myself.

was almost black, blue eyes, and a face, in the years I knew him, grooved by deep lines which his family called laugh lines. Carl Link, an artist who made a portrait of him, found these deep lines made drawing or painting his face difficult, for the slightest movement changed them and, therefore, his expression. His movements were quick and his manner direct—brusque though not unfriendly; the dominant first impression on meeting him was of a person who was frank, honest, vigorous. He had a sense of humor which showed itself in words and tone rather than in facial expression. An idealist, he once wrote a friend, "I am old-fashioned, and I am glad of it." He held to conservative ideas about women, politics, art, and literature; and thought fear "man's worst enemy."

Companionship with Linderman was refreshing. He loved to tell stories, and he told them masterfully. His publisher thought he had never heard a better storyteller. In his later years—the last eighteen of his life, when I knew him—he talked a good deal about his writings (although no doubt he talked more about them with me, an editor and professor of literature, than with other people), but seldom, unless urged, about his early experiences. Responding to openness of spirit, he disliked conscious sophistication. He attracted many friends, and it is strange that they do not figure more largely in his recollections.

Frank liked public appearances, though he may have seemed not to. For a number of years he told stories at an annual meeting of journalism students at the University of Montana; and he lectured at writers' conferences there as well as at other universities. In January, 1929, he wrote to Scribner's Sons: "Lately I have had fourteen invitations to lecture to schools and universities, all his [Dr. Ernest Horn's] doing, of course." He also told stories to many groups of school children in several states. Generous of his time and energy, especially when he could forward knowledge of the Plains Indian, he contributed to *Frontier* (later *Frontier and Midland*), without compensation, thirteen articles about life in Montana in the 1880's, and in many ways helped establish the success of the magazine. Frank became a Mason in Sheridan in

September, 1899, and received the Scottish Rite in the Helena consistory in March, 1911. During the rest of his life he was active in Masonry, and held a number of offices.

Frank's health had been rugged up to the time of the forest fire in 1919, when he exhausted himself trying to save his home at Goose Bay. After that, it was not so dependable as it had been. His letters to the family when he was in New York in 1929 and 1930 constantly mention his tiredness: "I get tired—the jam, the noise, the hurry take toll of me.... I feel as though I were a deer in a thorn thicket and needed rest." When extended time on a large hook-up of radio stations in New York City was arranged for him, he was unable to take advantage of it. After 1930 his health began to fail, although he would not report illness or even admit to feeling unwell. In 1937 he collapsed while speaking before a Masonic meeting in Helena and was hospitalized. In November of that year he wrote to Judge Lew Calloway in Helena: "This is the fourth time the medicine men have told me I was through, I fooled them three times and I may make it stick this time." He did not, however; in January, 1938, he went to Santa Barbara, where he died on May 12.

Two Montana schools—one in Kalispell and one in Polson—and a World War II liberty ship have been named for Frank Linderman. In 1927 the University of Montana awarded him the honorary degree of Doctor of Laws in recognition of his literary achievements.

II

From early boyhood Frank showed the interests which endured throughout his life. Although he submitted to wearing velvet suits with lace collars on Sundays and to being sent to dancing school, his real pleasure was in tramping off by himself into the Ohio woods to hunt squirrels with a sawed-off musket. He trapped animals and birds, and once, at least, tried his hand at taxidermy, ruining his freshly papered bedroom walls by mounting stuffed birds on them. His mother told of his filling the cistern with toads, water snakes, and fish. His pets died, and the cistern had to be drained. Frank himself recounted how he once took a long, black water snake into the kitchen and terrified the maid, who clambered up a door and clung there. Later in life he loved birds and animals in their free state; his aversion to killing grew over the years.

The Linderman family moved to Chicago in 1883, when Frank was nearly fourteen years old, and there, perhaps for only one year, he continued his schooling. He joined the Illinois National Guard, lying about his age to get in. His parents must not have objected, however, since they could easily have had him dismissed by informing the militia's officer of his correct age.

Frank's ambition had been to attend the Naval Academy at Annapolis, for he loved water as much as he loved the wilderness; but when he was quite young he lost the sight in one eye in an accident. Since going to the academy was no longer possible, he turned instead to the challenge of the western frontier. As he says in his recollections, he studied a map in search of the least civilized area in the United States, finally deciding on the Flathead country of Montana Territory. When his parents heard of his intentions, they seem again not to have raised serious objections, for his father accompanied Frank and his companion on the train for an hour out of Chicago.

Unfortunately, no letters between him and his parents exist from his days as a trapper. It is a safe assumption that they expected his return before many weeks passed; if so, they had to resign themselves to his absence. One wishes that Frank had told in more detail how he got along during those first weeks or months—how he developed the qualities of courage, self-reliance, and endurance necessary for survival in the wilderness; how he picked up sign language and learned the Indian's ways; what he did; and how he felt.

As a trapper from 1885 to 1891, he was happy, with "no more ambition than . . . an Indian." He probably would have remained an outdoorsman longer, had he not, as he states in his recollections, met Minnie Jane Johns, from New Richmond, Michigan, in

1891 in Demersville, where she was visiting her brother. He loved her at once, but he also loved his life as a trapper. He tried more than once to settle down, but each time he succumbed to the appeal of the streams and mountains. Finally, however, love for her conquered, and in 1893 they were married in Missoula. With his new responsibilities, Frank accepted any kind of employment he could find, happy in his family relationships, and satisfied with his work, but only in the way and to the degree that a conscientious man takes pleasure in doing his job well.

In the early years after his marriage—from 1893 to 1897—he worked in Butte, principally as an assayer, and there two of their daughters, Wilda and Verne, were born. But Frank was restless; he was not finding what he wished to do in life. Mrs. Linderman, a courageous and independent woman in her own right, remained, as always, his source of strength and spiritual renewal.

In 1897 they moved to Brandon, where their third daughter, Norma, was born. For several years Frank picked up only a scanty living for the family. Three or four years later he moved them to nearby Sheridan and ventured into newspaper publishing and furniture selling, with an assay office providing the principal source of support.

After serving in the state legislature as a representative from Madison County in the 1903 and 1905 sessions, Frank made another move, this time to Helena. For two years—from 1905 to 1907—he was Montana's Assistant Secretary of State; and then he became a very successful insurance agent for the Guardian Insurance Company of America, with the whole state as his territory. The family remained in Helena until 1917; by that time Frank had saved up enough money to build a house, ensure his daughters a good education, and embark on a career as a writer—a dream he had cherished for years.

As early as 1908 he had written "Frau" (his fond name for his wife): "I'll be on my way to where I used to listen to the ouzel and spread my blanket . . . . When I get among the birches I'm going to let a whoop out of my system that's been bewildered for years." In January, 1917, when he wrote her about acquiring Goose Bay on Flathead Lake, she replied: "Good news that you are sure of Goose Bay. . . . I am so glad you are going to have the place on the lake to live that you have always wanted." And later the same year: "We ought to have lots of pleasure planning and building our new home. After all, that is what life consists of, improving one's surroundings and having a personality that brings the right kind of friends. . . . I shall get pleasure through seeing you daily again [his insurance business had required him to travel all over the state] and listening to the people who will seek you for yourself in your new home." Although at first she had reservations about the welfare and happiness there of their three daughters— and Frank himself later wondered whether the move to Goose Bay had been entirely good for the family—they all loved the lakeside home.

Goose Bay was a lovely spot; Miss Verne Linderman has described it: ". . . a square bay on Flathead Lake. A wooded slope came down like sheltering arms from the hills behind the house. There was not a neighbor on either side; only virgin timber back of us, and, before us, the lake, rimmed on the far shore by the blue mountains, ten or twelve miles away." The house, built of tamarack logs according to the Lindermans' own plans, was on the center of the bay, a wide veranda running the length of its front, with eight or ten steps leading toward the beach. On the beach the family kept a rowboat equipped with a motor for cruising on the lake—cautiously, for storms blew up quickly on the water—and Frank built a sailboat in which he often caught winds to Somers, at the head of the Lake, to meet guests, friends "of the right kind"—Charley Russell, at least once a year; Dr. Horn; Hermann Hagedorn; and scores of others.

In the large living room of the house hung two old rifles over the fireplace, and on either side were crowded bookshelves. Down a hallway, where there was also a fine gun collection, Frank established his study, lined with Indian objects. Here he finished twelve of his thirteen books, as well as many other writings. Each morning Frank rose early and, following his preference, cooked breakfast for himself and his family. Then came writing. When he completed a story, he went eagerly into the living room and read it to any members of the family present. Later, when he took up sculpturing, he installed a workshop and a kiln in the basement. Jean P. Smith wrote in a *Frontier* article on Linderman: "A visit in the Linderman home on Goose Bay . . . is like stepping back into frontier days. Each bronze figure he has cast, each trophy, each picture breathes the beauty, the humor, the friendships, the hazards of an earlier life."[2]

III

Frank Linderman devoted a large share of his life to the Indians, both in learning and writing about their lore and in trying to help them in a material way. During his years as a trapper he had constantly encountered Plains Indians and had come to know many of them intimately. The first Indians he became acquainted with were Flatheads and Kootenais; somewhat later he came to know the Crows and Blackfeet, and, especially when he lived in Helena, the Crees and Chippewas. He was adopted into three tribes: the Blackfeet, who called him Mex-skim-yo-peek-kinny, meaning Iron Tooth; the Crees, who gave him the name Co-skee-see-cot, which means The Man Who Looks Through Glasses; and the Crows, who named him Mah-paht-sa-not-tsasa, meaning Great Sign Talker. He learned tribal legends from a number of full-bloods—Two-comes-over-the-hill, a Kootenai; Muskegon, a Cree; and especially Full-of-dew, a Chippewa medicine man, in addition to others. Only old full-bloods had his complete confidence; he trusted only their tales and descriptions of traditional customs and rites. He liked to tell of the young Blackfoot Indian entertaining tourists in Glacier National Park with sign language, who, when asked where he had learned sign language, answered, "From General Hugh L. Scott's book." This incident illustrated for him the reason for his distrust of the younger Indians' stories. He himself knew and used sign language, so that when he was

2 Jean P. Smith, "Frank B. Linderman: Sign Talker," *Frontier*, XI (November 1930), 59.

listening through an interpreter and watching the speaker he could check the translation.

Although Frank was always searching to form a conception of Indian life before contact with the white man, he was convinced, from his experience in his early days among Indians, that it was even then "far too late to study the Indian." In his preface to *Indian Why Stories* he expressed his sense of loss of knowledge about the Indian: "With his passing we have lost much of the aboriginal lore, rich in its fairylike characters and in its relation to the lives of a most warlike people." He asserted that Indian lore had been handed down literally and verbatim, not "changed and distorted as old-world folklore"; and he found "a beauty in the rites and ceremonies of the Indians," even though they were "surrounded by mists of superstition." A "poet by instinct," the Indian "framed old stories with which to convey his explanations to others."

Frank's desire to portray accurately the folkways of the Plains Indian—his concept of God, or Manitou; his respect for and co-operation with nature; his humor and fancy—amounted to a passion. He worked painstakingly, and was a bit rankled by the endeavors of some anthropologists to understand the Indian through writings about them or through questioning the younger, modern Indians. A perfectionist in details, he took great pains to correct any inaccuracies in his own writing that came to his attention. In December, 1934, for example, he wrote to his publisher: "I have learned by a long talk with Pretty-shield [the "red mother" of his book *Red Mother*] that she made a mistake in saying that Sitting-heifer was dancing the sun-dance when Plenty-coups shot her and I am anxious to make a correction. Can we have a sticker pasted in the books you have on hand, and then if the book goes into another printing add a note some place in the book? If I can afford it at all I'll pay for it. It is important that we make the correction."

In the sphere of action, Frank, along with others, did much to aid the homeless Crees and Chippewas, and eventually a reservation was set aside for them in Montana. His account in his recollections is inadequate, for it barely suggests the amount of time, energy, and money he spent on the project. The true importance of his role will not be known until the hundreds of letters and papers of his which have been deposited by the Linderman Estate in the archives of the Museum of the Plains Indian at Browning, Montana, have been studied; accounts heretofore have not assigned to Linderman due credit. It is safe to say that without his efforts the reservation would have been established years later, if at all.

Letters among the Linderman Estate papers reflect the appreciation of the Indians and their feeling of indebtedness to Frank. Day Child wrote, probably in 1931:

DEAR MR. LINDERMAN:

I am thinking of You today Why? its because you are the Man that got this Reservation for us. And all of the Rocky Boy Indians are thanking you. Now it look as if We the tribe of Rocky Boys do not have any Right in the Reservation. The Indian finally Decided to Be Allotted. In that Way they think they'll own their lands. We Decided to have You take the Matter up Because We know You are kind hearted and Smart.

Another letter from Day Child reads:

I want you to know how I like Frank Linderman, My father is dead. I loved him, but if my father came back and stood on one hill and I saw Frank Linderman on another hill I would not go to my father, I would go to Frank Linderman. You know I do not lie. This is the Truth.

Rocky Boy himself wrote Frank a long letter telling of the deplorable state of his reservation Indians, and added a postscript: "Walking Bear [Little Bear, chief of the Crees] told me that you told him to collect names for himself to be a Chief and that you are to make him a Chief, *You are Chief*."

On November 11, 1931, Frank wrote to one of the members of Congress from Montana:

. . . a delegation of Chippewas, from Box Elder, headed by old

Roasting-stick, whom I have known for 46 years, has just
visited me at Goose Bay.

These people wish to have their reservation allotted . . . I
finally sent them home to think again, promising that if they, or
a large majority of them, decided to ask for allotment I would
help them in the matter. . . .

He goes on to ask a number of questions regarding division of
land among the Rocky Boy Indians and says that the Indian
delegation traveled to Helena to see the governor and then came
straight back to Goose Bay, "hoping that I would advise a trip to
Washington." Again, Frank sought to aid the Indians; and
allotment was finally made.

Unfortunately, two possible opportunities for Frank to serve
the public with his knowledge of Indians failed to materialize. In
1929 the office of U.S. Commissioner of Indian Affairs became
vacant; and many of Frank's friends, especially Samuel McKelvie,
former governor of Nebraska, supported him for the position.
With his knowledge of and understanding of the needs of the
Plains Indian, he would have been the ideal man; and he was
challenged by the idea of the job. One of the reasons why he was
not successful may have been that Joseph M. Dixon, also a Montana Republican, had been made Assistant Secretary of the
Interior, and it was thought that another Montanan should not be
appointed to a high office in the same department.

In 1930 a plan was proposed under which two men, under the
auspices of the University of Chicago, would cover, in research
and writing, the history of the Northwestern Indian. An anthropologist, who had already been appointed, was to provide the
scientific, technical and cultural background; and Frank was
approached to undertake a biographical study of the personalities
and life of early-day Indians, with emphasis on the relations
between whites and Indians on the Northwestern Plains. In the
end, however, the project was never consummated.

IV

The idea of being a writer was in Frank's mind at least from his early days in Helena, and it gained strength when he dined Opie Read at the Montana Club there in 1911. He told Read of his desire to write, especially about Indian lore; and Read encouraged him to do so. Three years later, on insurance business in Forsyth, Montana, Frank found Opie Read lecturing at the Chautauqua. Read, upon seeing Frank again, said, "Thank God, the town is now redeemed." When they parted at midnight, after a long talk, Read again urged Frank, "Go to it . . . be sure to print the Indian lore." Frank immediately wrote "Frau" in Helena: ". . . I do wonder whether I could make a good living with my pen. . . . He said mine was by far the best western stuff ever written. . . . He said, 'Frank, I am never fooled, you are a real poet every inch of you . . . above all, print your book on Indian lore even if you have to pay for it because it will do well.'"

With this encouragement, Frank submitted a collection of tales to Charles Scribner's Sons; it was published as *Indian Why Stories* in 1915. The dedication, revealing the naïveté of the author publishing his first book (in later years Frank would never have written so profusely and sentimentally), read: "To Charley Russell, the Cowboy Artist, George Bird Grinnell, the Indian's Friend, and to all others who have known and loved Montana./ For I hold them all as kin/ Who have builded fires where nature/ Wears no make-up on her skin."

Scribner's Sons published all of Frank's books until 1929, a total of eight. Besides *Indian Why Stories*, they were: *Indian Lodge-Fire Stories* (1918), *On a Passing Frontier* and *Indian Old-Man Stories* (1920), *How It Came About Stories* and *Bunch-Grass and Blue-Joint* (verse) (1921), *Lige Mounts, Free Trapper* (a novel) (1922), and *Kootenai Why Stories* (1926).

As early as 1922 Frank was concerned because his books, although they showed a steady sale, were not selling in the numbers he had hoped they would. When one of his friends offered him a job selling insurance, however, he replied:

... Your offer is magnanimous and with your permission I will keep it in mind for possible future use, but up to now I have not thought of lessening my literary efforts, for I am getting along fairly well and my books are being well received. I found long ago that I could not write books and life insurance, and while I am sure that I could earn more money at the latter game I have long ago determined that there are more worthwhile things than dollars.

It is hard for some of my friends to believe that I feel it a duty to, in some way, preserve the Old West, especially Montana, in printer's ink, and if I can accomplish a small part of that duty I shall die contented. I have written six books and am half done with a seventh, besides finishing a dozen stories of old Marysville times, since I came here, and I am not half through. So you see, if I can live comfortably and complete my work I shall be doing what I believe I was intended to accomplish. I suppose it sounds foolish, but as Mark Twain has said, "I know I am a fool but I am God Almighty's fool and his works must be respected."

Nobody can tell what an author or his books can do until time has juggled both. Everybody knows that some of the best things have begged and some of the worst known worship for a limited time.

I want to do my work and I had rather do it *well* and up to the standard of the West itself as I know it than get money for flimsy or cheap literature. I am going to stick for a while, ... and play the string out or until I am in financial danger. ...[3]

Frank continued to write, often in discouragement and with a sense of frustration, although he was encouraged by the favorable reviews his books received. The Indian tales, one reviewer noted, "lift the curtain upon a different world, much as Hans Andersen lifted one from his Danish environment." The New York *Times* critic wrote: "There is nothing like them in our heritage of western Europe legends."

In 1924, seeing his capital dwindling and his income from writing not increasing, Frank bought the Hotel Kalispell, operated it for two years, and at the same time ran for the United States Senate. Fortunately for his writing, he lost the election.

[3] Letter to Harry Cunningham, June 22, 1922.

Selling the hotel at a profit, he returned to Goose Bay and resumed writing.

Through the 1920's, although they remained on good terms, both Frank and his publisher, Scribner's, were dissatisfied with the sale of his books; neither was able to understand why they were not larger. Both, of course, realized that the books were not of the best-seller type. Maxwell Perkins, the well-known Scribner's editor, wrote Frank on January 17, 1929, that royalty sales had been "disappointing—particularly so for 'Lige Mounts,'" adding that "it would be hard to write a better story than 'Lige Mounts.'" He recognized that Frank's books had "an intrinsic value far beyond their mere fictional value, which in itself is considerable . . . throwing great light on the quality of the Indian mind, and imagination, and on his ways of living."

In 1929 Frank made up his mind to change publishers. At the urging of his friends, he went to New York, taking along a few manuscripts, to visit publishers in person. There Hermann Hagedorn introduced him to Richard Walsh, of the John Day Company, who immediately showed an interest in Frank's work, especially the story of Plenty-coups, whom Frank had spent several weeks interviewing on the Crow Reservation in 1928. In an attempt to portray the life of the Indian before white-man influence came decisively upon him, Frank, who had known old Plenty-coups for many years, spent days drawing out his earliest recollections. The result was *American*, published by the John Day Company in 1930. Frederic van de Water thought it "not only a great book," but "one of those volumes," he wrote Frank in 1931, "too good for the present, that is due to be 'discovered' by someone long after you and I are dead." Reviewers noted that "nothing altogether comparable . . . has heretofore been added to our literature concerning the American Indian" (New York *Times*, April 27, 1930); that it "is a vivid and vital record set down by a recorder who is 'a creative listener' in the sense that he understands deeply . . . a clear, unadorned, moving history of a time and a people both gone" (Chicago *Tribune*, May 10, 1930); and that it "will interest ethnologists and historians" (Oliver La

Farge, in *Books*, April 13, 1930). The eminent ethnologist R. H. Lowie, an expert on the Crows, wrote in the *American Anthropologist* (XXXIV, 531–533) that he found in *American* "some absurdities and a great deal of value sprinkled through the book," adding that it "supplies some worthwhile facts for the ethnographer."

American, however, was published during the Great Depression, and the sale of the book did not come up to expectation, although it went into a third printing in January, 1931. Nevertheless, the John Day Company accepted more of Frank's manuscripts, reprinting *Lige Mounts, Free Trapper* under the title *Morning Light* in 1930, and publishing *Old Man Coyote*, a collection of Crow stories, in 1931. A New York reviewer found *Morning Light* "as fresh as a new-born colt" (*World*, August 24, 1930), and the *Saturday Review* commentator felt it "sincere in its picture of the interaction between human life and the land in which it is lived" (September 27, 1930). Frederic van de Water thought this novel and its successor, *Beyond Law* (1933) stand "in the first rank of novels of the West," perhaps because the author had been "a Doer before he became a Teller." The New York *Times* reviewer considered Linderman "as an interpreter of life on the western plains . . . second to none."

In 1932, with *Red Mother*, Frank tried to get a true picture of the Indian woman's life. It was somewhat less successful than *American*, probably because Pretty-shield, the Crow woman whom he interviewed, had a less accurate memory than Plenty-coups and possibly cared less. However, as the *Christian Science Monitor* noted, although *Red Mother* "lacks the substance and dignity of . . . *American* . . . the dash and romance of his *Lige Mounts* and the Hellenic beauty of the myths in *Old-Man Coyote* . . . it should dispel the misconception of the Indian woman as a wretched drudge" (November 26, 1932). And Professor Lowie, again in the *American Anthropologist* (XXXVI, 124–126), wrote that he had "learned a number of things from this layman's production" and that Linderman had made "in a very real sense a contribution to Crow source material." He found *Red Mother* "the most valuable of the three"—*American, Old-Man Coyote*, and *Red Mother*.

This book marked the end of Frank's writings about the Indian, with the exception of an essay in Winold Reiss's *Blackfeet Indians*, a book of paintings. The royalties from his later books were no more encouraging than from earlier ones, and Frank became increasingly frustrated. When he was in New York he had tried to break into magazine publication, but even with the help of Richard Walsh he was unsuccessful. The editors seemingly did not care for materials about Indians or early Montana. He thought that there must be some "tricks of the trade" in magazine writing, and at one time in 1933 wrote to his publisher about learning them. His letter brought this reply: "Frank, I hate to think of your trying to learn 'knacks' or bag of tricks merely for the sake of pleasing magazine editors. If you were a second-rater, that would be all right; but you are a first-rater, and therefore I believe you have got to continue to be yourself and do your own stuff, and if editors can't see it the way you write it, it is so much the worse for them; and it is tough on you. But I think it would be tougher on you to try to write in a way that is unnatural to you."

Frank determinedly went on writing in his own way, venting his bitterness privately to his close friends about the contrast between the slow sale of his books and the praise they received from the critics. *Stumpy*, a story about a chipmunk that played just outside his study window, was his last published book, although he wrote a number of articles, such as "My Kentucky Rifle and Other Rifles," and "Fur," "Gold," and "Grass," depicting the stages of Montana's development, and short stories in the popular vein like "Killing in Keep Cool," "Poker, Ponies, and a Girl," and "The Killing of Red Ranighan," that were never published.

By and large, Linderman was fortunate in the artists who illustrated his books. Charlie Russell, a lifelong friend, illustrated three of his early books—*Indian Why Stories*, *Indian Lodge-Fire Stories*, and *Indian Old-Man Stories*. *How It Came About Stories*, the single book of invented tales, was illustrated by Carle Boog, a Swiss by birth who was working in New York and was then painting animals, but was not western in experience. *Kootenai*

Why Stories used the services of Charles Livingston Bull, an artist nearer in spirit to the tales, for he had illustrated other western books, including Jack London's *Call of the Wild*. For *American* Frank found the artist who, along with Russell, pleased him the most—Herbert M. Stoops. All of his books after 1929, except *Morning Light*, which Joe de Yong, a young disciple of Charlie Russell, provided the drawings for (as he had for *Lige Mounts* earlier), were illustrated by Stoops.

Frank Bird Linderman left to posterity a worthy body of literature. Maxwell Perkins was right about the intrinsic value of his writings. The five volumes of Indian tales, all of which he learned directly from old tribesmen, are told in the manner and style of the Indian—simply, directly, and with suspense. His two characterizations of typical Plains Indian life, along with the legends, constitute a valuable contribution to ethnology and anthropology. Likewise, the two novels of early western life are authentic, based as they are on his own early experiences and those of his friends and acquaintances. And some of the selections in his one book of poetry, *Bunch-Grass and Blue-Joint*, are a good cut above much western verse. All of his writings, like his life itself, reflect the generous spirit of an era and a frontier that have since passed from the scene.

APPENDIX B

Linderman's Writings

Published

BOOKS

Indian Why Stories: Sparks from War Eagle's Lodge-Fire. New York: Charles Scribner's Sons, 1915. Illustrated by Charles M. Russell.
Later editions: New York: Charles Scribner's Sons, 1926; Scribner series of school reading, New York: Charles Scribner's Sons, n.d.; Cadmus Books, New York: E. M. Hale and Co., 1945.

Indian Lodge-Fire Stories. Scribner series of school reading. New York: Charles Scribner's Sons, 1918. Illustrated by Charles M. Russell.

On a Passing Frontier: Sketches from the Northwest. New York: Charles Scribner's Sons, 1920.

Indian Old-Man Stories: More Sparks from War Eagle's Lodge-Fire. New York: Charles Scribner's Sons, 1920. Illustrated by Charles M. Russell.
Later editions: New York: Charles Scribner's Sons, 1926; New York: Blue Ribbon Books, Inc., 1937.

How It Came About Stories. New York: Charles Scribner's Sons, 1921. Illustrated by Carle M. Boog.
Later editions: New York: Charles Scribner's Sons, 1926; New York: Blue Ribbon Books, Inc., 1937.

Bunch-Grass and Blue-Joint. New York: Charles Scribner's Sons, 1921. Verse.

Lige Mounts, Free Trapper. New York: Charles Scribner's Sons, 1922. Illustrated by Joe de Yong. Novel.

Later editions: New York: John Day Co., 1930, under the title *Morning Light*; London: Faber and Faber, 1931 and 1933, under the title *Free Trapper*.

Kootenai Why Stories. New York: Charles Scribner's Sons, 1926. Illustrated by C. L. Bull.

Later editions: New York: Blue Ribbon Books, Inc., 1937.

American: The Life Story of a Great Indian, Plenty-coups, Chief of the Crows. New York: John Day Co., 1930. Illustrated by H. M. Stoops.

Later editions: Yonkers, N.Y.: World Book Co., 1930; London: Faber and Faber, 1930, under the title *Plenty-coups, Chief of the Crows;* Bison Book, Lincoln: University of Nebraska Press, 1962, under the title *Plenty-coups, Chief of the Crows;* Magnolia, Mass.: Peter Smith, 1963, under the title *Plenty-coups, Chief of the Crows*.

Old-Man Coyote. New York: John Day Co., 1931. Illustrated by H. M. Stoops. Junior Guild selection.

Red Mother. New York: John Day Co., 1932. Illustrated by H. M. Stoops.

Beyond Law. New York: John Day Co., 1933. Novel.

Later editions: Corgi Books, London: Transworld Publishing Co., 1957.

Stumpy. New York: John Day Co., 1933. Illustrated by H. M. Stoops. Animal story. Junior Guild selection.

Later editions: Cadmus Books, New York: E. M. Hale and Co., 1933.

"Out of the North," in *Blackfeet Indians*, by Winold Reiss. St. Paul: Great Northern Railroad, 1935.

Recollections of Charley Russell. Ed. by H. G. Merriam. Norman: University of Oklahoma Press, 1962.

MAGAZINE ARTICLES, TALES, AND ANECDOTES

"Charles Russell, Cowboy Artist," *Outlook*, CXLV (April 13, 1927), 466–488.

"Morning Star, a Crow Indian Tale," *Frontier*, VIII (November 1927), 2–25.

"Two Animal Anecdotes," *Frontier*, VIII (March 1928), 83–86.

"Idioma, Things That Aren't So," *Frontier*, IX (November 1928), 55–56.

"Old Man Coyote and the Whirlwind," *Frontier*, IX (January 1929), 132–135.

"A Dog's Life: An Anecdote," *Frontier*, XI (November 1930), 65.

"The Bogie of the Box," *Frontier*, XI (January 1931), 160–161.

"Red Cloud: The Indian Sign," *American Legion Magazine*, (December 1931), 4.

"Through a Telescope," *Frontier*, XII (January 1932), 146–148.

"Partners, I," *Frontier and Midland*, XIV (November 1933), 62–64.

"Partners, II," *Frontier and Midland*, XIV (January 1934), 153–154.

"Who Was the Soldier Chief?" *American Legion Magazine*, (January 1934), 1.

"Chippewa Cross-Bows," *Frontier and Midland*, XIV (March 1934), 236–237.

"Secret of Keep Cool," *Frontier and Midland*, XIV (May 1934), 328–331.

"Lousy Hank," *Frontier and Midland*, XV (Spring 1935), 230–232.

"Yong Sing," *Frontier and Midland*, XV (Summer 1935), 313–314.

"A Little Flier in Wool," *American Legion Magazine* (February 1938), 18.

POETRY

"My Old Friend Pete Lebeaux," *Scribner's*, LXVI (August 1919), 170.

"The Trout Pool," "Luck," "The Old Cane," "The Old Frontier," *Scribner's*, LXX (August 1921), 144–146.

"To the Coyote," *Literary Digest*, LXX (September 1921), 34.

"Indian of the Screen," *Scribner's*, LXXIV (August 1923), 168.

"Old Bateese," *Frontier*, VIII (May 1928), 172–173.

"The Old Frontier," "Pete Lebeau's Lament," "Cabins," *Frontier*,
XIX (Spring 1939), 172–173.

Unpublished

Three articles: "Fur," "Gold," and "Grass," depicting Montana's
early development.*

Four Kootenai legends.

"Mike, the Story of a Trapper's Dog."

"Doctor and I" stories.

Five novels: "Henry Plummer," "Wolf and the Winds,"* "Iron
Shirt,"* "Chick of Last Chance Gulch,"* "Quartzville."

"Big Jinny, a Story of a Grizzly Bear."*

Uncle Billy Stories.

Three short stories: "Killing in Keep Cool,"* "Pokers, Ponies and
a Girl,"* "The Killing of Red Ranighan."

"My Kentucky Rifle and Other Rifles."

Note: Several of the short stories are not in finished form. In
writing the novel "Quartzville," Linderman used materials from
the "Doctor and I" stories.

   * Written after Linderman's visit to New York in 1929–1930.

Acknowledgments

I am indebted especially to Norma Linderman (Mrs. Roy) Waller, and Misses Wilda and Verne Linderman for permission to edit their father's recollections; to Doris F. Merriam; to Mr. Michael Kennedy, Montana Historical Society, Helena; to Dr. A. Barry Braunberger, Kalispell; to Dr. Alan P. Merriam, Indiana University; to Dr. Claude Schaeffer, Museum of the Plains Indian, Browning, Montana; to Mr. William K. Converse, Helena; to E. E. McGilvra, Butte; to the reference librarians at the University of Montana and the Missoula Public Library; and to Miss Mary Dempsey, Montana Historical Library, Helena.

H. G. MERRIAM

219

Index

Index

224